D0576903

WITHDRAWN

COLONEL
TOM PARKER

ALSO BY
JAMES L. DICKERSON

Faith Hill: Piece of My Heart

Dixie Chicks: Down-Home and Backstage

*Last Suppers: If the World Ended Tomorrow,
What Would Be Your Last Meal?*

North to Canada: Men and Women Against the Vietnam War

*Dixie's Dirty Secret: The True Story of How the Government,
the Media, and the Mob Conspired to Combat Integration
and the Vietnam Antiwar Movement*

*Women on Top: The Quiet Revolution That's Rocking
the American Music Industry*

*That's Alright, Elvis: The Untold Story of Elvis' First Guitarist
and Manager* (with Scotty Moore)

*Goin' Back to Memphis: A Century of Blues,
Rock 'n' Roll, and Glorious Soul*

Coming Home: 21 Conversations about Memphis Music

I'm So Sorry: The Stories Behind 101 Very Public Apologies

Country Music's Most Embarrassing Moments

Adult
92
PARKER
Tom

COLONEL
TOM PARKER

The Curious Life
of Elvis Presley's
Eccentric Manager

JAMES L. DICKERSON

Cooper Square Press

WITHDRAWN
Beverly Hills Public Library
444 North Rexford Drive
Beverly Hills, California 90210

First Cooper Square Press edition 2001

This Cooper Square Press hardcover edition of *Colonel Tom Parker* is an original publication. It is published by arrangement with the author.

Copyright © 2001 by James L. Dickerson

All rights reserved.
No part of this publication may be reproduced, stored in a retrieval system, or transmitted in any form or by any means, electronic, mechanical, photocopying, recording, or otherwise, without the prior permission of the publisher.

Published by Cooper Square Press
An Imprint of the Rowman & Littlefield Publishing Group
150 Fifth Avenue, Suite 817
New York, New York 10011

Distributed by National Book Network

Library of Congress Cataloging-in-Publication Data

Dickerson, James.
    Colonel Tom Parker : the curious life of Elvis Presley's eccentric manager / James L. Dickerson.
        p. cm.
    Includes index.
    ISBN 0-8154-1088-3 (cloth : alk. paper)
    1. Parker, Tom, 1909-   . 2. Concert agents—United States—Biography. I. Title
    ML429.P33 D53 2001
    782.42166'092—dc21

                                00-052321

Printed in the United States of America

⊗™ The paper used in this publication meets the minimum requirements of American National Standard for Information Sciences—Permanence of Paper for Printed Library Materials, ANSI/NISO Z39.48-1992.
Manufactured in the United States of America.

Beverly Hills Public Library
444 North Rexford Drive
Beverly Hills, California 90210

To my mother, Juanita Dickerson Caldwell

and

To my sister, Susan Dickerson McCaskill

CONTENTS

ACKNOWLEDGMENTS

I would like to thank the following people and organizations for helping me with this book: Ed Frank of the Mississippi Valley Collection at the University of Memphis; my former research assistant, Ginger Rezy; the Jean and Alexander Heard Library at the Vanderbilt University Library; Frances Preston, Brenda Lee, Marshall Grant, Bobbie Moore, Paul Lichter, Al Dvorin; Diane Grey at the *Tampa Tribune*; Carl Sedlmayr Jr., Laura Sedlmayr, Hal Kanter, Evelyn Black Tuverville, James Reid; John Bakke at the University of Memphis; the Public Library of Nashville and Davidson County; the Federal Bureau of Investigation; Joan Jacka at the Nevada Gaming Control Board; Debbie Taylor at the Tampa Humane Society; Sharon Toon at the Selective Service System; the Tampa-Hillsborough County Public Library; Loretta Bowman, county clerk, Las Vegas, Nevada; Ave M. Sloane and Marian Smith at the U.S. Immigration and Naturalization Service; Mark Medley at the Country Music Foundation; Frank Coffey, Chips Moman, D. J. Fontana, Donna Presley Early; Sgt. Dan Grossi of the Tampa Police Department; Claudia Anderson at the Lyndon Baines Johnson Library; my editor at Cooper Square Press, Michael Dorr; and special thanks to Scotty Moore.

THE SECOND GREATEST
SHOW ON EARTH

Tampa shone like a beacon in the night to young Tom Parker.

It was the Las Vegas of its time: A place where you could buy anything for the right price, where vast financial empires could be built
on one-trick ponies, midnight hustles, and high-stake shell games,
where all it took to make a big score was a dream grand enough to
capture the imagination.

Nature has joined Tampa and St. Petersburg at the hip with an
enormous inland saltwater bay, but they are two very different cities.
St. Petersburg, with its sandy Gulf of Mexico beaches, has long been
Florida's west coast playground for the rich and famous. Tampa has a
more austere, working-class foundation. For most of its early history,
it was best known as a landing port for Colombian banana boats.

From the time the region was first explored in the 1500s by Juan
Ponce de León and Hernando de Soto, Tampa has had a dual reputation: First, as a natural paradise fed by mineral springs with miracu-
lous healing qualities, and second, as a wide-open port city, where
gambling, prostitution, and drinking were tolerated at sensible levels,
as long as they were kept a respectable distance from the well-mani-
cured neighborhoods of polite society.

For Tom Parker, Tampa offered everything a young man could possibly want. By the early 1930s, when he first appeared on the scene

in the Tampa Bay area, the Florida land boom of the 1920s had sub-
sided, leaving behind a flood of new arrivals, some with fortunes to
invest, others desperate for work. It was the ideal time and place for
Parker to put down roots. With the exception of the Tampa/St. Petersburg area, the entire west coast of Florida was a desolate waste-
land.

Since Tampa offered the only major port between Key West and
Pensacola, illegal immigrants who wanted to bypass the mainstream
ports on the west coast heavily favored it. Cubans arrived by the thousands to work in the area's cigar factories, and it was the port of choice
for those Germans, Italians, and Russian and East European Jews
who preferred a backdoor entry into the United States. Of all the
ports in America, it was the one that asked the fewest questions. It
was the place to go if you were without papers, and had a past and
wanted a new start.

When Tom Parker first arrived in Tampa in the early 1930s, he had
not been using that name for long. There is no documented record of
his existence in America prior to his arrival in Tampa. Everything
about his life before that is an historical blur. It would be decades before anyone determined that his real name was something other than
Tom Parker.

According to one theory, later accepted by a Tennessee probate
court and encouraged by Tom Parker himself, he was born Andreas
van Kuijk in Breda, Holland, on June 26, 1909.[1]

When he came into the world, goes that theory, five brothers and
sisters greeted him; four additional siblings would arrive before he
reached the age of ten. His parents were Adam and Maria van Kuijk.
From all indications, he had a fairly normal childhood. His maternal
grandparents, Johannes and Marie Ponsie, made a living as itinerant
peddlers hawking trinkets as they traveled the waterways of the
Netherlands.

Andreas was sixteen when his father died, sending his family into
turmoil as it attempted to adjust to the loss of its primary breadwin-
ner. Where would they live? What would Maria do to feed the family? Andreas began to disappear for short periods of time. Later it
was discovered that he was hanging out at the shipyards. One morning he left home and never returned.[2]

A second theory, favored by the author, has it that Parker was born in Russia to Jewish parents and acquired his Dutch identity during his teen years while living with the van Kuijk family. At the time he arrived in Tampa, Jews lived in closely knit, insular groups that afforded protection from non-Jews who often looked upon them with suspicion and disapproval. The 1920s and the 1930s were not good times to be visibly Jewish in America, so many preferred to live in anonymity.

There were few patterns in Parker's life, but the one that stuck with him the closest was his propensity to gravitate to other Jews. It began in Tampa and continued throughout his life. Whether you believe Parker was born in the Netherlands or in Russia, the fact remains that there is no documentation to substantiate either claim. In carny lingo, "you pays your money and you takes your chances."

All we know for certain is that Andreas dropped out of sight in Holland in the late 1920s and early 1930s. Somewhere between Holland and the United States, he shed his old identity and reinvented himself. As Andreas discarded his Dutch identity, Tom Parker was being birthed, fully grown and sporting a gigantic Cuban-rolled cigar. "Hello," he said upon his arrival in Tampa. "My name's Tom Parker and I'm from Huntington, West Virginia."

As the world's second immaculate conception in only two millennia, it would forever mystify residents of Huntington, West Virginia, where the name Tom Parker exists only in the mind of its creator.

Throughout the 1920s and early 1930s, dozens of midway carnivals crisscrossed America, providing entertainment for fairs, circuses, and independent promoters. The Johnny J. Jones Exposition was one of the best known, but there were many others, including the Rubin & Cherry Shows, Beckman & Gerety's C.A. Wortham Shows, and John M. Sheesley's Mighty Midway.

One of the most aggressive was the Tampa-based Royal American Shows, which had begun operation in the early 1920s. It played catch-up throughout the decade, but by the early 1930s, it was the dominant midway attraction in the country, a distinction it enjoys to the present day.

Essentially, the midway shows were refinements of the traveling medicine shows that were popular from the 1880s into the new century. The Kickapoo Indian Medicine Company was representative of that type of show. Typically, its ten-act program offered dancing Indians, contortionists, a trapeze act, rifle and handgun exhibitions, and a tightrope walker.[3]

As more glamorous midway shows grew in popularity, the medicine shows dwindled in number, so that by the mid-1960s they had pretty much vanished. But by the time Tom Parker arrived in Tampa, they were still very much in evidence, particularly in the South, where they offered the only live entertainment available.

The routine seldom varied: the medicine show would set up its tents on the outskirts of town and the show's pitchman would go into town with a "Jake" and an Indian and do a series of routines on highly traveled street corners. The skits were done to lure people to the tent shows, which normally lasted a couple of hours. The real purpose of the medicine show—and later the midways—was to sell products, not offer entertainment.

Throughout the 1920s, the godfather of American midways was Johnny J. Jones, a mild-mannered man of diminutive stature who had a reputation for savvy business decisions and compassion toward his employees. He was well liked among the carnies. When word passed along the midway circuit in December 1930 that he had died, the first reaction was sadness, for it was said among carnies that Jones never intentionally inflicted an unkindness among his own kind, but that sorrow quickly turned to apprehension over who would assume the mantle of leadership.

Carnies need a figurehead who can offer spiritual leadership. Someone who can cut the big deal with the straight world. They have their own language, their own code of conduct, their own expectations of the non-carny world. With the passing of Johnny J. Jones, the carny world was thrust into a void. Top carnies are not chosen by democratic vote. Nor are they anointed by divine intervention. They rise to the top by demonstrating a natural ability to lead.

In 1931, the man destined to assume that leadership role was Carl J. Sedlmayr, who owned and managed (along with the Velare Brothers) the Tampa-based Royal American Shows. Sedlmayr, who was born on October 20, 1886, in Falls City, Nebraska, was forty-five when Jones died. He was not born into a carny family, a fact that made his rise to prominence even more impressive, but rather to a family of German ancestry.

Sedlmayr's childhood was uneventful until his father died in 1897, at which time he was sent to Kansas City, Missouri, to live with relatives. By the age of fourteen, what he wanted more than anything else was to become a pharmacist. That dream was dashed when he applied for a position as a pharmacist in Omaha and Council Bluffs, Iowa, only to have his application rejected.[4]

Sedlmayr then responded to a newspaper advertisement soliciting salesmen for a new writing instrument called the fountain pen. Dazzled by its flashy appeal, he took the newfangled invention out on the road and found immediate success as a traveling salesman. During his travels, he met several medicine show pitchmen and became interested in a lifestyle that was then the epitome of American show business. In 1907, at the age of twenty-one, he jumped headlong into the carny life by taking a job as a ticket seller at Chicago's Riverview Park. Before long, Sedlmayr had saved enough money to purchase his own sideshow attraction.

With the idea that "Royal" would be attractive to Canadians and "American" would be appealing in the United States (to be successful, a midway operator had to do equally well in both countries), he renamed his business the Royal American Shows.[5] By 1925, Sedlmayr had taken on two partners, Elmer and Curtis Velare. Together, they built the Royal American Shows into a first-rate operation.

Motion pictures and radio were a constant threat to the carnivals, but the carnies were able to be competitive by capitalizing on the "hands on" nature of their shows. You could see the entertainers up close. You could smell the grass and the popcorn and the candied apples. Plus, carnivals had girlie shows that provided a level of titillation missing from radio and movie theaters (unless you got really lucky in the balcony).

Sedlmayr was a master showman, not that he ever climbed atop a stage to perform. His talent lay elsewhere. He had the ability to go into a town and by the sheer force of his personality convince everyone that Royal American was the greatest show on earth. Most carny operators know more about the cities and towns they visit than do the people who live there. They quickly learn who is honest—and, more importantly, who is not.

If a town is under the control of a mafia-style family that operates its own girlie shows and gambling halls, then the carny operator will hear from them in quick order. Carnies scoff at the charge that they cannot be trusted. To them, it is the world-at-large that runs the biggest scam, with its hidden hometown agendas and ruthless centers of power.

Typically, Sedlmayr arrived in a town three days ahead of the show. The first order of business was to introduce himself to the authorities, the political leaders, and those businessmen whose opposition he most wanted to avoid. Once that was accomplished, he would go to the field where the carnival was scheduled to set up and he would walk off the location of every attraction. He had a step that was precisely three feet. He knew the measurements of every attraction in his show and he took pride in his ability to step off markers for each stake and support post that would be needed.

By 1935, Sedlmayr was the undisputed king of the carnival circuit. The Royal American caravan filled ninety railway cars and offered the largest assortment of midway rides, sideshow attractions, and entertainers on the circuit. Royal American received an unexpected boost in 1938, when workers for the Barnum and Bailey circus went on strike. During the down time, Royal American, which often supplied the midway for the circus, was able to expand its allotted space, so that when the strike ended and the circus went back out on the road, Royal American had more space than the circus.

For as long as anyone could remember, "The Greatest Show on Earth" had always been P. T. Barnum's claim to fame, but after 1938, Carl Sedlmayr's Royal American midway was clearly the second greatest show on earth.

Throughout the 1940s and 1950s, Royal American expanded its influence, and by the late 1990s it was still the undisputed leader. Carl Sedlmayr never received the public recognition—or notoriety—that Barnum did, but that was because he decided early in his career that he wanted to remain behind the scenes. His name is largely unknown outside the carnival business, but within the business he is a deity.

With the end of the 1965 season, the Royal American train returned to its winter quarters in Tampa and all the equipment was unloaded and placed into storage. Sedlmayr and his son, Carl Sedlmayr Jr., agreed to meet the following evening at the son's house for dinner. When the father didn't show up as arranged, Carl Jr. became concerned and went to his house to check on him. He found him in his bed, where he had passed away quietly in his sleep.

More than 1,200 showmen descended upon the Greater Tampa Showmen's Club to attend Carl Sedlmayr's funeral. In keeping with the king's ecumenical lifestyle, services were conducted with full Masonic Rites by both a rabbi and a Protestant minister. His body was interred in a mausoleum at Showmen's Rest in Tampa and the Royal American torch was passed to his son, who at age forty-six had ridden his share of carnival circuits.[6]

☆   ☆   ☆

Carl J. Sedlmayr Jr. first met Thomas A. Parker in 1931 or 1932. He was twelve or thirteen, at an age when he was just learning the ropes of the carnival business from his father. The twenty-two-year-old Parker was hard to miss: A six-footer, with a pudgy, pear-shaped midsection, he stood out in a crowd. He had a round, friendly face and blue eyes that had a mischievous glint to them.

Sedlmayr's recollections of Parker are still vivid.[7] He doesn't recall what city they were in, but he remembers walking the grounds one day when he looked up and saw a new face. He paid attention because carnivals are families, and new members are always scrutinized. Tom Parker was behind the counter of a concession stand, standing tall amid the crowded hurly-burly of the midway, selling candied apples with all the fervor of a tent-show evangelist.

Sedlmayr is not certain what month Parker signed on with Royal American because all their early records were destroyed when the roof of a show wagon sprang a leak and soaked everything inside with rain water. He recalls the approximate year he met Parker because he recalls what age he was. "It was a small community," he said of Royal American. "We were close because we worked and lived together."

Traditionally, the carnival train pulled out of Tampa in March or April. For as long as anyone can remember, the season always began the first week in May at the annual Cotton Carnival celebration in Memphis, Tennessee, and ended the last week in October at the Louisiana State Fair in Shreveport—two cities that would prove to be critical in the careers of both Tom Parker and Elvis Presley.

Usually, each booking was for one week, but some venues, such as the Annual Spring Festival in St. Louis, Missouri, and the Calgary Exhibition and Stampede in Alberta, Canada, lasted for ten days to two weeks. Other stops along the way from Memphis to Shreveport included the Annual Shrine Jubilee in Davenport, Iowa, the Edmonton Exhibition in Alberta, Canada, the Regina Exhibition in Saskatchewan, Canada, the State Fair of Wisconsin in Milwaukee, the State Fair of Minnesota in St. Paul, the Kansas State Fair in Topeka, and the Mid America Fair in Topeka.

Memphis was the first city in which Parker sold candied apples. The occasion was a festival named Cotton Carnival, a not-too-subtle imitation of the New Orleans Mardi Gras. Cotton Carnival began with the arrival of the "royal barge," which came in off the Mississippi River to dock on Monroe Street in the heart of downtown Memphis. There followed a parade with gaily decorated floats and marching bands.

The king and queen, who were inducted from the families of successful cotton merchants, donned regal apparel and tossed candy to the children and adults that lined the downtown streets. In later years, they used elaborate motorized floats, but in the early 1930s the floats were constructed out of old wagons discarded by the ice company and drawn by horses and mules. [8]

The one thing that Tom Parker shared with his traveling companions was a healthy distrust of authority. Carnival staffs are not composed of nine-to-five, button-down-collar types who thrive on regimentation and a sense of social responsibility. Carnies come in all shapes and sizes, colors, ethnic backgrounds, sexual orientations, and talents, but the one thing they all share is a distrust of traditional society. It is that common perception that binds them into a family unit. The first thing Parker would have done upon arriving in Memphis, especially since it was his first outing with the carnival, would have been to find out who the bosses were. Not that he would have had any desire to schedule a meeting: The idea was to stay out of trouble's way.

In the early 1930s, Memphis was home to one of the most powerful crime cartels in the country. For more than two decades, the Prudential Insurance Company had labeled Memphis the "murder capital" of America, based on a study of homicide rates across the country. It was a title that would stick with the city throughout the 1930s and 1940s, and one that would reappear periodically up until the present day. There were many complex reasons why Memphis was a dangerous city, but the underlying reason was a subterranean crime culture built on cocaine distribution, prostitution, gambling, and, in later years, sophisticated white-collar scams that milked the government and private industry of millions.[9] In the early years, many of these criminal activities were conducted out of storefront operations on Beale Street.

Running parallel to the underworld was a political organization fronted by the notorious E. H. "Boss" Crump. He not only controlled the politics of Tennessee, he often influenced national policy. For nearly four decades, he dictated selections for political candidates, including president, federal judgeships, and a wide range of local jobs, everything from U.S. marshal to draft board memberships.

Memphis was the talk of the nation in the 1930s, and magazines regularly sent reporters into the city to report on the nefarious activities that many editors considered a threat to the health and safety of the entire nation. Whatever impression Parker had of Memphis when he arrived in 1931 with Royal American, what he almost certainly left with was a clear understanding that it was the most dangerous city in America.

Sedlmayr is not certain how long Parker worked for Royal American. He says it may have been only for a year or two. However, it is more likely that Parker worked for the carnival for six or seven years. Parker himself suggested as much in later years. If so, he would have been at the Cotton Carnival opener in 1934 when a riot broke out after it was announced there were no more tickets available for a performance of the Guy Lombardo Orchestra at the city auditorium. A mob of disappointed fans formed a ring around the auditorium and kept ticket holders from entering the building. During the ensuing riot, windows were smashed and doors were kicked in. The incident would have given Parker his first glimpse of the destructive power, and limitless financial potential, of musical stardom.

With time, Parker did more than sell apples with the carnival. He liked to tell the story of his dancing chicken routine, in which he put a hot plate under a metal sheet covered with sawdust. He placed several chickens on the sawdust and whenever he wanted them to "dance," he juiced up the hot plate and scalded their feet. Other times he captured wrens and painted them yellow and sold them as canaries. Oscar Davis, his assistant in later years, told Elvis biographer Jerry Hopkins that Parker told him he was responsible for food preparation on the train—carnies called it the "pie car"—and sometimes did a little palm reading on the side.

One story has Parker operating a hot dog stand. There is no inherent challenge in selling hot dogs. People buy them because they like them. The challenge is in selling hot dogs without actually selling them. Parker's hot dogs contained small bits of meat at each end of the bun, with globs of mustard and cheap fixings in between. If anyone ever looked at their hot dog and complained that they had been cheated, Parker pointed to a wiener he had tossed into the sawdust earlier in the day. "Why, you dropped your meat, boy," he said, pointing to the well-worn wiener on the ground.

Another story has it that when one of the carnival's food concessions was doing poorly, there was talk among the carnival management of reducing the price of a meal from fifty cents to twenty-five cents. Parker said he had a better idea. He painted a sign that said, "Admission one dollar. If not satisfied, half your money back." Of course, the concession was flooded with customers who wanted to take advantage of a good deal.

When the makings for a particular concession commodity were in short supply, such as enough lemons for lemonade, Parker would go to the nearest drugstore and purchase packages of citric acid to give his concoction the right color. Once he had the sugar-water brew properly mixed, he topped it off with a slice of lemon. It tasted like hell, but it looked like lemonade and that was all that mattered.

In the early 1930s, the Royal American Shows were usually jam-packed with high-energy entertainment. For someone of Parker's sensibilities it was exhilarating. Midgets, bearded ladies, contortionists, trapeze artists, expert marksmen, knife throwers, animal exhibits with gorillas and snakes and lions, and games of chance of every description imaginable. Anyone with a unique act could find a home with the carnival. The only requirements were that it had to be an oddity of one kind or another or be based on an undetectable scam.

Some acts were remarkably simple. White Wing was an African American man who dressed in a mock military uniform, complete with white trousers and shoes. He patrolled the midway with a pointed stick, a bag, and a whistle. If he saw a piece of paper on the ground, he blew the whistle as loudly as he could and rushed wildly toward the paper, stabbing it with a dramatic flourish. Midway patrons gladly gave him fistfuls of money for presenting such an unexpected and stellar performance.

One of the most popular attractions was Leon Claxton's "Harlem in Havana." Claxton was the most successful black carny on the circuit. Unlike minstrel shows, which were primarily made up of whites using blackface, Claxton's shows were composed of African Americans who danced and sang and performed skits for a sit-down audience. Claxton had an extraordinary talent for high-quality productions and many of his theatrical inventions were later incorporated into early rock 'n' roll revues.[10]

All midways had girlie shows, and Royal American was no exception. It would have been a natural draw for a twenty-one-year-old single man like Parker, but there is no indication that he was the slightest bit interested in women at that time. Whatever his vices at that age—later it would be food and gambling—women were not included.

One of the things that impressed Parker about Royal American was its commitment to new technology. In Carl Sedlmayr's eyes, bigger was always better, particularly if it was enhanced with some new gadget or invention. In 1932, he started using gigantic navy searchlights to fill the night skies with dazzling shafts of light that could be seen for forty miles. The following year Royal American was the first to group four Ferris wheels together into one mammoth attraction.

There wasn't much associated with the carnival that could be categorized as highbrow entertainment. One of the first lessons that Parker learned as a carny was that when it comes to American entertainment, the formula for success always rests with the lowest common denominator. People could laugh at carnies all they wanted, but when it came to making money in entertainment, carnies wrote the book.

As always, the Royal American tour ended in Shreveport. After leaving Memphis, Tom Parker must have thought that city's wickedness and wide-open lawlessness—on Beale Street he could have purchased "dime" boxes of cocaine and enjoyed the company of prostitutes while listening to the best blues offered anywhere—was an anomaly, because the other stops along the tour were tame by comparison.

Shreveport brought him back to reality. The population of Shreveport in the early 1930s was less than half that of Memphis, but it was caught up in the same underworld machinations, with one major difference: While organized crime in Tennessee was pretty much confined to the Bluff City (as it was called because of its location overlooking the Mississippi River), the entire state of Louisiana was under the control of strong-arm bosses, beginning with Huey "Kingfish" Long, who was elected governor in 1928 and United States senator in 1931, the year Tom Parker rolled into town aboard the Royal American show train.

Parker most likely played his first slot machine in Shreveport. Since the state fair lasted an entire week the carnies had to look for ways to entertain themselves in their off-hours. Shreveport was not a wide-open city like New Orleans. While it offered much the same types of entertainment, the venues were tucked away out of sight, especially the after-hours dives that offered bootleg whiskey and gambling.

In the early 1930s, the slot machines in Shreveport were owned by New York Mafia don Frank Costello. How they got there is now part of Louisiana political lore. At the time Costello wanted to put slots into Louisiana, New Orleans Mafia boss Sam Carolla already had that franchise for New Orleans. The rest of the state was slot-free. Costello went to Huey Long and cut a deal with him, whereby Long agreed to use the state police to protect the slots statewide, including those owned by Carolla. That sounded like a good idea to Carolla, who agreed not to oppose Costello's entry into the state. To distribute and service his slots, Costello chose Carlos Marcello, the owner of a jukebox distribution company named Jefferson Music.[11]

All that would have been made clear to Parker during his first visit to Shreveport. For all its secrecy, organized crime was not shy about informing business owners that it was part of a Mafia network under the protection of Huey Long. It was exactly that sort of admission that coerced the cooperation of independently owned nightclubs and restaurants that did not want trouble with the mob.

By the time Parker returned to Tampa in November 1931 or 1932, he had received an education in the dark underbelly of American politics and business that would stay with him for the remainder of his life. His biggest problem lay in his legal status. If there were no criminal convictions on his record or if there were no outstanding warrants out for him, he would have had no problem obtaining American citizenship after living in the country for five years. Naturalization was not complicated. The first requirement would have been for Parker to announce his intention to become a U.S. citizen three years before actually applying for citizenship. That announcement, called presenting "first papers," could have been made to a United States District court clerk.[12] For some reason, Parker never made an effort to obtain United States citizenship.

As a carny, Parker had a job that kept him on the road for most of the year. He could be anything—or anyone—he chose while working the midway. To his way of thinking, citizenship would be more of a burden than an asset. What he needed more than anything else was a family, a *real, honest to goodness* American family that would allow him to blend into the community. Unfortunately, he didn't know many women.

One of the many concessions that traveled with the Royal American tour was a booth owned by the Have-a-Tampa cigar company. The booths were usually operated by attractive young women with inviting, oversized smiles. All of the women behind the counter were appealing (that was why they were hired), but one in particular caught Parker's attention. Her name was Marie Mott.

Twice married, Marie was one year older than Parker, which would have made her twenty-seven when they met in 1935. One of her marriages had produced a son, Robert Ross. At the time she met Parker, she and Robert were living at home with her parents and her brother, Bitsy Mott.

Whether it was true love, or based on the economics of survival, Parker and Marie moved in with each other that same year. Not only did the union provide him with a ready-made family, it gave him a place to live when he wasn't on the road: He moved his belongings into the home of Marie's parents. Whether they were actually married has never been established. There is no record of a marriage in Tampa of a Tom Parker or an Andreas van Kuijk, so if they were married it may have been under another name. The most likely scenario is that they were never married.

Bitsy Mott told author Dirk Vellenga that he recalled the household being in an uproar whenever his sister and her new husband came in off the road. Said Bitsy: "I remember they used to move my Daddy and Momma out of their bed and use the bed themselves. Daddy and Momma would sleep wherever they could. That would irritate me a little."

Parker may have wanted companionship and a place to live, and his motivation may have been as simple as that. But if he expected his marriage to Marie to provide him with American citizenship, he was mistaken. Female aliens who married American men were afforded citizenship, but the reverse did not necessarily apply.

A male illegal immigrant could not marry an American female and automatically obtain citizenship. Prior to 1922, an American woman who married an illegal alien actually lost her American citizenship. By the time of the Colonel's marriage, the law was changed to allow American women who married aliens to keep their citizenship, provided their alien husbands were able to qualify for citizenship; but throughout the 1930s and 1940s it remained a somewhat gray area with the courts.[13]

Apparently, authorities never challenged Marie Parker's legal status, but if for some reason her husband was not eligible for citizenship, then their marriage would not have provided him with it.

Carl Sedlmayr wasn't the only master showman in the Tampa Bay area. Across the bay in St. Petersburg was a businessman whose grandiose style and tactics garnered him a national reputation. James

Earl Webb was no run-of-the-mill businessman. He owned the most famous drugstore in the world—Webb's City.

Webb bragged that he sold a thousand prescriptions and five thousand ice-cream cones daily. That wasn't difficult to do with a store that occupied ten city blocks and attracted sixty thousand customers a day. The size of the store itself made it a curiosity, plus the fact that it sold everything from automobile tires to televisions and dinette sets to Swiss watches, but it wasn't size that kept it packed with customers: It was Doc Webb's incomparable showmanship.

A gaudy dresser, the five-foot-five King of Promoters dressed in suits that would have made Liberace envious. He told friends he owned over a hundred suits and fifty sport coats, all of them dazzling to the eye. Webb had a style of his own, one that Parker would later appropriate for Elvis Presley, almost to the finest detail. Although it was style that grabbed everyone's attention, it was his genius for sales promotions that made him one of the richest men in Florida.[14]

During one promotion, Webb advertised a sale on dollar bills. He promised to sell two thousand one-dollar bills for the low price of ninety-five cents. Webb's City was mobbed by thousands of customers who grabbed up the ninety-five cent dollars and then spent them on merchandise there in the store.

The following day, he ran a second promotion: This time, he sold twenty-five-hundred dollar bills for eighty-nine cents each. Again, the store was mobbed. On the third and final day, he offered to buy back any outstanding dollar bills at a dollar and thirty-five cents each. However, there was a catch—the bills had to have the right serial numbers. Again, the store was packed with people eager to take a chance that their dollar bill would have the correct serial number and earn them an easy thirty-five cents. Of course, there were no matching serial numbers, since Doc Webb had all those bills at home in his safe.

If dollar-bill promotions didn't do the trick, Doc Webb tried something else. *Cosmopolitan* magazine once sent a reporter to Webb's City. The resulting story told of a hoochie-coochie show in the cafeteria, of sales people hawking women's underwear at the cigar counter, and an outdoor show that featured Doc Webb himself in a three-ring circus "cavorting in a high wire act with a galaxy of pretty and daring young ladies."

It is impossible to measure the combined effect that Carl Sedlmayr and Doc Webb had on Tom Parker. He soaked it up, every nuance, taking some ideas intact, merging others with bits and pieces of his own experiences, throwing away nothing. Without the inspiring influences of Sedlmayr and Webb, it is unlikely there ever would have been a Tom Parker, at least not the one who later revolutionized the entertainment industry.

By 1938 Parker had tired of traveling with Royal American. The work was hard and offered little financial security. He notified the front office that he would not be returning for the next season. Not much is known about Parker's activities between 1938 and 1940, except that he was successful in getting work promoting personal appearances for a variety of performers, including California-based pop singer Gene Austin, motion picture star Tom Mix, and country artist Roy Acuff.

For the most part, that meant passing out leaflets, schmoozing with radio announcers and newspaper reporters, and coming up with ideas for ticket giveaways or in-store, Doc Webb–like promotions in which the artist made appearances to sign autographs. That was hardly enough to qualify for a full-time job, so he took on a variety of day jobs of a more mundane nature.

With news of the Nazi defeat of the French, Congress passed a law in 1940 that must have shaken Parker. The Selective Service Act established the first American military draft since 1918. All men between the ages of twenty-one and thirty-six were required to register with local draft boards. In time, each man would be ordered to report for a physical examination. Those who passed the examination would be inducted into the armed forces for one year of military service.

On October 16, 1940, Parker went to the Selective Service office in the First National Bank Building and filled out the required registration papers. On the form he described himself as having brown hair, blue eyes, and a light complexion. He said he had no obvious physical characteristics that would aid in identification. Required to list an employer, he gave singer Gene Austin of Hollywood, California.[15]

At that time, he and Marie were still living with her parents at 1210 West Platt Street, so after four years there must have been considerable pressure from his in-laws to find a job and support his family. The newly enacted draft law was an added incentive. Working as a part-time promoter was hardly the type of job that would keep him out of military service. He needed a job that would make him appear useful to the community.

Early in 1941, he found a job with the Tampa Humane Society as its field agent. The most attractive aspect of the offer was the free apartment that went with the job. Parker, Marie, and Robert moved into the apartment, which was located on the second floor of the shelter, and set up housekeeping.

What Parker really wanted to do was to become a full-time entertainment promoter. The animal shelter was conveniently located on North Armenia Avenue and afforded him a base from which to pursue his other interests.[16] His first challenge, which he apparently issued to himself, was to come up with a promotional scheme to help the shelter obtain more public support. His best idea was for the Humane Society to provide a pet cemetery for area animal lovers who wanted to give their pets a dignified resting place. Whether Parker created the concept himself or stole it from someone else is unclear, but it proved to be a very successful promotion.

Throughout 1941 it was uncertain whether the United States would enter World War II. Parker did not hear from the draft board again all year. Then, on December 7, 1941, the Japanese attacked Pearl Harbor, an act that ensured the entry of the United States into the war. One month after the attack, on January 8, 1942, the Tampa draft board sent Parker another questionnaire to complete. Coincidentally, it was mailed on the very day Elvis Presley was celebrating his seventh birthday in Tupelo, Mississippi. Parker waited nearly two weeks to return the questionnaire.

Based on the information he provided, the board assigned him a III-A classification. That meant he was being deferred because he was married and had a child to support. Parker didn't hear from the draft board again until the following February when he was reclassified I-A, which meant he was now considered available for military service.[17]

Why the draft board would reclassify him is a mystery. All married men with children were exempt. At the end of 1943 that exemption would be eliminated for everyone, but at the time Parker was reclassified it was still in effect. The most likely explanation is that the board checked out his questionnaire and was unable to find proof that he and Marie had been married as he had claimed. There is no record of their marriage in Tampa, and to this day no one has ever found a marriage registration for Thomas and Marie Parker.

The next time Parker heard from the draft board, it was to report for his pre-induction physical.[18] War casualties mounted rapidly throughout 1943 and the end of hostilities was nowhere in sight. Parker had a wife and a child to support, and he was working day and night to save the lives of poor defenseless puppies. Surely, that would be enough to keep him out of the army. He was much too old to be playing war games.

2

ON THE ROAD WITH
HANK AND EDDY

In the winter of 1943, Tampa was invaded by an MGM film crew that had come to shoot scenes for an upcoming Spencer Tracy movie, *A Guy Named Joe*. Tracy portrays a wartime pilot who dies and then becomes the guardian angel to a younger pilot. Also starring in the film were Irene Dunne and newcomer Van Johnson.

At that time, Tracy was just about the only major star left in Hollywood. Clark Gable, Robert Taylor, James Stewart, and Robert Montgomery had all volunteered for the army. With so many actors in uniform, MGM cut back its production log to only two dozen movies a year. Tracy turned down many scripts that year before he read Dalton Trumbo's screenplay for *A Guy Named Joe*. It was a sentimental, flag-waving story that appealed to Tracy's sense of patriotism.

Although Trumbo was the "king" of patriotic movies (later that year Tracy, Johnson, and Trumbo worked together on *30 Seconds over Tokyo*), he was subsequently called before the House Committee on Un-American Activities and grilled about his alleged ties to the Communist Party. He refused to answer the committee's questions and was convicted of contempt of Congress. After he got out of jail, he was blacklisted for years, and wrote screenplays under assumed names.

MGM chose Tampa for *A Guy Named Joe* because MacDill Air Force Base was located on the southern perimeter of the city.

MacDill was the only primary army training center in Florida and the military was eager for movie companies to use its facilities. It was good publicity and helped the army in its recruiting efforts.[1]

One day the movie's production manager strolled into the Tampa Humane Society and asked Tom Parker if he had any dogs he could borrow for a few scenes. Parker was elated. Not only would he not charge him for the use of the dogs, he would accompany them to the base and make sure they stayed in line and obeyed orders. Although he was only the lowly dogcatcher in the eyes of the movie people, the experience gave Parker his first glimpse of big-time show business, and set his soul on fire.

As 1944 began, it looked as though Tom Parker would be drafted. The fighting in Europe and the Pacific was fierce, chewing up men by the boatloads. The Tampa draft board looked at its quotas for March and April, and dug deep into its rolls. On March 3, 1944, the board sent Parker a letter ordering him to report for his pre-induction physical.[2]

The following week he reported to the examining station along with dozens of other men. Records don't indicate where the examining station was located, but it was probably at MacDill. Once he arrived, he was weighed, his height was measured, and he was given rudimentary eye and hearing examinations. An army physician checked his blood pressure and listened to his chest, and took a health history.

Thus far, he had a one-on-one relationship with his examiners. All that was about to change. After leaving the cubicle where the physician had examined him, he was told to take a seat and wait until his name was called. He sat down on a metal folding chair in a roomful of men, most of whom were younger by several years. He wasn't there long before the names started flying . . . *Thomas Andrew Parker*. He fell in line with the other men and went to yet another sparsely furnished room.

The men were told to form two rows, one behind the other, and stand shoulder to shoulder. An army physician barked out orders for the men to drop their pants around their ankles. They were told to spread their feet apart.

Unless the physician had unusually long arms, Parker was confronted by a man whose face was only inches away from his own. Without explanation, the physician began the routine he would carry out dozens of times before the day was over. "Turn your head to the left," the physician said.

Parker felt the physician grab him by the testicles.

"Cough," the physician said.[3]

The purpose of the examination was twofold: First, to determine if the movement of his testicles during his cough indicated he had a hernia; second, to find out if any of the men acquired erections when they dropped their pants in the presence of other men. Before he left the examining station that day, Parker knew he had one of the most sought-after classifications a man could get. He was classified 4-F, which meant he was rejected for military service for "physical, mental or moral reasons."[4]

A physical disqualification would have been based on any number of ailments. Mental disqualifications were based more on emotional problems than actual mental deficiencies, although those with exceptionally low IQs were usually passed over. The "moral" disqualification usually was based on the perception that the inductee was homosexual. The reason for Parker's disqualification has been lost to history, since the law requires the Selective Service System to destroy those records after a specified time. However, if Parker was rejected for physical reasons, the physician must have been unusually inept, for Parker lived another fifty-three years after the examination.

Parker's draft board sent him a letter on March 16, officially notifying him of his 4-F classification. In September of the following year, his classification was amended to 4-A, which meant he was considered, at thirty-six, to be too old to serve in the armed forces.[5] Parker had dodged a bullet.

In 1944, one of the most promising up-and-coming country artists was a guitarist from Henderson, Tennessee, named Eddy Arnold. He wasn't a star yet, but he was well on his way. In those days, the career path to success in the music business often began with a stint at a local radio station. Live music was a staple at most stations and it was usually not difficult for an aspiring singer to get a booking.

Arnold made his radio debut in 1936 at a station in Jackson, Tennessee. From there, he went to stations in Memphis and St. Louis, and then back to Jackson, where he became a regular at WTJS for six years. Radio stations did not pay entertainers to perform live; they were expected to do it for the experience it offered them.

To support himself, Arnold played club dates whenever possible, and took a part-time job as a mortuary assistant. His primary job was to drive the ambulance. The undertaker gave him a place to sleep in the funeral home and paid him twenty-five cents for every corpse he could bring in. He was paid fifty cents for each funeral he worked and was paid extra if he put on a suit and acted as a pallbearer.

By 1943, Arnold had attracted the attention of Dean Upson, an executive at radio station WSM, which operated a booking agency named Artists' Service Bureau. In return for a fifteen percent commission, the agency booked Arnold for live performances and allowed him to bill himself as a "Grand Ole Opry" star. Upson told Arnold he wanted to become his personal manager. He offered him a five-year contract, but the singer didn't want to be obligated for that long and signed with him for only one year.[6]

That year *Radio Mirror* ran a feature on Arnold that said the singer was "increasing in popularity with every appearance." Tom Parker read the story and made a mental note to keep his eye on the singer. Arnold didn't have a record contract yet, but there was a definite buzz on the twenty-five-year-old, and Parker thought he had the looks and voice to be a recording star. The following year, Arnold, who began billing himself as the Tennessee Plowboy, proved him right by inking a recording contract with RCA Victor.

Inspired by his brush with the movie business, and relieved that he had escaped the clutches of the U.S. Army, Parker took a few days off from his job at the animal shelter to travel to Nashville. Everyone he talked to in the business had told him that if he wanted to have a full-time career as a promoter he needed to go to Music City and schmooze with the heavy hitters of country music. He had done some promotional work on a small scale in Tampa for "Grand Ole Opry" stars Ernest Tubb and Roy Acuff, and that was enough to get him in the door of the Ryman Auditorium.

The "Grand Ole Opry" had been on the air since 1925, though when it first started, it was named the "WSM Barn Dance." Because WSM was an NBC affiliate, it received several hours of programming from New York. In return, the radio station fed several shows a week to the network, all of which featured popular music and big orchestras. The most popular show was "Sunday Down South," which featured Dinah Shore and Snooky Lanson.

On Saturday night, NBC's big offering was its "Music Appreciation Hour," which featured classical music and opera. As a counterpoint, WSM offered "Barn Dance" immediately after the network feed. One night, while making fun of the serious music featured on the network show, the WSM announcer introduced the "Barn Dance" as the "Grand Ole Opry." The name stuck, and when WSM later increased its broadcasting power from 1,000 watts to 50,000 watts, the "Grand Ole Opry" could be heard in homes across most of the nation.

WSM station owners caught a lot of flack from their friends for airing the show, since many people in Nashville thought it presented the city in a bad light; but the show proved to be enormously successful outside the Nashville area and soon country music fans were flocking to the city to hear their heroes in person. For that reason, the "Opry" quickly outgrew the radio station facilities. WSM tried out several new locations, including the War Memorial Building, before finding a permanent home for the "Opry" at the Ryman Auditorium.

As luck would have it, on the Saturday evening Parker visited the Ryman, Eddy Arnold was scheduled to perform in a pre-show program that preceded the "Grand Ole Opry" broadcast. Or maybe it wasn't luck. Maybe Parker planned his visit to coincide with Arnold's performance. Whatever the logistics of the meeting, Parker introduced himself to Arnold and told him that he thought he could do the singer some good as a promoter. Arnold was impressed by Parker, but sometimes found his guttural accent hard to follow.[7]

While in Nashville, Parker found out that the "Opry" planned to sponsor a traveling tent show to promote the program and its sponsors in small towns across the South. The show would feature four acts, including Eddy Arnold, and would take place in a circus-type tent. Parker told the "Opry" management that type of show was right up his alley, for he had been trained in the art of carnival entrepreneurship by the master himself, Carl Sedlmayr.

Parker was hired on the spot. He returned to Tampa, quit his job at the Humane Society, and acquired a secondhand truck that was large enough to carry the equipment he needed—posters, glue buckets, brushes, etc.—and comfortable enough to sleep in while he was out on the road. Then he hired his assistant at the shelter, a man named Bevo, to be his assistant promoter.

When the tent show arrived in Florida, Parker pulled out all the stops and worked tirelessly to promote the entertainers. His job was to arrive in town several days ahead of the show and plaster posters anyplace they would be noticed. He was also expected to establish relationships with local radio stations and newspapers, and to stimulate interest in the show. If there was a good turnout, Parker would take credit for it. If the crowds were sparse, he would have an explanation ready about how it was someone else's fault.

Traveling with him in the rambly-shambly old truck, which he had painted bright yellow, was his assistant Bevo, who overnight had gone from assistant dogcatcher to assistant concert promoter. In his autobiography, *It's a Long Way from Chester County*, Eddy Arnold described Bevo as a circus roustabout who impressed him as a real character. "He thought he was a real dude, a ladies' man, and he'd show up wearing all kinds of odd things other people had thrown away, like pants that were too big or too short, jackets with shoulders that almost drooped down to his elbows, or colors that didn't go together," Arnold said. "He was a real ladies' man, too, just the way some men are drinkers and some gamblers, and that used to get him in all kinds of trouble."

Bevo's job was to collect the posters that Parker had put up so that they could be recycled. Sometimes he would disappear for days at a time. Usually it had something to do with some woman he met on the road. Bevo liked to tell women that he was Eddy Arnold's manager; sometimes the women believed him and ran off with him to the next town, only to run back home to mother when they discovered he had lied and was little more than an assistant roadie.

All of which aggravated Parker to no end, for he always needed the posters for the next town; but, according to Arnold, Parker had a hard time staying mad at Bevo. Each time he pulled one of his disappearing acts, Parker yelled at him and told him how he was letting everyone down. Then, because Bevo obviously wasn't carrying a full load, Parker ended up patting him on the shoulder and telling him to get back to work.

By all reports, Parker was a fearless promoter. In one town, so the story goes, he drove past a live radio broadcast where a local band was performing at an outdoor remote. In between songs, Parker dashed from his truck, leaped up on the stage, took over the microphone, and told the listening audience that they were missing a *really* good entertainer named Eddy Arnold at the tent show across town. By the time the microphone was wrestled away from him, he had said everything he wanted to say, stealing minutes of valuable air time for his client.

Arnold appreciated his efforts and told him so.

When the two-week tour was over, Parker told Arnold he wanted to be his manager. Arnold said he already had a manager, but the contract was running out next year. Parker asked if he was happy with his management. Arnold said he had signed a recording contract with RCA but had not yet recorded anything. His income with a manager was not much different than it had been without a manager.

Parker told him what managers have always told potential clients, that people all up and down the line were robbing him blind, stealing nickels and dimes that added up to real money. If he were Arnold's manager, Parker would cut out the middlemen and look after the singer's money. *"Boy, I'll make you a star!"* That sounded just fine to Arnold.

In December 1944, RCA booked a recording session for Arnold. The two songs recorded that day, "Mommy, Please Stay Home with Me" and "Mother's Prayer," were released the following month. The record did very well by 1945 standards, selling out all 85,000 copies pressed. Arnold was elated. Two other records released that year, "Many Tears Ago" and "Cattle Call," did not sell as well, but Arnold was off to a good start with his recording career, and he knew it.

☆   ☆   ☆

Throughout 1944 and into 1945, Parker continued to work as a freelance promoter for the "Opry" acts that toured Florida. During that time, the "Grand Ole Opry" management pressured him to move to Nashville, but he always had a reason to decline. Not until September 1945, when the Tampa draft board sent a letter notifying him that he had been reclassified 4-A—too old for military service—did he feel free to leave Florida.[8] The last thing he wanted to do at that point in his life was to make waves with the draft board.

The 4-F classification he had throughout 1944 was a good one to have, for it kept him out of the army, but it was a classification that was subject to change. Once a man was classified 4-A, there was no going back: Too old was too old.

In the latter part of 1945, Parker and Arnold struck up a management deal. Parker and Marie moved to Nashville, and actually moved into the house with Arnold and his wife, Sally, for a while. To the Tennessee Plowboy, Parker was an earthy, uneducated man who seemed to have a knack for dealing with people.

"A lot of times people think they're dealing with a rube," Arnold wrote in his autobiography. "'Oh, I can take him,' they decide. They don't take him. He's ahead of 'em before they even sit down across a table. He's sharp with horse sense; he fools 'em. They think, because his English might be faulty (he might say a word wrong here and there), 'Oh, I'll handle him.' They walk right into his web."

Right off, Parker proved he had a knack for being a manager. He took Arnold out of the tent shows and the beer halls, and booked him in quality venues. He arranged for him to host a "Grand Ole Opry" segment and made deals right and left for him, little deals that added up to big money. For example, when a theater owner agreed to book Arnold only if the theater received a cut of the sales from his souvenir book, as actually happened, Parker responded by saying that was fine as long as the theater gave Arnold a cut of the popcorn sales. He could always see the angle.

Theater owners were accustomed to dealing with rubes, but they weren't used to dealing with a genius who only looked and talked like a rube. Parker proved during his first year as Arnold's manager that if he had a genius for nothing else, it was as a manager. As a carny, he had learned the importance of two things—details and eye-to-eye contact with the "mark."

He knew that the success of every scam ever devised depended on the manipulation of minute details. He knew that whatever management paid the entertainers on the carnival circuit was peanuts compared to what they earned off the sale of concessions. The same principle governed the music business. For every singer who felt like a big shot because he made a hundred dollars for singing his heart out, there was a concession operator or theater owner who made twice that amount.

Theater owners were not used to dealing with carnies, especially those representing country acts, so if Parker offered to give them a cut rate on Arnold's performance fee in exchange for a cut of the food concessions, most agreed on the spot, thinking they had put one over on him and on the theater owner in the previous town who had not received the same deal.

The first thing Arnold and his band noticed that was different about Parker was his willingness to go out on the road and deal with people in person. Most Nashville managers made deals and set up tour dates over the telephone.

Not Parker. He didn't want to give concert bookers and theater owners time to think about one of his offers. He wanted to be there in person, making eye contact, intimidating them with his size and his take-it-or-leave-it readiness to walk out of a meeting. When you got down to it, Parker was one hell of an actor.

Eddy Arnold was one of the hottest new stars in country music. For the next several years, it was not unusual for him to have two or three records in the Top 10 at the same time. In 1948, he had nine Top 10 records on the charts, five of which went to number one. Money poured in from record sales, from his concerts, from his souvenir sales, and from his song publishing.

Unlike most of the country artists of his day, Arnold wrote many of his own songs. He had learned that the real money in the music business lay in song publishing. That was a side of the business Parker did not understand when he arrived in Nashville, but he was a quick study, and what he learned from Arnold about the publishing business benefited him greatly in later years when he managed Elvis Presley's career.

One of the first things Parker did when Arnold's records started to make the Top 10 was to wean him away from the "Grand Ole Opry." There was no money in it. Why do it? Besides, not only was the show not making them money, the "Opry" management asked for a fifteen percent commission on all personal appearances done by artists who appeared on the show. They reasoned that the performer would not have the personal appearance without the Opry association.

Parker persuaded Ralston Purina to sponsor a fifteen-minute daily radio show, hosted by Arnold, called "Checkerboard Square." The show aired at noon each day on the Mutual radio network. Mostly he sang the entire time, but sometimes he had guests such as Hank Williams and Ernie Ford, and they chatted on-air and took turns performing.

The radio show gave Arnold celebrity status beyond the confines of country music. Ever expanding his client's career, Parker made his first trip to Las Vegas and booked Arnold into the plush Hotel El Rancho Vegas for a two-week engagement. Arnold was stunned when Parker told him. He had played plenty of state fairs, rodeos, and beer joints, but never had he played anyplace as sophisticated as the El Rancho.

At first, he was concerned that the booking would offend his Southern Baptist fans. He had heard that Vegas hotels tried to get entertainers to gamble away their earnings and he told Parker to make sure they understood he would not gamble in the hotel casino. To Arnold's delight, his Vegas show was a success.

He reveled in the attention and in meeting movie stars like Robert Mitchum and Clara Bow. At the end of his engagement, the hotel issued a press release congratulating him on his performance. "He has proven a new theory in our entertainment policy that his folk songs are very much accepted by the Las Vegas public as entertainment," said the press release. "During the past year he has proven our best find and has done top capacity business."

Vegas was everything Parker had ever dreamed of in a city, a true carny's paradise where money talked and kickbacks were an accepted way of doing business. The chrome-plated slots, elegant blackjack tables, and mesmerizing roulette wheels made the dingy, backroom slots of Louisiana look like cheap imitations. Of course, gambling was only the outward manifestation of what made Vegas tick. At a deeper level was an economic system based on P. T. Barnum's dictum that there's a sucker born every minute. For Parker, it was the beginning of a long, satisfying relationship.

The first time Tom Parker went to Shreveport with the Royal American tour, Jimmie Davis was teaching history and social studies at Dodd College, a girls school. Davis had set his sights on a teaching career at an early age, and had earned a master's degree in education at Louisiana State University, but his first and only love was music. He was good enough to pay his way through college by working as a street troubadour.

Shreveport radio station KWKH featured country music on Friday nights. Sometime around 1930, Davis became a Friday-night regular; he was different from many of the other performers because he wrote his own songs. Before long, a talent scout for Decca Records heard him and offered him a recording contract.

Davis's first record, "Nobody's Darling But Mine," was a modest success and enabled him to form a band to perform in country music venues across Louisiana and Texas. Since Davis could hardly support himself on his meager earnings as a performer, he took a job as the Shreveport city clerk. While serving as city clerk, he continued to perform with his band and continued to make records for Decca. His biggest strength was as a songwriter; in the course of his career he composed over three hundred songs, including the still popular "You Are My Sunshine."[9]

At the urging of his wife, Davis entered politics and was elected Shreveport's commissioner of public safety. Four years later, he was elected public service commissioner for the North Louisiana district, a state office that provided oversight to electric and gas utility companies.

In 1943, he ran for governor, and, to everyone's astonishment, was elected to a four-year term. At the end of the 1944 session of the legislature, Davis joined the lawmakers in singing a rousing rendition of "You Are My Sunshine" from the floor of the House of Representatives. As their booming voices echoed throughout the august chamber, one of the lawmakers released two pigeons named Peace and Harmony. Davis left the chamber to the cheers of the lawmakers, an exit that would have made P. T. Barnum—or Tom Parker—stone-cold proud.[10]

Exactly when Davis and Parker first met is unknown. Parker's yearly visits to Shreveport had stopped by 1938, and he did not move to Nashville until 1945 (where Davis went periodically to take care of business). It seems likely that they met in the early 1930s, when Davis, who had a passion for show business, would have been drawn to the Royal American midway, or Parker, who had the same passion, would have been drawn to Davis's KWKH performances.

Parker and Davis shared more than a mutual interest in entertainment. They shared a fascination with the dark underbelly of American society. Davis's political ascent coincided with the arrival of the Frank Costello–Sam Carolla slot-machine empire in Louisiana. As commissioner of public safety in Shreveport, it would have been impossible for Davis not to have been aware of the slots and of their ownership. The way it worked, Carlos Marcello did the legwork for Costello, finding locations for the machines and collecting the proceeds. Once he put the machines in place, it was his responsibility to compensate local officials for their cooperation and silence.

Senator Huey Long protected the machines by using state troopers to keep disgruntled local officials in line. When Long was assassinated in 1935, the political hierarchy was shifted about, but not much changed for the lords of the underworld, who saw their power increase with each passing year.

By the time Davis became governor, the boss with the most political clout was Leander Perez, better known as the "Boss of the Delta," and the boss with the most underworld clout was Carlos Marcello, whom Tennessee Senator Estes Kefauver once dubbed "the evil genius of organized crime."[11]

Jimmie Davis was a close associate of Perez and a longtime friend of Marcello. Shortly after he became governor, Marcello, Costello, and Florida mobster Meyer Lansky, opened two full-fledged gambling casinos in Jefferson Parish, southwest of New Orleans. Parker would have been especially interested in Lansky. Not only was he the financial genius behind the mob's investment in Las Vegas casinos, he was linked to the Santo Trafficante family of Tampa, considered by federal authorities to be the most powerful crime family in Florida.[12]

From 1937 up until the time Parker left Tampa, the city underwent what the feds and newspaper reporters labeled the "Era of Blood." For eight years, Trafficante and his six sons fought off rival gangs for control of the Tampa Bay area. By the time Trafficante emerged the clear winner in 1946, his namesake, Santo Jr., had moved to Cuba to set up a string of casinos. That was where he met Marcello, a five-foot-two, barrel-chested pit bull who spoke with a hybrid Sicilian–New Orleans drawl and passed himself off as a simple working man. When Fidel Castro came into power, he closed down the casinos and put both Santo Jr. and Marcello in jail for a short while.

After the death of his father, Santo Jr. formed a partnership with Meyer Lansky and introduced him to Marcello. The three of them pretty much had a lock on illegal gambling from Texas to Florida and up into the Mississippi Delta. With Lansky on their team, they could claim a foot in the door of legalized gambling in Las Vegas.

Of the three, it was Marcello who had the most fearsome reputation. Legend has it that New York Mafia don Vito Genovese, who could travel anywhere in America he chose without difficulty, always made it a point to telephone Marcello before traveling to New Orleans.[13]

In those days, it was customary in most southern states for the governor to bestow the title of "Colonel" upon his biggest supporters. It was an honorary title, but, depending on the state in which it was issued, it opened doors for those who held it. In Tennessee, it had little meaning, but in two states—Louisiana and Mississippi—it carried considerable weight, particularly with law enforcement officers. If you were a Colonel in either of those states, you could pretty much get away with anything just short of murder (and even that was not out of the question).

In 1948, the final year of his first term, Governor Davis knighted his friend Tom Parker as an official Louisiana "Colonel." It was a public way of saying "My friends are your friends." On the way to the investiture, Parker, recognizing the public relations value of the commission, told an associate, "From now on, see to it that everyone addresses me as the Colonel."

The "colonelization" of Tom Parker was not the only historically significant event of 1948 in Louisiana. It was also the year that Governor Jimmie Davis's musical alma mater, Shreveport radio station KWKH, launched a weekly show named "Louisiana Hayride." It was broadcast on Saturday evenings from the Shreveport Municipal Auditorium, a 3,800-seat building on the fringe of the city's business district.[14]

Patterned after the wildly successful "Grand Ole Opry," the "Hayride" offered three hours of live entertainment in a variety show format that featured up-and-coming country artists, comics, and an emcee with a bag full of well-written ad-libs. They performed from a traditional auditorium-style stage in front of a backdrop that featured a swampy, bayou landscape that was in keeping with the state's tourism theme.

A regular feature was a quiz segment called "Beat the Band." Contestants were pulled from the audience and asked to identify a tune played by the house band, the Lump Lump Boys. If they could name the tune before the music stopped, they won a prize. Since sponsors did not want anyone to go away empty-handed, those contestants who failed to guess the right tune were given a second chance. The second song played was always "You Are My Sunshine."

The strength of the show was its musical talent. Typically, the "Hayride" chose newcomers eager for the exposure. They were signed for one year at union scale and brought back every weekend. In its first year of operation, the "Hayride" signed a large cast, including Johnny and Jack and the Tennessee Mountain Boys with Miss Kitty Wells, Tex Grimsley and the Texas Playboys, and the Four Deacons.

Then one day the "Hayride" hit paydirt.

Four months into the show, a young man pulled up in front of the auditorium in a battered old car that was filled with all his belongings. Also in the car were his wife and stepdaughter. All he wanted, he said, was the opportunity to show folks at the "Hayride" what he could do. That man was Hank Williams, and before going on to bigger and better things, he gave the "Hayride" a musical identity that allowed it to be competitive with the "Opry." His raw musical style and emotional honesty made him an immediate audience favorite and resulted in packed auditoriums. Williams stayed with the show until June 1949, then moved to Nashville and joined the "Opry."

With 50,000 watts of broadcast power, the "Hayride" could be heard all the way to New Mexico to the west and up into Arkansas and Mississippi to the north. That was a good start, but KWKH producers were ambitious and soon put together a network that extended the show's influence even further. Eventually, CBS picked it up, giving them one show a month at first, then putting it on weekly for half of its three-hour show.

Dropping in that first year to perform as a guest star was a Canadian artist named Hank Snow. He had been a successful artist in Canada since the mid-1930s, when he signed a recording contract with RCA Victor, but he was just beginning to make inroads into the American market in 1948. Until the mid-1940s, RCA Victor had released his records only in Canada.

Because American country artists performed extensively in Canada, they came into contact with new talent that was often totally unknown south of the Canadian border. Ernest Tubb discovered Hank Snow, who performed under the name "Hank the Singing Ranger," while touring in Canada. His talents so impressed Tubb that he put out an industry buzz on the singer and arranged for him to perform in Dallas.

With Tubb promoting Snow at every opportunity, RCA Victor had no choice but to distribute his records in the United States, though they continued to release them in Canada and to promote him as a Canadian artist. With the modest success of "Brand New Heart," RCA Victor took a second look at Snow and by the late 1940s had decided to release his records in the United States.

Two years after his first "Hayride" performance, Snow was a bona fide *American* country music star. He had two smash hits in 1950, "Golden Rocket" and "I'm Movin' On," and, that same year, was asked to become a regular cast member of the "Grand Ole Opry." As a result of his sudden success, Snow moved to Nashville and eventually became an American citizen. He was well thought of in country music circles, and had a reputation for honesty and fair play.

Under Colonel Tom Parker's guidance, Eddy Arnold's career soared. Concert bookings were going so well that Parker took out an ad in *Variety*: "Eddy Arnold and I regret that we have no available personal appearance dates for the season of 1949." That wasn't exactly true. Arnold was heavily booked for the year, but his promotion-conscious manager—Arnold adamantly refused to call him Colonel—always managed to squeeze in a date or two for panicky callers who were afraid they had missed the bandwagon.

It was during this period that the Colonel first met Al Dvorin, the Chicago talent broker who specialized in performing artists, midgets, and trained-animal acts. His office manager was Tom Diskin, whose two sisters sang with Pee Wee King, a popular country artist Dvorin booked. When King went out on the road with Eddy Arnold, Diskin gave Dvorin four weeks' notice and joined his sisters. That was when Diskin met Parker and decided to work for him.

Pee Wee King was not the only Dvorin act that the Colonel booked to travel with Arnold. Bobby Powers and Donna Dempsey were a midget act that caught the Colonel's eye. Bobby played the accordion and Donna danced. "They were a cute midget team," says Dvorin. "Just beautiful!"[15] Parker thought they added pizzazz to the show.

At that time, Arnold's personal appearances were bringing in $4,000–$8,000 a night; his song book, which sold for fifty cents, was bringing in about $40,000 a year; and his record sales were among the highest in country music (in 1948, he earned $250,000 in record royalties). By 1949, he was raking in a cool $500,000 a year. "Bouquet of Roses" became his first million-seller, a remarkable feat for a country artist. With the birth of his second child in January 1949, his personal life was equally satisfying.

Shortly after Arnold terminated their management deal, Dean Upson left WSM Artists' Service Bureau and went to Shreveport to help KWKH start up the "Hayride"; but that did not last for long and soon he was back in Nashville, where he opened an advertising business. As Arnold's success leapfrogged each month, making him the talk of Nashville, Upson grew more and more resentful. Finally, he filed a lawsuit against Arnold, alleging that their management contract was still in force. He said Arnold owed him ten percent of everything he had earned since their contract was signed in 1943.

The lawsuit devastated Arnold, not just because he was a man of his word and was appalled that someone would publicly charge him with a failure to pay his bills, but because he was becoming increasingly uncomfortable with his relationship with Parker. Mixed in with that apprehension was probably an element of self-loathing, for he had agreed to give Parker twenty-five percent—not ten percent—of his earnings, based on Parker's agreement to represent him exclusively.

Arnold had no doubts about Parker's effectiveness as a manager, for that was indisputable, but it was the way in which Parker was effective that concerned him. Whenever the Colonel ran ads—and there were plenty of them—he always put his name next to Arnold's. Everything was always signed "Eddy Arnold and Tom Parker."

Despite his nickname as the Tennessee Plowboy, Arnold was urbane, considerate of the feelings of others, and respectful of authority, a true believer in the southern concept of how a gentleman should present himself in public. He was everything Parker was not, and slowly, year after year, the differences began to grate on him.

Parker was brash, boastful, and at times downright obnoxious. He was a carny through and through, and never pretended to be otherwise. At meetings with RCA Victor executives, he slapped them on the back, stuck funny hats on their heads, and erupted into fits of laughter.

Arnold's explosive laugh was every bit as raucous and unpredictable as his manager's, but it was Parker, not Arnold, who played the part of the country bumpkin. Arnold never knew what to expect, and all he could be certain of was that Parker was out there somewhere in the dark, wheeling and dealing, backslapping and glad-handing, devising new schemes to make his "boy" more money.

Country music had never seen anything quite like the success of Eddy Arnold. No other country artist had ever crossed over to pop and sold records in such large numbers. No other country artist had ever had so much success with love songs. No other country artist had ever enjoyed a reputation as a sex symbol. Women were going crazy over Arnold out on the concert circuit. He was a heartthrob.

Parker was always two steps ahead of everyone else. To get Arnold into the movies, he persuaded the William Morris Agency to open doors for the Tennessee Plowboy. Two movies, *Feudin' Rhythm* and *Hoedown*, were filmed shortly after Arnold's first Las Vegas engagement, and both were released in 1950 to mixed reviews. That led to a half-hour television show for NBC, *The Eddy Arnold Show*. It was little more than an extension of his radio show, but it put his name and face out there for millions of television viewers to discover.

Throughout it all, the Upson lawsuit plagued Arnold. It dragged on year after year, one deposition after another. Fighting with a previous manager made him more aware of his present manager. That twenty-five percent commission was getting bigger all the time. Arnold was making plenty of money, but he had one manager who wanted ten percent and another manager who wanted twenty-five percent, and the federal government was demanding more than half for taxes. It was beginning to look like everyone owned a piece of Eddy Arnold except Eddy Arnold.[16]

Sometime during that period, Parker went to Shreveport and— backed by unknown investors he most likely met through his association with Jimmie Davis—tried to muscle in on the "Hayride." He told the stunned owners that he wanted to take over the show for himself. He offered to buy the show outright, but they wouldn't sell. Parker wasn't used to being told no. He left in a huff. No act of his would ever again play the "Hayride," unless the money was just too damned good to turn down.

☆   ☆   ☆

Tom Parker reveled in Eddy Arnold's success. He had proved all the doubters and critics wrong. He really did know what he was doing. They could call the old Colonel a carny if they wanted to—although he was only forty-two in 1951, he looked much older—but they couldn't argue with success, and his client was one of the biggest stars in America. To Parker's way of thinking, he was the reason for that stardom.

Why wouldn't he think so? Wasn't it he who went to industry conventions and draped a banner saying "Never Forget Eddy Arnold" over a rented elephant's back and paraded the animal back and forth for all to see? Wasn't it he who rented a herd of trained ponies to entertain music executives? And wasn't it he who thought up the multipage, trade-magazine advertisement that depicted Eddy Arnold as a plowboy ankle-deep in mud behind a team of horses?

Arnold had a string of Top 10 records in 1951 and 1952, including "Kentucky Waltz," "I Wanna Play House with You," and "Call Her Your Sweetheart," but he began to spend less time in the recording studio and in concert, and more before television cameras. He spent two weeks on the *$64 Question*, a top-ranked quiz show; made several appearances on Perry Como's popular network show; and hosted *The Chesterfield Show*, its summer replacement. In August 1951 his picture appeared on the cover of *TV Guide*, a clear indication that he had made the transition from country crooner to pop entertainer, something no other country artist had ever done.

As Arnold's celebrity grew, so did his management frustrations. Mixed among his television and personal appearances, and his recording sessions, were stressful meetings with lawyers over Upson's lawsuit. By 1953, it had been four years since the lawsuit had been filed, and with each passing year the depositions and legal confrontations grew progressively more fractious.

When the case finally went to trial, Upson's lawyer made Arnold look foolish for not keeping better financial and tax records, and for a time it appeared that the entertainer was in big trouble. Then the pendulum swung back in his favor when the judge ruled that Upson had altered, without Arnold's knowledge, the contract to make it appear the agreement ran for an indeterminate period instead of for one year.

Finally, in 1953, the judge disallowed the major claims made by Upson and instructed the deputy court clerk to determine what Arnold owed Upson, if anything, for the one year the management agreement was in effect. When the ruling was made, Arnold was in Las Vegas, where he had been booked for a two-week engagement at the Las Vegas Sahara Hotel. Although he did not yet know how much he would have to pay Upson, it was clearly a victory for the entertainer.[17] Booking Arnold at the Sahara was Bill Miller, who had just begun his new job as entertainment director at the hotel. Miller and Parker hit it off right away. That may have been because both men had similar personalities or it may have been because Miller, like Parker, was a Russian Jew, born in 1904 in Pinsk, Russia. Miller, who emigrated to the United States at a young age with his parents, David and Lena, never knew his Russian name. When they entered the country at Ellis Island, New York, immigration officials gave them the name "Miller."

In the beginning of his adult career, Miller thought his niche was as a dancer, but after finding no success as a performance artist, he retired his dancing shoes in 1945 and purchased a nightclub in Fort Lee, New Jersey, named the Riviera. He renamed it "Bill Miller's Riviera" and set out to make it the showplace of the East Coast. Soon he was booking new artists such as Frank Sinatra, Joey Bishop, Dean Martin and Jerry Lewis, and Sammy Davis Jr. It was one of the hottest nightspots in the country.

Bill Miller's Riviera had a good run until 1952, when the nightclub was closed so that a new highway could be built through Fort Lee. When Milton Prell, who had opened the Las Vegas Sahara in 1952, learned of the nightclub's closing, he called Miller and offered him a position with the hotel. Miller bought a ten percent interest in the hotel in 1953 and was named entertainment director. Over the years, Miller became one of Parker's closest friends and most trusted confidants.[18]

The Upson experience soured Arnold on the concept of even having a manager. He had trusted Upson, taking him at his word, and, to Arnold's way of thinking, his former manager had turned on him and put him through legal hell. If a man he had trusted without question would alter a contract, as the judge ruled, what might a man he had never trusted, in this case the Colonel, do to him behind his back?

It all came to a head during the Las Vegas engagement. Arnold, Parker, and his assistant, Tom Diskin, were in the entertainer's room discussing business, when Parker and Diskin decided to take a break and go down to the coffee shop. While they were gone, the telephone rang. The caller asked for Parker, but, according to author Michael Streissguth, when Arnold said he wasn't there, the caller, not knowing it was Arnold who had answered the phone, asked him to give Parker a message: "Just tell him that the show we got together with Hank Snow is doing great."

Arnold hung up the telephone and stormed down to the coffee shop. He was furious. He was paying a twenty-five percent commission for exclusive representation. It was a betrayal of the highest order for Parker to be involved in Hank Snow's career. As he approached the table where Parker and Diskin were seated, he saw them push the papers they were looking at under the table in an attempt to hide them. Arnold delivered the message about Snow and then returned to his room.

"I just ignored him for several days," Arnold said in an interview with Streissguth. "I wouldn't talk to him. But then we came home, and he went away on a trip . . . I sent him a wire."

The telegram told Parker that he wanted to sever their relationship. He asked Parker to meet him at his attorney's office to work out the details. Parker didn't argue with Arnold, but let him know that it took more than a telegram for an artist to terminate a contract with his manager: It took hard, cold cash.

On September 4, 1953, Parker and Arnold met in the attorney's office and formally dissolved the management contract, although Arnold agreed to allow Parker to continue to book him on an independent basis. Exactly how much the entertainer paid Parker to terminate the management contract has never been disclosed, but it must have been a substantial amount for Parker to roll over without a fight.

Afterward, Arnold had nothing but praise for Parker, telling reporters that they had split because they were different personalities. Parker took the same line in his comments, telling *Billboard*, "I'm very sorry to lose Eddy. He's a fine boy. I'm glad that we were able to part pleasantly."[19]

Early the following year, the judge handed down his decree in the Upson case. Based on the calculations of the deputy court clerk, the court ordered Arnold to pay Upson the princely sum of $782.94.[20] Within the space of a few months, Arnold was able to divest himself of two enormous burdens. It was a pivotal moment, but not for the reasons he hoped.

With Parker partly out of his life, Arnold asked Joe Csida to manage him. Csida was a former *Billboard* editor who had left the magazine to try his hand at management and television production. Csida was an able manager, but within a year after Arnold terminated his agreement with Parker, his career had taken a downward turn. By the end of the decade, the Tennessee Plowboy's stellar career was in ruins.

With Tom Diskin as his assistant, Parker set up an office inside the lobby of the WSM studios, though station executives didn't know it at the time. It was the perfect place for them to do business. There was a telephone in the lobby that they could use free of charge and, certainly, there was plenty of office furniture that could be utilized for business meetings with new clients.

Oscar Davis, who had made a name for himself as Hank Williams's manager, also used the lobby as his business office. He had been thrown for a loop by Williams's sudden death in January and, like Parker, was eager to attach himself to new clients. He ended up attaching himself to Parker by agreeing to do promotional work for him.

Actually, Parker had an office in the garage behind his house in Madison, Tennessee, but it was off the beaten path of the Nashville music industry; the radio station lobby served his purposes for the time being. He and Davis took turns answering the telephone. They would respond to the caller by announcing the telephone number. If the call was for Davis, and Parker answered, he would say, "Just a minute," and then hand the telephone to Davis, who repeated the same routine when he answered.

After his experiences with Eddy Arnold, Parker decided the best way to proceed would be to start his own booking and management company, and to sign a number of acts, so that if one of them went south on him, he would have others. He named his new company Jamboree Attractions and put a covered-wagon logo on his stationery that proudly proclaimed, "We cover the nation."

Within a few months, he put together a roster of new talent and started booking shows for Cousin Minnie Pearl, Whitey Ford (also known as the Duke of Paducah), and a young country singer named Tommy Sands who would later find success as a pop star. It was a good lineup, for starters, but what he needed was another headliner.

Always generous to the "old" Colonel, fate stepped in and delivered unto him one of the top solo acts in the city—all without Parker ever lifting a finger. In the fall of 1954, Hank Snow started looking around town for a new manager. He wanted someone who could not only arrange bookings for him, but open doors with television and radio.

Snow was well aware of the success Parker had with Eddy Arnold, so when he heard that they had severed their management contract, he decided to approach Parker about taking over his management. He would later regret not checking into the reasons for the failed business relationship, but, at the time, it seemed like a good idea.

Parker was at home when Snow called, and since the singer lived just a short distance away, the Colonel suggested that they meet in his garage office. When Snow arrived and entered the office, he got the first surprise of what would prove to be a long string of surprises. "Hello, Tom," Snow said cheerfully.[21]

Parker stiffened. "At all times from here on out, you refer to me as Colonel Parker," he admonished the startled entertainer. The meeting lasted about two hours. Much of that time, according to Snow's later recollections, was spent with Parker detailing all the great accomplishments he had with Eddy Arnold. If what Hank Snow wanted was to become a national star like Eddy Arnold, then he had certainly come to the right person, Parker assured him. He would make Snow a star, putting his name up in lights.

In record sales, Hank Snow was one of the top five country performers in the nation. He was just a notch or two below where Eddy Arnold had been at that point in his career, but he wanted more. He wanted to move beyond the pack and challenge Arnold for the top position. Who better to do that with than the Tennessee Plowboy's former manager?

No agreement was reached during their first meeting, but after several more discussions, Parker agreed to act as his exclusive manager on the condition that Snow pay him a flat fee of $2,500 to cover "special services rendered" for the remainder of the year. The commission clause of their contract would go into effect on January 1, 1955.

As the start-up date approached, Parker, who already had pocketed $2,500 from Snow without lifting a finger, offered a new proposal.

Why didn't they merge their two companies, Hank Snow Enterprises and Jamboree Attractions, into a single partnership in which each owned a fifty percent interest? The way Parker explained it, they would make a killing by combining their companies and by using Snow as the headliner for the shows they booked. That sounded like a good idea to Snow, so he agreed.

Then Parker dropped the other shoe. He told Snow that his assistant Tom Diskin owned twenty-five percent of Jamboree Attractions and Snow would have to buy him out before the deal could be consummated.

Snow wrote Diskin a check for $1,225, an amount that represented a twenty-five percent share of Jamboree Attractions. Parker then explained that since the buyout left the company valued at $3,750, Snow needed to write him a check for $1,775 in order for them to become fifty-fifty partners. He wrote the check.

That day, Hank Snow walked out of the garage office the proud co-owner of Hank Snow Enterprises–Jamboree Attractions. He knew in his heart that he was well on his way to mega-stardom—and it had only cost him $5,500.[22]

Parker looked at the same $5,500 and saw something else.

That Saturday, it was oppressively hot, with the temperature hovering near the one hundred degree mark all afternoon. Not until after 6 p.m. would the temperature drop below ninety-three degrees. Most Memphis teenagers, at least those who had the twenty-five-cent admission fee, made a beeline for the city's air-conditioned movie theaters on Saturday afternoons. Few homes in Memphis were air conditioned in 1954, and movie ads that read "Keep Cool and Comfortable" were as effective in attracting patrons as were the movies themselves.

Nineteen-year-old Elvis Presley was no exception. He spent the afternoon in a movie theater, where he caught the mid-afternoon show and blended into a crowd of youngsters in which the median age was probably twelve, if not younger. He had graduated from Humes High School the previous year and, after a couple of false starts, had found a job as a truck driver for Crown Electric. Elvis was out of place in the movie theater.

In those days, it was unheard of for anyone over eighteen to attend a matinee. It was just understood that Saturday afternoons were reserved for the kids. That would not have bothered Elvis, for he was immature for his age and often sought the company of younger kids.

When he got home that day, it was around supper time and his mother, Gladys, told him that he had received a telephone call from a man named Scotty Moore. He had told Gladys that he represented Sam Phillips's Sun Records studio and wanted to talk to Elvis about coming over to his house for an audition.

Elvis didn't need anyone to explain what that meant. He had been by Sam's Union Avenue studio several times in an effort to attract his attention, but thus far had only managed to attract the attention of his pretty secretary, Marion Keisker. Unknown to Elvis, she had been trying for months to persuade Sam to give Elvis an audition.

Sam always had an excuse not to do so, and it was not until earlier that afternoon, when Marion and Scotty went next door with Sam for a cup of coffee, that he finally relented and told Scotty that he had his permission to give the boy with the funny name an audition. Sam had released a record earlier in the year that Scotty and his band, the Starlite Wranglers, had recorded, but the record, a country tune titled "My Kind of Carryin' On," had not done well and Scotty was eager to return to the studio for a second chance.[23]

When Elvis returned Scotty's call, it was Scotty's wife, Bobbie, who answered the telephone. Scotty and Elvis spoke briefly, just long enough to set up a meeting for the following day. The audition would take place on a holiday, the Fourth of July, but Scotty and Bobbie had no special plans, and apparently neither did Elvis.

Bobbie was the first to spot Elvis coming up the sidewalk. He wore a white, lacy shirt, white buck shoes, and pink slacks that had a black stripe down each leg. His hair was slicked back into a ducktail. She let him in the front door, then called out to Scotty, who was in the back room playing his guitar, "That guy's here!"[24]

Scotty asked Bobbie to run down the street and ask Bill Black if he would come over and sit in on the audition. Black played stand-up bass in the Starlite Wranglers with Scotty and was in the habit of leaving his instrument at Scotty's house, where there was more room and no children to torment the strings.

Scotty and Elvis were already strumming their guitars when Bill arrived. Elvis wasn't terribly proficient on the guitar, but his voice was strong and it seemed like he knew every song that had ever been written. Elvis had been singing around town, trying to find a direction for his voice, but he hadn't yet found it and jumped from blues to pop to country. "He sang everything from Eddy Arnold to Billy Eckstine—you name it," Scotty says. "It was uncanny to me how he knew so many songs."

Bill listened for a while, then got up and left.

When Scotty thought he had heard enough, he told Elvis that he would talk to Sam and get back in touch with him. After Elvis left, Scotty and Bill got together to critique his performance. Bill was blunt. "Well, he didn't impress me too damned much," he said. Bobbie, who had been turned off by his appearance, agreed with Bill. "I don't think anyone was real impressed," she says. "He had a good voice and he could sing, but the type of stuff he was singing, he was just like everybody else."[25]

Scotty had a more favorable impression, though nothing about Elvis jumped out and demanded attention. What most impressed him was Elvis's timing. He was able to pace his voice to the music in a way that made Scotty take notice.

Later that day, Scotty called Sam and told him about the audition. He was complimentary of Elvis's singing and of his repertoire, but didn't hype his potential. Sam had two options: He could bring the Starlite Wranglers into the studio and cut a record with Elvis doing the vocals, or he could ask Scotty and Bill to come in with Elvis and repeat the audition so that he could hear his voice on tape. He chose the latter and asked Scotty to have everyone at the studio the following night.

Since they all had day jobs—Scotty worked for his brother at a dry-cleaners; Bill worked at the Firestone plant; and Elvis worked at Crown—they went about their normal routine on Monday. After work they went home, had supper, and washed up, then met at Phillips's studio. It was still hot when they arrived, with the temperature just beginning to fall below ninety degrees. No one seems to remember if the studio was air-conditioned then, but if it was, the noisy cooling units would have been turned off so as not to distort the tape. The studio was hot as blue blazes.

They did it the same way they had at Scotty's house, only this time with Bill playing bass. They started out with "Harbor Lights," a song Bing Crosby had recorded several years ago. Then they did Ernest Tubb's "I Love You Because." Nothing seemed to click. They sounded like a bunch of kids playing what they had heard on the radio.

The more they played, the worse it seemed to get.

Finally, around midnight, they took a break. Scotty went outside for a cigarette. Union Avenue was one of Memphis's main drags, so even at midnight there was a steady stream of traffic past the studio. The last dozen songs they had played had been ballads. Scotty didn't have anything against ballads, but his natural impulse was toward more up-tempo music. It always had been, even when he was a child first learning the guitar.

Back inside the studio, they sat around on the floor, tired, not sure what to do next. Suddenly, in a moment of inspiration, Elvis jumped to his feet and started playing his acoustic guitar, singing "That's All Right, Mama," a blues song recorded by Arthur "Big Boy" Crudup in 1940. But he wasn't exactly "playing" his guitar, he was slapping the strings, going more for a rhythm than a sound.

Bill, who had been sitting on his bass, exhausted, jumped to his feet and joined in. Hearing Elvis's up-tempo riff, Scotty's ears perked up and he cut in with his electric guitar. When they finished the song, Sam stuck his head out of the control room door. "What ya'll doing?" he asked.

"Just foolin' around," Scotty said, not sure whether their sudden moment of madness would meet with Sam's approval.

"Well, it didn't sound too bad," Sam said. "Try it again."

This time, Sam turned on the tape.

After several takes, they listened to the playbacks. No one knew quite what to say. It was good, they knew that much, but it didn't sound like anything else on the market. Finally, Scotty said, "Well, you said you were looking for something different."[26]

Sam didn't say anything right away. He was just as stunned as they were. They looked at him, waiting for him to let them know if they had recorded a record or had merely wasted their time. Finally, Sam told them what he thought, though he didn't say it outright. "Okay, we've got to get a back side," he said. "I just can't take one song down to the disc jockey."

When they went home that night, they were excited about "That's All Right, Mama," but apprehensive about their ability to record another one like it for the flip side. As it turned out, that apprehension was justified. When they returned two days later to Sam's tiny eighteen-by-thirty-two-foot studio, everything they played sounded flat and uninspired.

They left the studio that night without a B-side, but Sam was not overly concerned. He called a friend, Dewey Phillips (no relation), and asked him to stop by the studio. Dewey was the hottest disc jockey in Memphis, known for his weird sense of humor and his obsessive behavior on the air—sort of a milder, 1950s version of Howard Stern.

Dewey loved the song and took a tape copy back to play during his show. And play it, he did—over and over again. By the time Scotty, Bill, and Elvis returned to the studio, Sun Records had received orders for 5,000 records that had not yet been pressed.

Now they knew they had to come up with a B-side—and fast. Based on Dewey's airplay alone, they had become local celebrities. This time around it was Bill who set the creative monster in motion. They were sitting around the studio, talking about what they would do next, when Bill suddenly jumped to his feet and started singing "Blue Moon of Kentucky" in a high, falsetto voice, thumping his bass with all the maniacal energy he could muster.

"Blue Moon of Kentucky" had been recorded as a ballad by bluegrass legend Bill Monroe, but Bill Black sang it fast, driving the lyrics along with a foot-thumping engine. As had happened with "That's All Right, Mama," they knew in an instant they had a record. Elvis took over the vocal, Scotty revved up his guitar, and Sam beamed as he sent the tape rolling. They had their B-side.

Now they were ready to rock 'n' roll.

Marion wrote out a contract for Elvis to sign, but Scotty and Bill were not offered contracts. Sam suggested they work out a separate deal with Elvis. Excited over the release of their record, Scotty and

Bill didn't think too much about the legal niceties of what they were doing. The three of them got together and decided that Elvis would receive fifty percent, with Scotty and Bill each receiving twenty-five percent. Since they needed a name, they called themselves the Blue Moon Boys. Later, it would evolve into Elvis and the Blue Moon Boys.

That same week, Sam expressed concern to Scotty that someone might sign Elvis to a management contract. It was common practice in those days for disc jockeys to demand management of an artist they broke on the air. Sometimes they also asked for a percentage of the song royalties. Sam suggested to Scotty that he become Elvis's manager, at least for the first year.

That sounded like a good idea to Scotty, so he talked it over with Elvis and had a lawyer draw up a management contract. On July 12, 1954, seven days after they recorded "That's All Right, Mama," Scotty went to Elvis's home, where he, Elvis, Gladys, and Vernon Presley signed the future King of Rock 'n' Roll's first management contract.

"Take good care of my boy," Gladys said.[27]

The contract referred to Elvis as a "singer of reputation and renown," and Scotty as a band leader and booking agent. Under the terms of the one-year agreement, Scotty would receive a ten percent commission of Elvis's earnings from personal appearances. Even that was misleading, for ten percent of Elvis's fifty percent amounted to only an extra five percent for Scotty. The contract did not prohibit Elvis from accepting bookings from other sources, which meant Scotty received zero commission if someone else did the booking. Oddly, the contract made no mention of Elvis's earnings from records.[28]

Scotty and Bill were too excited at the time to notice, but all they could hope to get out of the arrangement was their share of the money received from concert appearances. Neither would ever be paid for playing on the Sun Records recording sessions and only Elvis would receive royalties from the records.

That meant they were not entitled to any compensation for the work done on "That's All Right, Mama" and "Blue Moon of Kentucky," or for any other recordings done at Sun Records. As far as Sam Phillips was concerned, Scotty and Bill were persona non grata. His deal was with Elvis, and Elvis only. If Elvis understood that, he never let on to Scotty or Bill, who both assumed they were charter members of a 50-25-25 partnership.

More and more, Tom Parker's makeshift garage office was becoming his refuge. A shake-up in management at WSM resulted in a ban on long-distance calls from the lobby telephone. Although Parker, Oscar Davis, and some of the other promoters who worked the "Opry" talent pool were still allowed access to telephones in the back offices, being stuck in the back wasn't nearly as much fun for Parker, who viewed the lobby as a stage upon which to play the role of the fast-talking manager.

Besides, with Hank Snow writing him checks right and left, he didn't see any reason to knock himself out at the radio station. When he wasn't smoking cigars alone in his office, he spent most of his time networking with music executives and other managers. He didn't go out on the road like he used to, which was a clear deviation from everything he had learned at Royal American. It might have been because of his age, for at forty-five his metabolism wasn't what it once was, but, more likely, it was because most of his work centered around booking artists, not managing their careers.

Hank Snow was the only artist he had agreed to represent as a manager, and that contract wasn't due to kick into operation until January 1955. Parker was in no hurry to begin a more intimate working relationship with Snow. From the beginning, Parker clearly felt an antagonism toward him, though the reason why is not apparent. It may have been a personality conflict, or it may have been because Snow had a green card to live and work in the United States—and Parker did not—and the sight of him only reminded the Colonel of his own secret life and how vulnerable he was to deportation.

Whatever the reason, he played Snow for the sucker, using him, manipulating him for his own purposes, all the while glad-handing him and complimenting him on his wonderful God-given talent. Snow never sensed the contempt Parker felt for him, and was eager to follow his new manager's game plan, doing whatever he asked without question.

Exactly when Parker first heard Elvis Presley's name is unclear, but on July 30, 1954, the Blue Moon Boys played a concert at Memphis's Overton Park Shell, an outdoor amphitheater that catered to family entertainment. The headliner that night was Slim Whitman, one of several country acts booked by Parker's Jamboree Attractions.

Audience reaction to Elvis that night was so strong, with young girls screaming and rushing the stage, that Whitman could not have missed the excitement if he had wanted to, especially with the audience still screaming for Elvis when he took the stage. That type of reaction had happened in the 1940s with pop crooner Frank Sinatra, but he had played large venues in big cities; for it to happen on the country circuit with an unknown singer with a strange first name was astonishing.

Most likely, Whitman communicated directly or indirectly with Parker about what he had witnessed. It wasn't the sort of thing an artist would keep to himself. Another possibility was Oscar Davis, who sought out Memphis disc jockey Bob Neal to get the inside scoop on Elvis. Neal played Elvis's records for Davis and accompanied him to a live performance.

Subsequently, Parker credited Davis with telling him about Elvis, though he was always evasive about when. However Parker first found out about Elvis, whether from Whitman or Davis, it is apparent he knew what was happening in Memphis as early as August, when "Blue Moon of Kentucky" entered *Billboard's* regional charts at Number Three, just behind Hank Snow's "I Don't Hurt Anymore."

Parker knew then he wanted to lure Elvis into his managerial web. Based on the success the Blue Moon Boys had experienced at the Shell, Sam Phillips called Jim Denny, the manager of the "Grand Ole Opry," and talked to him about booking them on the "Opry." Denny told him that he had heard the record and it really wasn't appropriate for the "Opry." Even so, he promised to keep an open mind about the group and said he would stay in touch.

Phillips turned his attention to the "Louisiana Hayride," which by then was also broadcasting from a 50,000-watt sister station in Little Rock, Arkansas. The "Hayride" was interested in booking the Blue Moon Boys, but they required new artists to guarantee weekly performances and to sign a year-long contract. Things were happening so fast, Phillips wasn't sure he wanted to commit Elvis to a long-term contract, so he stalled, not saying no and not saying yes.

Meanwhile, Parker worked behind the scenes to get Elvis booked at the "Opry." He talked to Hank Snow about Elvis, suggesting that he might be a good addition to their joint booking company. Since Snow hosted his own segment of the show, "Opry" management would be hard pressed to turn down someone he wanted to feature, so why didn't he talk to Denny about putting him on the show?

Denny agreed to add Elvis and the Blue Moon Boys to Snow's segment of the October 2 show, but only for one song—and only on the condition they perform "Blue Moon of Kentucky," and not that other song that sounded like something African Americans would listen to on Saturday night.

When Phillips got the call from Denny, he was speechless, a rare condition, then and now, beyond comprehension to those who know him. It had only been a month since Denny had turned him down. Why had he changed his mind?

Well, never mind why . . . the "Grand Ole Opry" was the big time. Aside from a call from the Lord himself, there was no telephone call that could possibly mean more to a Memphis performer than one from the "Opry." Elvis, Scotty, and Bill were beside themselves with excitement when they loaded up the car on the morning of October 2 and headed out for Nashville, a drive of about four hours.

Over the years, much has been written about their performance that day, mainly that it was a disaster that sent Elvis home in tears; but Scotty Moore doesn't remember it that way at all. According to Scotty, the audience was restrained but polite, and while there were no crowds of screaming teenagers rushing the stage, no one in the band felt their performance had been greeted by hostility. Neither did Elvis leave in tears, says Bobbie Moore, who went to Nashville with Bill Black's wife, Evelyn: "He seemed pretty happy to me."

When Sam Phillips returned to Memphis, he called Pappy Covington, the booking agent for the "Louisiana Hayride," and accepted his offer of an eighteen-month contract. Elvis and the Blue Moon Boys—already the name had changed, with Elvis moving out front—would be expected to be there every Saturday night. They would be paid forty-two dollars, with Elvis receiving eighteen and Scotty and Bill each receiving twelve.

Elvis's first performance at the "Hayride" was on October 16. The only thing different about their show for the "Hayride" that night was the addition of D. J. Fontana, a drummer who played directly behind them, hidden from the audience by the backdrop. Drummers were not acceptable to country music audiences at that time, but since some country acts used them when they recorded and needed a drummer to make their performances sound like their records, the "Hayride" kept D. J. on call.

When he wasn't hanging around the "Hayride" on Saturday nights, waiting for his cue to slip quietly behind the curtain, D. J. played the Shreveport nightclub scene. Country music wasn't his first choice, for he had grown up listening to big-band music and the jazz and Dixieland of New Orleans, but a gig was a gig, and he gave every country group that he backed the best that he had. He derived most of his income from the honky tonks and strip joints in and around Shreveport, the clubs that Carlos Marcello controlled from New Orleans.

The announcer who introduced them that night was Frank Page, one of the "Hayride" staffers—Norm Bale being the other—who pressured KWKH program director Horace Logan into offering Elvis and the Blue Moon Boys a contract. "Horace was not in favor of it," says Page. "He didn't see it as country music. We didn't either, but we thought, why not give it a try? We knew they were attracting attention and selling records. We had heard the records. We cajoled Logan into it."[29]

Elvis, Scotty, and Bill met with D. J. backstage before the show. Their newest release was "Good Rockin' Tonight," their most uptempo tune to date. They listened to the record and D. J. decided that what he needed to do, musically, was just stay out of their way. Their music had a natural groove to it and D. J. didn't want to disrupt it.

What surprised D. J. most about the group was that it was comprised of only three people. The first time he heard the record he thought he could hear five or six pieces in the group.

That night, the "Hayride" audience was enthusiastic, though not as boisterous as it would get as Elvis's fame spread. The following month, Bob Neal, who had done some bookings for the group, talked to Sam Phillips about taking over Elvis's management from Scotty. Neal was a big bear of a man, with a broad smile and an easygoing manner, and everyone in the band, Scotty included, liked and trusted him. The possibility that Neal might be running interference, even unwittingly, for a great white shark lurking ominously in the background, never occurred to anyone.

3

THE COLONEL SURVEYS
HIS WILD KINGDOM

January 1955 began prophetically enough, as Memphis was shaken by a minor earthquake. The city rests on the southeastern edge of the New Madrid fault, a ticking geological time bomb centered in New Madrid, Missouri, and extending south to Marked Tree, Arkansas, just across the Mississippi River from Memphis.

Mention earthquake and most people think of California, but the fault with the most violent history is in Missouri, not California. When the next big one comes (and it was overdue in 1955 and is still overdue today), Memphis will be leveled and reclaimed by the surging Mississippi River, say the people who study such things. Memphians understand that their city, for all its past glories, is little more than a temporary state of mind. It could disappear, literally, in the blink of an eye.

By contrast, Nashville is located two hundred miles away and is practically immune to the geological rumblings of the New Madrid fault. Residents there never knew about the 1955 Memphis quake, and even if they had felt its baby tremors, or later heard about it, they would not have cared. The affairs of the two cities have never been closely intertwined.

Tom Parker had delayed, dragged his feet, found excuses, and dreaded it, but the start of the new year meant he was now officially

Hank Snow's manager. He apparently never had any intentions of offering his talents to Snow, as he had to Eddy Arnold, but Snow did not know that and was excited about the new partnership.

Parker's thoughts were on Elvis Presley. As Parker's management contract was kicking in with Snow, Elvis's new contract with Bob Neal was about to begin. Scotty's management contract with Elvis still had six months to go.[1] For the past several months, Neal had been arranging bookings for the band in Texas and Arkansas.

Sam had mentioned Neal as a likely successor, so Scotty knew a change was coming. He had mixed feelings about that. He didn't like being the manager, and never once asked for his commission, but it was the only thing he had in writing that linked him to Elvis and the records they were making. He wanted to be the manager and he didn't want to be the manager. Mostly, he just wanted to play his guitar.

Sometime around Christmas, Scotty found the name and address of a booking agency in Chicago. Whether he wanted to be the manager or not was immaterial. If he was going to hand the contract over to Neal, then he wanted it to be on the heels of a victory, not because he couldn't get the job done. That is the reason he wrote to the booking agency in Chicago. With Neal booking them in Texas and Arkansas, it would be a feather in Scotty's cap if he found a booking for them in a large venue outside the South. He sent a letter to the agency, along with their most recent record, and waited for a response.

In mid-January, he received his answer. "Thank you so much for your letter regarding your artist and while we are a booking and promotion agency I don't have anything at present where I could place your artist," said the letter writer. "There are few outlets for hillbilly entertainers in this area around Chicago."

The letter was neatly typed on Jamboree Attractions letterhead and was signed by Tom Diskin.[2] Not knowing anything about Tom Parker or Jamboree Attractions, Scotty had sent his letter to the office in Chicago, thinking it was the main address for a large booking agency. Actually, the Chicago address wasn't so much a branch office as it was an attempt by Parker to placate his associate Diskin, who lived in Chicago.

At about the same time that he received the rejection from Jamboree Attractions, Scotty relinquished his managerial contract to Bob Neal. Sam had convinced him that it would be the best thing to do for the band. No one offered him any money to give up the contract. No one bought him out. He just handed it over.

Bob Neal's full name was Robert Neal Hobgood, but the shortened version worked better for radio, where he hosted two programs daily for WMPS. He was a well-known personality about town, someone who could help your career if you were in the music business. Like his competitor Dewey Phillips, he was a constant target of promoters and record executives who wanted to get as much publicity as possible for their concerts or records.

One favorite ploy of promoters was to pay radio announcers to host shows in which their artists were performing. That way, they could be certain the announcer would mention the show during his regular radio shift.

Neal first met Parker in the mid-to-late 1940s, when Parker came to Memphis to promote shows for Eddy Arnold. Parker purchased legitimate spot announcements to promote the shows, but he also slipped Neal fifty dollars or so to host the show and to plug it when he was on the air.

"There were maybe three or four who were known as real old-fashioned, hustling promoters—the Colonel, Oscar Davis, J. L. Frank, and Larry Sundrock," Neal said. "My knowledge of [Parker] was that he was always completely straight, not like some of the others who'd promote on a wing and a prayer. The Colonel's philosophy was if you're gonna do something, be able to pay for it when you start . . . His background was as a carnival worker. He was a real hustler and he knew how to get the people out."[3]

Without a doubt, Neal ran interference for Parker in getting Elvis's contract away from Scotty. Whether he knew he was doing it, or Parker simply manipulated him into doing it, is still an unanswered question. Almost everyone who knew Neal liked him as a person. He had a warm personality and an ability to make other people feel important.

The fact that he would take fifty dollars from Parker to host and promote a concert, and see nothing wrong with it, indicates that he would have seen nothing wrong with doing Parker other favors, especially if he was convinced it would be in Elvis's best interests.

Although Parker always denied seeing Elvis perform in the weeks immediately following the Overton Park Shell concert, clearly the Colonel did see him perform. Equally clear is the fact that he became obsessed with Elvis during that time. What Parker saw while lurking about in the background, watching and waiting in the shadows, was the same thing that D. J. Fontana saw when he first met Elvis and the Blue Moon Boys. What struck D. J. about the group was the way in which Elvis, who was four years younger than Scotty, deferred to his bandmate and manager. He trusted Scotty fully, and when questions arose, he made it clear that Scotty—or "Old Man" as he was fond of calling him—was in charge. To this day, that still stands out in D. J.'s memory.[4]

If D. J., who was in his early twenties, would pick up on that, so would the wily Parker, even if watching from a distance. On top of Elvis's respect for Scotty was the fact that he was a navy veteran and had served in China during the bloody days of the Communist Revolution and later during the Korean War.[5] Anyone associated with the military was a threat to Parker. He would never take on a veteran in a head-to-head confrontation. He preferred to work behind the scenes, to defeat his adversaries with guile and cunning, always operating from a safe distance.

On February 6, 1955, Elvis and the Blue Moon Boys were booked for a Sunday performance at Ellis Auditorium in downtown Memphis. It had only been a week or so since Bob Neal took over the management contract, but he wasted no time in setting up a meeting for Sam, Elvis, and the boys with the man he had decided, in his capacity as manager, would be perfect to do the booking for the group—Colonel Tom Parker.

They met at Shorty's Grill, a hole-in-the-wall eatery within walking distance of the auditorium. Neal, Sam Phillips, Parker, and his assistant Tom Diskin were already seated in the cafe when Elvis, Scotty, and Bill arrived. When they were introduced, Scotty didn't say anything about the rejection letter he had received from Diskin a couple of weeks earlier. He could have asked Diskin why he was interested now—and not two weeks ago—but that might have instigated a whole new set of problems, and taking credit for a failed booking attempt was the last thing Scotty wanted to do. Diskin had his own reasons for keeping his mouth shut. He didn't want Parker to know that he already had passed on Elvis. Scotty and Diskin began their relationship with a secret that neither man would ever acknowledge.

Parker and Diskin were there, Neal explained to the boys, because he wanted them to take over the booking and wanted to make sure that everyone was comfortable with that arrangement. Parker, his flinty blue eyes sparkling as he stole furtive glances at Elvis, made a spiel about his past success with Eddy Arnold and his future prospects with Hank Snow, and Diskin backed him up.

Together, Parker and Diskin worked their captive audience like a team of carny barkers peddling a five-cent bottle of snake oil. Bill sat through the introductions, then excused himself after listening to the opening spiel, saying he needed to get back to the auditorium to take care of some business. It didn't take long for Scotty to size up Parker. He had seen hucksters like him by the dozens in Shanghai and scores of rat-infested ports on the South China Sea. He knew nothing about Parker, other than what Neal told them, but there was something in his demeanor that made his skin crawl.

Elvis and Scotty stayed a while longer, then they, too, left to return to the auditorium. Scotty didn't have a good feeling about the meeting, and for the first time he began to wonder about the future of the band. In their absence, Neal, Parker, Diskin, and Sam took care of business. Parker said he wanted to book them for an upcoming series of performances with Hank Snow. Everyone agreed that was a good idea.

Scotty wasn't the only one to leave the meeting with an uncomfortable feeling in the pit of his stomach. Parker had much the same reaction to Scotty, though for entirely different reasons. Scotty wasn't like most of the musicians that he knew. There was something dangerous, wholly unpredictable, about Scotty.

Raised in rural West Tennessee, Scotty was hardheaded and single-minded, the way southern farm boys are apt to be, and while that suggested the potential for a certain amount of down-home gullibility, it also suggested a potential for righteous rage, the likes of which was familiar to every carny who has ever worked the southern circuit.

However, that wasn't what bothered Parker the most: It was Scotty's experience in the real world beyond the shores of the United States that made him uneasy. That, combined with the deference Elvis displayed toward Scotty during the meeting, convinced Parker that Scotty was a threat. The sooner he could be forced out, the better.

Parker wasted no time in getting Elvis out on the road with Hank Snow. Seven days after their meeting in Shorty's, Elvis and the Blue Moon Boys were in Lubbock, Texas, performing on a country music bill with the Duke of Paducah, Bill Myrick and his Rainbow Riders, and Jimmie Rodgers Snow, Hank's nineteen-year-old son.

Two days later, Elvis and the Blue Moon Boys joined the Hank Snow Jamboree in Abilene, and Snow saw for the first time what all the fuss was about. The audience went crazy when Elvis performed—screaming, waving their arms, rushing the stage, doing things he had never seen country audiences do. All of which made him glad he had formed a partnership with Parker. He knew Elvis was under contract to Bob Neal, but with the Colonel now doing the booking, Snow knew it would only be a matter of time before they had the entertainer under full contract.

When Parker suggested they put together a tour featuring Snow and up-and-coming rocker Bill Haley and the Comets, Snow jumped at the idea. The only problem with that, said Parker, was that they needed money to promote the tour. He suggested they each put $15,000 into a special joint account and then settle up after the tour. Snow wrote Parker a check for $15,000. The show was booked in six or eight cities, and sold out for every performance, but when Parker gave him a financial statement afterward, it did not indicate where Parker had contributed his share of the start-up money.[6]

Snow felt he had been cheated, but he let it ride, partly because he was so busy, doing about 250 performances a year, and partly because he simply didn't want to believe the worst. Denial is the first refuge of road-weary musicians out on tour, most of whom would rather sleep than fight.

The success Elvis was having with the Hank Snow Jamboree overshadowed whatever reservations Snow had about Parker. That success was an amazing thing to watch. Despite being the headliner, Snow was as impressed as everyone else by Elvis's strange ability to connect with the audience, even when it got to the point where he had to take a backseat to Elvis and allow him to close the show.

Talent aside, Elvis was just a kid—the same age as Snow's son Jimmie—and it was impossible not to like the boy, especially the way he fielded every question with a polite "yes sir" or "no sir." In the months that followed, Snow often had Elvis over as a guest at his Nashville home, and memories of Elvis and Jimmie out in the backyard taking turns tossing a knife into a tree, a favorite pastime of teenage boys in the South, remained with Snow long after the music had stopped playing.

Once Parker got Elvis and the Blue Moon Boys on the road, he started working on Elvis, telling him that he deserved better than what he had. Once the Colonel had gained Presley's confidence, he hinted that perhaps the young singer needed a better band. Elvis would have none of that, for he, more than anyone else, knew just how important Scotty and Bill were to the creation of the music they made in the studio. But Parker had targeted the band, and even though he wasn't yet the manager, he was plotting and scheming to get Scotty and Bill out of the way.

They had only been out on the road a few weeks when Parker approached the members of the Hank Snow band and asked them if they would be interested in becoming Elvis's band.[7] It wasn't the first time he had done something like that. In 1945, he tried to generate trouble among the members of Eddy Arnold's band, and, when that didn't work, he put them on salary, which led to the resignation of two members.

Hank Snow's band wasn't interested in Parker's suggestion, and told him so. It was a ludicrous suggestion to make to a hardcore country band anyway. They didn't play rock 'n' roll. The band members told Scotty and Bill about Parker's overture, quickly confirming their suspicions about Parker. Said Scotty: "We knew from day one the Colonel didn't want us around. It became obvious as it went along. I had Elvis's ear, and he didn't like Elvis's friends being around."

Hank Snow's band also gave Scotty and Bill another interesting bit of information: They had heard rumors that the Colonel was an illegal alien. For some reason, that news didn't surprise either of them. As long as he got them bookings, they didn't care what country he was from.

What Scotty and Bill—or anyone else, for that matter—didn't notice at the time was how skittish Parker was about Memphis. He was
fearful of the city. He didn't go there any more than was absolutely
necessary to take care of business. You could probably count his lifetime visits to the city on two hands, with five or six of those visits being with Royal American during his carny years. There is no record of
him ever taking his wife Marie there during the fifty-plus years of
their marriage.

In one of those ironies that are so dear to historians, E. H. "Boss"
Crump died in 1954 at more or less the precise moment that Elvis
and the Blue Moon Boys stepped onstage for their first performance
at the "Louisiana Hayride." While it signaled a cultural changing of
the guard, it had no effect on the powerful Memphis underworld,
which remained as strong as ever. By the mid-1950s, Memphis was no
longer branded the "murder capital of America," but the sheer volume of crime in the city was staggering.

What Parker had not learned about Memphis during his visits with
Royal American, he would have learned from the Dixie Mafia in
Louisiana. Any city that could stop Carlos Marcello and Santo Traffi-
cante at an imaginary line drawn across the middle of the Mississippi
Delta could do what it wanted with the likes of a Tom Parker—and
he knew it.[8]

What made the Memphis underworld unique was its ability to use
political influence to have the government act as its enforcer. Want
trouble with the IRS? Then tangle with the Memphis group. Want
someone deported? The Memphis group will take care of it for you.
Do you have a rival who has a large shipment of heroin coming into
the country? Someone you'd like to see the feds bust? Well, everyone
knew who to call.[9]

By contrast to the growing influence of the Memphis group, the
Dixie Mafia was undergoing hard times. Mostly as a result of Tennessee Senator Estes Kefauver's hearings on organized crime, Marcello was issued his first deportation order in 1953, though he was still
successfully fighting it two years later. That event, more than anything
else, made Parker cautious in his dealings with Memphis, especially
now that his good friend Jimmie Davis was no longer governor of
Louisiana.

☆   ☆   ☆

The first few months of 1955 were some of the most exciting times Elvis would ever know, if for no other reason than that they gave him his first taste of success on the road. Accompanying Elvis and the Blue Moon Boys on many of the early road trips were Bobbie Moore and Evelyn Black, both of whom were stunned by the frenzied adulation Presley received from the women in the audience.

Evelyn recalls one time when she and Bobbie were sitting on the steps of a high school gym, watching the performance from a safe distance, they thought. But when the show ended, all hell broke loose. "[The fans] were swarming and we started down the steps and we barely made it," she says with a laugh. "They were like a herd of cattle. It was fun, though. When Elvis said good-bye, they pulled his shirt off and all that stuff. He signed one lady's boob."[10]

Tom Parker didn't make a good first impression on either of the wives. "He was a hard-boiled man, I thought," says Evelyn. "I don't think he associated with too many people on a personal level. I never saw him sit down and talk to Scotty or Bill."

"I thought he looked like a clown," says Bobbie. "He used to be a carnival barker and he dressed the part. He looked like a carnival guy, but acted like a businessman. I never saw him laughing or having a good time. He told Scotty he was paying a lot of income tax. The more he had to pay, the better he liked it."[11]

When the Hank Snow Jamboree tour ended, Parker put Elvis in shows with other artists he was booking—the Duke of Paducah, and Mother Maybelle and the Carter Sisters. June Carter, who later married Johnny Cash, has memories of sitting backstage and changing Elvis's guitar strings. He was rough on a guitar, the way he flailed away at it, and it was rare to see him end a set without at least a couple of busted strings.[12]

It was at one of those shows that Parker first met Gladys and Vernon Presley. Elvis and the Blue Moon Boys had swung through Arkansas and played dates in Camden, Hope, and Pine Bluff before arriving for a Friday night show in Texarkana. The next morning they would head down to Shreveport for their weekly booking on the "Hayride."

Apparently, it was a brief meeting, just long enough to say hello and to evaluate them. He just wanted to get his foot in the door. The first part of his plan had already been set in motion. Noticing the friendship developing between Elvis and Hank Snow, he asked his partner to put in a good word with Elvis about him as a manager.

Snow did as he was asked, and at every opportunity he praised Parker as a manager, telling Elvis how successful the Colonel had been with Eddy Arnold. Snow told him that, when his contract with Bob Neal ran out, he hoped Presley would sign with their agency, Hank Snow Enterprises–Jamboree Attractions. Elvis said that anything Snow and Parker could work out with his parents would be fine with him. That was all Parker needed to hear.

One of the few acts not affiliated with Colonel Parker to join Elvis out on the road was Johnny Cash and the Tennessee Two. Cash was tossed into the pot by Sam Phillips, who had signed him to a recording contract. His first release, "Hey Porter," backed by "Cry, Cry, Cry," was a big regional hit, as was the follow-up, "Folsom Prison Blues."

June Carter remembers Elvis playing "Cry, Cry, Cry" on the jukeboxes every time they stopped for lunch or dinner out on the road. Elvis liked the record so much, she says, that he used it to tune his guitar. June hadn't met her future husband yet, but the fact that Cash's music fascinated Elvis was enough to make her want to meet him; later that year she encountered Cash for the first time at the "Grand Ole Opry," and they've been together ever since.

The bass player with the Tennessee Two was Marshall Grant. As a result of touring with Elvis during those first few months of his career, they became close friends and stayed in contact over the years. Grant went on to become a top-ranked manager in his own right, and has directed the careers of the Statler Brothers for many years.

The energy Elvis generated onstage impressed Grant. It was a sight to behold. The person who did not impress him was the man lurking in the background, Tom Parker. "He should have been with some circus act somewhere," Grant says. "That's where he started, with dancing chickens or turkeys. I think he ought to have stayed there. He always had that hat on and that cigar stuck in his mouth and he walked around sort of cocky, and frankly I never did pursue a friendship with him. When I was there, he was there, and that's the way it was. . . . When Elvis started having to close the show with Hank, that was what started it all. The Colonel saw something in Elvis then. He was knocking the people out of their seats and selling the majority of the tickets on the Hank Snow tour. That's when [Parker] started working on Vernon."[13]

The Parkerization of Elvis Presley had begun in earnest by summer, with the Colonel coordinating a series of sly moves, the execution of which demanded consummate skill and precision. His first challenge was to endear himself with Vernon and Gladys. He got off to a good start in Texarkana, then faltered in subsequent encounters out on the road.

At one meeting in Tampa, he had papers prepared for Vernon and Gladys to sign making him a "special advisor" to Elvis. Vernon was ready to sign, but Gladys put him off, saying she was in no hurry. All of which disturbed Elvis, who told his mother that Colonel Parker was just the type of person he needed to manage his career.

To get over the hump, Parker enlisted the aid of Hank Snow. His public image was as a clean-living Christian man who knew right from wrong, and endeavored to do the right thing in both his public and private life. That was the way most people saw him, including Vernon and Gladys. And it was pretty close to the truth.

Parker's second challenge was how to extricate Elvis from Sam Phillips and Sun Records. Logically, the Colonel would want to see Elvis sign with a larger label, one based in New York, and that certainly figured into the equation. More to the point was his fear that the Memphis underworld, for which he had a healthy respect, would decide to add Elvis to its trophy case. If that happened, Parker knew he was history.

That summer, he received a visit from Arnold Shaw, the newly named manager of the E. B. Marks Music Corporation in New York. They met at the Andrew Jackson Hotel in Nashville to talk business and Parker was impressed enough to invite him to his house for dinner, something he rarely did. He liked to keep his wife, Marie, away from his professional contacts, and she was seldom involved in his business affairs.

Parker played Elvis's records for him on a phonograph in his garage office, but Shaw had never heard of the singer or Sun Records. One of the records the Colonel played for him was "Mystery Train," a song that had been recorded in July. Shaw listened to the record with interest and expressed surprise that the singer was a white kid. He thought it sounded like a blues song and naturally assumed that the person singing it was black. That confused him, but no more than the fact that a successful manager of country music acts spoke with a Dutch accent.

Parker told him that Elvis was under contract to Bob Neal of Memphis, but he expected to have control of the contract before much longer. "No one's heard of him north of the Mason-Dixon line, but I'm not snowin' you when I tell you that he's the biggest thing that's hit the South in years," he told Shaw in a conversation Shaw reconstructed years later for *Billboard's The World of Country Music*. "In Florida and Georgia, the girls are tearin' the shirt off his back."

Parker had Vernon and Elvis in his corner, but Gladys was concerned about all the criticism Elvis had received during the Florida tour and she wasn't convinced that the fast-talking Parker had her son's best interests at heart. That was the reason Parker was trying to get them to agree to a contract making him "special advisor." By doing it in increments, he felt he had a better chance of winning over Gladys.

Hank Snow was Parker's ace in the hole, and he knew that if anyone could counteract the "evil influences" of the music industry that concerned Gladys, it was Snow with all his talk of faith, redemption, and the everlasting love of a forgiving God. Parker was a manipulative genius, but he knew that convincing a mother of his own godly virtues was beyond even his considerable talents.

As early as July, according to Snow, Parker was talking with RCA Victor executive and producer Steve Sholes about getting a recording contract for Elvis. Snow himself telephoned Sholes several times about Elvis. Sholes was a large, friendly man with a round face who had made talent excursions to Nashville from New York on a regular basis for RCA since the 1930s. Before he succeeded in persuading

RCA to open an office and a studio in Nashville, he shared studio space with the Presbyterian Church. That relationship ended abruptly when a church member found an empty vodka bottle in the studio and accused Sholes of being a Communist.

Sholes liked what he heard about Elvis. In one memorandum signed by Parker, Snow, Bob Neal, and Parker's assistant Tom Diskin, all four men agreed to a proposal that would have Parker and Snow paying $10,000 in exchange for Elvis's release from Sun Records and another $30,000 paid to unspecified persons for unspecified purposes.

If Hank Snow and the others who talked to Parker during this period are to be believed, he was telling people within months of Neal taking over the contract from Scotty that he was the person to talk to about Elvis's future. Only a fool would have negotiated with a record company for an artist he was not certain he controlled, and no record company executive would have risked civil or criminal prosecution for unfair business practices, by negotiating with someone he felt was not empowered to speak for the artist—and, certainly, neither Parker nor Sholes was a fool.

It is possible, but not likely, that Neal and Parker told Elvis of their plans, and asked him not to tell his mother, Scotty, or Bill until they had everything in place. It is equally possible, but not likely, that Snow would contact RCA Victor, his own label, on behalf of an artist that was not signed to him.

Obviously, Snow, RCA Victor, and everyone else involved were convinced that Parker, who didn't have a signed contract with Elvis, was in control of his destiny. The only person who could have assured them of that was Bob Neal. To Elvis, Scotty, and Bill, Neal was just about the nicest man they had ever met. He had a son Elvis's age and he played the role of a father to all of the boys in the band. To this day, Scotty is convinced that Neal backed out of the picture because he felt the pace too strenuous, not because of any prior arrangement he made with Parker.

The first evidence that Parker was controlling Neal came in August, when D. J. Fontana was asked to join the band. The arrangement Scotty and Bill had with Elvis was that Elvis was to receive fifty percent, and Scotty and Bill would each receive twenty-five percent.

Scotty and Bill felt that D. J. added depth to the band, and since they had started using a drummer in the studio, they needed D. J. with them out on the road full-time. He performed every week with them at the "Hayride" and did some tour dates.

Elvis's response was that he could not afford to pay D. J. out of his fifty percent, but would agree to do it if Scotty and Bill agreed to pay a share of D. J.'s $100-a-week salary out of their own pockets. Scotty and Bill agreed to do that, and D. J. was hired as a salaried, full-time band member.[14]

No sooner was that done than Neal sat Scotty and Bill down for a little talk. In what will go down as the biggest betrayal in popular music history, Neal informed the stunned musicians that they, too, would have to go on salary.

"But we're partners with Elvis in this!" they said.

"No," Neal answered. "You're not."

"But what about our percentage?"

"Doesn't exist," he told them, reminding them that they had nothing in writing. Scotty and Bill didn't know about the side deals going on among Parker, Neal, and Snow, but, even so, they blamed it on Parker, telling Neal that they knew the carny was behind it. Neal denied that it was Parker's doing. "It became obvious [the partnership agreement] wasn't fair, because Elvis was the star, regardless of the fact they contributed largely to it," Neal explained in 1971 to biographer Jerry Hopkins. "My contract was with Elvis, not with Scotty and Bill. They weren't contracted to me—or to Sun."

Scotty and Bill threatened to quit, but since it was clearly a take-it-or-leave-it offer—and they were having the time of their lives out on the road with Elvis—they finally agreed to go on salary. They would receive $200 a week when they were working and $100 a week when they were not. "That may not have been a decent salary for what we were doing, but at that time it was [decent] for the guy on the street," says Scotty. "The problem was, the guy on the street didn't have all the responsibilities we had."

Neal's assertion that it was his, not Parker's, doing would be more convincing if he, Parker, and Snow had not been acting in concert in other activities, such as approaching RCA Victor. Also pointing toward Parker was the fact that he had done much the same thing to

Eddy Arnold's band. But there was a difference between putting Arnold's band on salary and putting Elvis's band on salary. Scotty and Bill were instrumental in developing the sound that made Elvis unique and they had started out as equal partners.

One can only imagine how Scotty and Bill felt at that moment. For more than a year they had been playing on Elvis's records, sharing in the excitement of soaring record sales, even though they were not paid a penny by Elvis or Sun Records for playing on the records. That did not concern them since they felt they would make money from their twenty-five percent share of the performance fees.

In the back of their minds was a conversation Scotty had earlier in the summer with Elvis, during which Elvis offered to pay them a share of the royalties he received from record sales. That promise, along with a percentage of the performance fees, had been enough to sustain them over some hard times out on the road.

Now all that was gone. They were nothing more than salaried employees and could never hope to financially benefit from the success they knew was on its way. Only one person they knew of was capable of grand larceny at that level, and his name was Colonel Tom Parker. Scotty and Bill never confronted Elvis over their partnership downgrade. It was not in their nature to be confrontational over money issues. Instead, they suppressed their feelings, allowing them to fester.

It took some doing, but the same month that Scotty and Bill got the shaft, Parker succeeded in getting Vernon and Gladys to sign a contract designating him as a "special advisor" to Elvis and Bob Neal for a period of one year. The document stated that his fee would be $2,500 per year, payable in five installments.[15] As a "special advisor" he would be empowered to negotiate on Elvis's behalf. It was the agreement he should have had before he approached RCA Victor earlier in the summer. It was the agreement he had to have to move Elvis over to RCA Victor. At least now the Colonel's courting of RCA was legal and out in the open.

It was at this juncture that Parker probably informed Gladys of his Jewish ancestry. Why would he tell Gladys, who had disliked him at first sight, his deepest, darkest secret? The only explanation is that he had learned Gladys had a secret of her own. She herself was of Jewish ancestry, according to author Elaine Dundy, who based her conclusion on anecdotal information that Gladys's maternal grandmother, Doll Mansell, was the daughter of a Jewish mother.

Elvis's supposed Jewish ancestry was often the subject of debate, sometimes heated, among the entertainer's inner circle. Consider the following exchange among Elvis's cousin Billy Smith, Lamar Fike, and Marty Lacker, himself a Jew.

Fike: "Since, by Jewish orthodoxy, the mother continues the heritage, Elvis was Jewish. If you want to believe that."

Lacker: "Maybe she was a Jewish Indian. No, really Billy could be forgetting there's such a thing as a French Jew. Jews are everywhere."

Smith: "I'm not forgetting nothin'. She's just not. I wouldn't be ashamed of it. There just wasn't any Jewish blood in our family."[16]

As Tom Parker was squirming his way into Elvis's life, Sam Phillips was doing some maneuvering of his own. At the time he started up Memphis Recording Service, he was working as an engineer at radio station WREC. Working with him at the radio station was Marion Keisker, an on-air personality and host of a popular talk show, *Meet Kitty Kelly.*

For a time, Phillips tried to hold down both jobs. When it reached the point where it was apparent he could not do both without risking a complete emotional breakdown, he left his job at the radio station to work full-time at his recording studio. Coming to his aid was Marion, who left the radio station to work for him at the studio.

Marion's official title was secretary, but she was more of a partner when it came to the operation of the business. It was Marion who first discovered Elvis, and it was Marion who used her popularity and media experience to promote the artists who were signed to Sun Records. She was very much a team player, and, according to some people, was head-over-heels in love with Sam.

The one person Marion couldn't stomach was Tom Parker.

When Elvis and his parents signed the "special advisor" contract with Parker, warning bells went off inside Marion's head. "Colonel Tom had been working on the family at least a year, in the most polished and Machiavellian way," she told Jerry Hopkins some years later. "You couldn't believe it. Mrs. Presley, God rest her soul, she was just a mother, was what she was, you know. The Colonel'd go to her and say, 'You got the finest boy in the world and it's terrible the way they're making him work.'"

Exactly when Parker first set his sights on Elvis was hard to pinpoint. Marion said: "I know he started following him around to all his shows and he spent a great deal of time with Mr. and Mrs. Presley, particularly after that show in Jacksonville."[17]

That summer, as his business relationship with Elvis was obviously nearing an end, Sam Phillips decided to start up the nation's first all-female radio station. He had a new slate of artists who were creating a stir of their own—Johnny Cash, Jerry Lee Lewis, and Carl Perkins—but he seemed to want something more out of life.

Kemmons Wilson was a local entrepreneur who, after a successful run as a homebuilder, decided to build a string of motels named Holiday Inn. After all these years, the exact nature of Wilson's friendship with Sam is a bit fuzzy, but sometime that summer Wilson offered to loan Sam money to start up the radio station.

Sam and Wilson housed the new station, which was given the call letters WHER, in a Holiday Inn on Third Street south of Crump Boulevard. To Marion's surprise, Sam moved her from the studio over to the radio station to work as an announcer and news reporter.

Marion wasn't happy about the move, but other than tearing down the front door of the studio, which she had purchased with her own money, she kept her thoughts to herself and relinquished her role as the heart and soul of Sun Records.[18]

☆   ☆   ☆

With everything in place, Tom Parker made his move.

Because of his contacts with RCA Victor, he had approached the record company first about obtaining Elvis's contract from Sun Records. They were interested, but there was opposition within the label from executives who didn't think Elvis was anything other than a flashy hillbilly singer, so they left the decision up to Steve Sholes, their country-and-western specialist.

When it became apparent that Sholes couldn't offer the type of money Parker wanted, he talked to executives with other record labels, most notably Columbia Records. Actually, after picking up a buzz on Elvis, Columbia sought Parker out.

Mitch Miller—a well-known orchestra leader who had made a name for himself as a record executive and producer with popular artists such as Pattie Page and Frankie Lane—was head of the artist and repertoire department of Columbia Records. As the talks about Elvis began, Miller had a Number One record of his own on the charts, "The Yellow Rose of Texas."

With the admonition not to offer more than forty thousand dollars for Elvis's contract, Miller sent Bill Gallagher, Columbia's marketing director, and Dick Link, another executive, down to Nashville to talk to Parker. They met in the lobby of the Andrew Jackson Hotel, a favorite meeting place of the Colonel.

Gallagher and Link made their pitch, pointing out Columbia's history as an industry leader, and Miller's ability to top the charts, even with records of his own. Parker listened attentively, then suggested they meet again the next day.

When Parker arrived the next morning at the hotel coffee shop, Elvis accompanied him. They sat around and talked for a while, then Parker abruptly excused Elvis, saying he needed to talk business with the boys. After Elvis left, Gallagher told Parker that Miller had authorized a forty-thousand-dollar advance if Elvis signed with Columbia. Parker nodded politely, let out a laugh, then told Gallagher that he was way off base. The Colonel, however, would think about it and get back to him. He never did.

Parker didn't know much about music and didn't really seem to care for it. What he did know were deals and percentages—and, of course, whether or not the pea was under the shell. The first lesson Parker learned after moving to Nashville was that the real money was in publishing. He watched Eddy Arnold make as much, if not more, from the publishing rights to his songs as he did from his record sales.

The number Parker had to work with was $40,000—a $35,000 payment to Sam Phillips and a $5,000 advance to Elvis. Columbia had offered $40,000. Atlantic had offered $25,000, and RCA had offered $25,000. Columbia's offer would cement the deal, but Parker received nothing on the side.

Parker went to Hill and Range, a New York song publisher with whom he had dealings while working as Arnold's manager. Since he knew that Hill and Range was in tight with RCA, he made a side deal with them. If they would put up some or part of the remaining $15,000 needed to close the deal with Sam Phillips, Elvis would agree to record only songs that their company owned. In addition, Elvis would agree to sign with them as a songwriter.

Hill and Range agreed to the deal, although how much of the remaining $15,000 they put up and how much was actually put up by a behind-the-scenes investor is still debatable. With what he had learned in Nashville, Parker was thinking ahead, for he knew that if he then set up a publishing company with Elvis and required the songwriters who wrote the songs to list Elvis as a co-author, he could make millions.

In retrospect, Parker's decision to accept RCA's offer was the best thing that could have happened for Elvis's career, though he could not possibly have known that at the time. From September 1955 until December 1959, RCA placed fourteen Number One songs on the pop charts, many of those recorded by Elvis, while Columbia placed only four. A contract with Columbia might have been the kiss of death.

On November 21, 1955, everyone involved in the deal—Colonel Parker, Elvis, Vernon and Gladys, Steve Sholes, Bob Neal, a representative of Hill and Range, and Hank Snow—gathered at Memphis Recording Service to ink the deal. A photographer got shots of Gladys tightly clutching her black handbag while kissing Elvis on the cheek, and another with Elvis standing between Hank Snow and Colonel Parker.[19]

It was not the biggest deal Parker would ever make, but it was the smoothest. As summer turned to fall, all Parker had to show on paper for his association with Elvis was a $2,500-a-year advisor's fee and a percentage of the bookings. But he was set for life—and he knew it. He had big plans for Elvis. Parker was not unlike a chess master who can think three steps ahead of the opposition.

Sam Phillips was in the same situation.[20] He had lost Elvis in the deal, but from the time talks began and the signing took place, he had earned $35,000 in cash, obtained a loan for a radio station from Kemmons Wilson, and was given the opportunity to acquire stock options in Holiday Inn that would make him a millionaire many times over.

The night before the signing took place, Parker called Snow and asked him to come to Memphis so that he could meet with Vernon and Gladys and allay any fears they had about their son signing a new contract. Whether Hank Snow was told Elvis would be signing a new management contract with Hank Snow–Jamboree Attractions that day, or simply assumed it, is unclear, but he went to Memphis with the understanding that he and Parker were entering into a partnership with Elvis.

After the signing, Parker asked Snow if he wanted to ride back to Nashville with him instead of spending the night and catching a plane the next morning. During the three-and-a-half-hour drive, Snow asked him how the signing had gone. Parker told him everything had gone fine. He said he went into the meeting with two different contracts, one in each side pocket of his coat. Luckily, he had just the contract for the occasion. He told Snow they would make so much money they would be able to retire.[21]

Snow went home that day thinking that Parker had signed Elvis to a contract with Hank Snow–Jamboree Attractions. In truth, the RCA contract was the only one Elvis signed that day. The contract Parker had referred to was an agreement he had asked Bob Neal to sign stipulating that out of the forty percent in combined commissions he and Neal were taking from Elvis, there would be an even split until Parker took over the contract in March 1956. As it was, Neal received twenty-five percent and Parker received fifteen percent.

The more questions Snow asked him about the deal, the more defensive the Colonel became, repeatedly saying, "Don't you trust the Colonel?" When Parker dropped him off at his house, Snow had a very uneasy feeling. After thinking about it for a while, he made an appointment with his lawyer and showed him the financial statements Parker had prepared for him. The lawyer told Snow that he was concerned because Parker had not formed a corporation to shield their partnership. Snow showed him the statement for the Jacksonville engagement, and the lawyer suggested they initiate an investigation into Parker's activities. Snow reluctantly agreed.[22]

After they obtained the documents they needed from Jacksonville, they went over the figures, concluding that gross ticket sales had been altered and were not included in the final gate receipts. The lawyer advised him to meet with Parker immediately for the purposes of establishing a corporation.

In his autobiography Snow recalled his lawyer saying, "Parker is a dangerous man, and you could be headed for serious trouble with the IRS, since you are a fifty-percent partner of this agency." Snow telephoned Parker and asked him to come over to his house. When the Colonel arrived, Snow confronted him with his concerns and urged him to set up a corporation. Parker would have none of that. According to Snow, the Colonel flew into a rage and suggested they dissolve their partnership. Snow pondered that suggestion for a moment, then asked the obvious question: "What happens to our contract with Elvis Presley?"

"You don't have any contract with Elvis Presley," Snow recalls the Colonel saying. "Elvis is signed exclusively to the Colonel."

The Colonel was telling the truth, but only half the truth. Elvis was not signed to Hank Snow, that was true. But neither was he signed to the Colonel, though he soon would be. As a result of that confrontation, Parker and Snow severed their business relationship. That may have been the reason Parker offered to let Snow ride back with him to Nashville, so that he could plant seeds of doubt in Snow's mind and provoke Snow into ending their relationship before any contract was signed with Elvis. Snow walked away from that meeting thinking that he would simply sue Parker and get his share of the contract, but his lawyer advised against it. You can sue someone for cheating you, but you can't sue someone for tricking you into believing they have cheated you. By the time Parker signed Elvis, the Colonel and Snow's partnership has already been severed.

Parker may have cheated Snow, but he did it fair and square, under rules set down generations ago by members of the International Carny Convention. The incident understandably left Snow embittered. In his autobiography he wrote that when Elvis died in 1977, Snow watched a videotape that Vernon had prepared to thank everyone for their kindness during his grieving. "His words carried a lot of emotion, and I thought they were well spoken—until he said, 'Tom Parker was an honest man,'" Snow wrote. "With that, I got cold chills."

☆   ☆   ☆

In December 1955, less than four weeks after the historic changing of the guard at Memphis Recording Service, Parker's Louisiana
friends descended upon Memphis, along with dozens of high-ranking
political leaders from all twelve southern states. They gathered at the
Peabody Hotel, a posh watering hole for Delta planters, located on
Union Avenue just up the street from Sam Phillips's studio.

Senator Strom Thurmond of South Carolina was there. Senator
James Eastland of Mississippi was there. Current and past governors
from most of the states were present. It was the largest known gath-
ering of right-wing political leaders and white supremacists ever as-
sembled.[23] The meeting itself was top secret, and newspaper reporters who tried to crack it were treated roughly by guards posted
outside the doors. Before the week was out, the Memphis newspapers and the *New York Times* broke the story, identifying the organization behind the meeting as the Federation for Constitutional Government. What they did not uncover was the true purpose of the
secret meeting. That would not become apparent for more than forty
years.

As the pieces fell into place in the late 1990s, it was learned that
the group met in Memphis to develop a plan to combat racial integration in the south. To accomplish that, they created super-secret
government agencies with the capability to undertake covert mis-
sions. The first state to do so was Mississippi, which created the Mississippi Sovereignty Commission in the spring of 1956.[24]

Louisiana later followed the lead set by Mississippi. Former agents
of the Federal Bureau of Investigation were recruited to organize and
later run the commission. They used the Central Intelligence Agency
as a guide and, for a period of nearly twenty years, operated in almost
total secrecy with the clandestine help of a nationwide network of
white supremacist journalists. One Mississippi lawmaker once described the CIA as a "kindergarten" compared to the commission.[25]

Tom Parker's friendships in Louisiana and his Colonel's title automatically put him in good standing with the commission. There is no
evidence that Parker was ever a financial contributor to the commission or an active participant in its illegal activities, but he knew that

the commission had the power to disrupt Elvis's career, and he made certain that Elvis did nothing to offend commission members.

Namely, that meant tempering Elvis's fascination with African American culture. If Elvis was ever aware of what was occurring behind the scenes, he never confided in his band members. He left the dirty work to the Colonel. He was much too busy learning how to become a superstar.

After signing with RCA, Elvis and the band went back out on the road, playing to screaming fans whose adoration seemed to multiply with each passing day. Parker also went out on the road, only not with Elvis. At the end of November he went to Chicago to attend the Showmen's League of America convention.[26] He never severed his ties with his carny background and continued to attend the conventions for the remainder of his life. In Chicago, he visited with his old friend Carl Sedlmayr and his son Carl Jr., who had himself become a close friend of the Colonel.

While Parker was at the convention, all hell broke loose in Toledo, Ohio, where Elvis slugged it out in a hotel bar with a jealous husband. When the man who started the fight was released by authorities, he told reporters that he had been paid by Elvis to stage the fight. It wasn't true, but it grabbed national headlines and embarrassed Elvis.

Reporters tracked Parker down at the convention and demanded to know if Elvis was paying people to start fights so that he could get publicity for his concerts. Parker blew his stack and screamed at the reporters, his blustery red face blowing up like a balloon as he denied that the entertainer was involved in any kind of publicity stunt. Once he calmed down, he broke out into a smile, rolling that big cigar around between his lips as the silver lining came to him in a showman's epiphany. Said Parker: "Anyway, they've got Elvis's name spelled right."

The first three months of 1956 were chaotic for Elvis as he undertook his first recording session with RCA and made his first network television appearances on CBS's *Stage Show*. Parker saw his boy as prime material for television and the movies, and wasted no time using the connections he had made with Eddy Arnold to open doors in Hollywood for Elvis.

First, he had serious business to take care of. Bob Neal's contract with Elvis ran out in March and Parker had a new one drawn up designating himself as the entertainer's sole manager. The contract specified that Parker would receive a twenty-five percent commission for his efforts.

Incredibly, Neal meekly stepped away from the contract, giving credence that he and Parker had planned it that way all along. Neal explained it this way to Jerry Hopkins: "I simply let it go. The only further thing I received was some small amount of commission and royalties from the initial period. There wasn't anything involved in a continuing commission or share. I hadn't asked for anything and hadn't tried to negotiate anything. I could have, but I didn't."

Once he was firmly in the driver's seat, Parker tightened the vice on Scotty and Bill. RCA was instructed to stop referring to Scotty, Bill, and D. J. as the Blue Moon Boys. Their photographs were dropped from the promotional literature. The Colonel also informed the news media, fan magazines in particular, that if the band members were ever pictured with Elvis in any of the layouts, they could count on losing his cooperation for future projects.

As if all that were not enough, he took the photo concession away from Bill Black, who had been selling pictures of Elvis and the band for twenty-five and fifty cents apiece, making about a nickel profit on each photo. Parker took that nickel and put it in his own pocket.

Parker may have dropped the Blue Moon Boys, but Elvis did not. He continued to introduce them to the audience by that name when they were out on tour. "We knew [Parker] didn't want us around," says Scotty. "It tickled him to death when we decided we wanted to stay in one hotel and Elvis could stay in the other, simply because of the fans coming around. He knew I had Elvis's ear from the beginning. It became more obvious as it went along."[27]

Once asked to describe his relationship with Parker, D. J. said, "I didn't have any relationship with him. . . . We didn't deal with the Colonel. If we needed something, we went directly to Elvis, but he didn't like that. Elvis would say, 'Don't worry about the Colonel.' Elvis would take care of what he said he would. We didn't care what the Colonel did." The band accompanied Elvis to San Diego, California, where they did *The Milton Berle Show* from the deck of the USS *Hancock*, an aircraft carrier similar to the one Scotty had served on offshore from Korea.

Prior to the show, Elvis did his first screen test in Los Angeles. Parker had arranged for him to test with movie producer Hal Wallis, who was famous for films such as *The Maltese Falcon* and *Casablanca*. After the test, Parker and Elvis flew to San Diego for the Berle show. Berle met them at the airport, and as they were driving away, he pulled the contract from his pocket and handed it to Elvis. Before Elvis could take the piece of paper, Parker snatched it from Berle's hand, admonishing the startled entertainer that he had no business giving contracts directly to the Colonel's client.

It was one of Parker's busiest periods. Not only did he steer Elvis toward a movie contract, he booked the young singer on the best television had to offer—in addition to Milton Berle's popular progam, he booked him on *The Steve Allen Show* and *The Ed Sullivan Show*. He also booked Presley for his first appearance in Las Vegas.

With Elvis quickly becoming the hottest recording artist in America, Parker took action to sever the old ties that he felt would hold the entertainer back. The first was the contract with the "Louisiana Hayride." It was unreasonable for the "Hayride" management to expect a star of Elvis's magnitude to honor a contract that tied him down every Saturday night for almost no pay. To get out of the contract, Parker agreed to allow Elvis to play a benefit performance at the Shreveport Coliseum, with most of the proceeds going to the "Hayride."

Elvis and Parker were not the only busy people during this time: in the spring the FBI opened its first file on Elvis Presley.[28] That action was initiated by a Memphis businessman, whose identity the FBI continues to protect. The man wrote to FBI Director J. Edgar Hoover to complain about Elvis and to encourage him to use interstate commerce statutes to take action: "There are minds who will scarcely stop short of complete indecency to exploit their wares upon the public, and youth is not able to discriminate between the right and wrong of it."

Hoover responded that the FBI really didn't have the authority to do what the letter writer advocated. He brushed off the complaint, but there would soon be a flood of complaints from all over the country, some of which ended in death threats against the entertainer. Before the year was out, the FBI would be very much involved in Elvis's career, with FBI field agents firing off coded messages to the director on a regular basis.

☆   ☆   ☆

Less than a week after Elvis's performance on *The Milton Berle Show*, Parker announced that his boy had signed a three-film contract with Paramount Pictures. For the first picture, Elvis would receive $100,000, with the price increasing to $150,000 for the second picture, and $200,000 for the third. Hal Wallis had wanted an exclusive commitment, but Parker retained the right for Elvis to do one picture a year for other movie companies. For his efforts, Parker pocketed $112,500 in commissions, which meant that Elvis was essentially doing the first movie for free.

After a couple of weeks on the road, performing primarily in Texas and New Mexico, Elvis and the band pulled into Las Vegas for a two-week booking at the New Frontier Hotel. The headliner of the show was Freddy Martin and his orchestra, who planned to do a stage show version of the Broadway musical *Oklahoma!* Also included for the dinner crowd's amusement was comedian Shecky Greene.

By any standard, it was a bizarre booking, one only an ex-carny with his thoughts on the midway could envision as being appropriate. The name under which Parker booked Elvis added to the surreal quality of the engagement. To Las Vegas audiences, he would be America's first "Atomic-Powered Singer."

Elvis and the band knew it was going to be a *long* two weeks. Audiences in the 1,000-seat room were polite and applauded each time the music stopped, but there were no screaming girls or rowdy boyfriends stomping their feet and raising hell with the band. The audience was mostly composed of middle-aged tourists who had come to the show to eat a good steak and hear their favorite songs from *Oklahoma!*

Sitting in the audience at Parker's invitation was his friend from the Sahara, Bill Miller, although by that time he had moved over to the

Dunes Hotel. In later years, Miller told reporters that he had recognized Elvis's talent from the beginning: "I said, 'Boy, some day I'm going to fire up this guy's career.'"[29]

Writers often referred to the engagement as a failure, but neither Scotty nor D. J. remember it that way. To Scotty, no show was a failure if the house was packed and the audience applauded at the end of each song. D. J. felt the same way. "They just weren't used to that type of entertainment," he says of the audience's polite response. "We tried everything we knew. Usually, Elvis could get them on his side. It didn't work that time."

Parker salvaged the public relations aspect of the engagement by asking the hotel to allow Elvis and the band to do a special Saturday matinee for teenagers, with proceeds going to a local youth baseball park. It worked like a charm. The room was packed with screaming teenagers who charged Elvis at the end of the show, ripping his shirt to shreds. One reporter noted that a young girl clutched a button from his shirt as if it were a diamond.

Since Elvis didn't drink or gamble, he found little to do in Las Vegas and spent most of his time going to movies and hanging out with friends. At the end of the engagement, he left the city thinking that perhaps "Sin City" was not the best showcase for his talents. The entertainment media seemed to agree. "Doesn't hit the mark here," declared *Variety*.

Parker could not have disagreed more.

After shows in Minnesota and Wisconsin, Elvis and the band returned to Memphis, where Parker had booked them for a show at Ellis Auditorium as part of the annual Cotton Carnival celebration. It doesn't appear that Parker attended the concert, which also featured Hank Snow and the Jordanaires, but apparently the Colonel did take Elvis by the Royal American midway that night to meet his friends the Sedlmayrs.

"People gathered around, and [Parker] told them that the first job he had in show business was on Royal American Shows selling candy apples," recalls Carl Sedlmayr Jr., who was pleased to see a midway alumnus make a name for himself in mainstream show business. "He didn't try to put it [his carny experience] down or anything."

Perhaps taking advantage of the Colonel's personal introduction to the world of carnydom, Elvis made it a point in the years that followed to visit the Royal American midway on a regular basis. "He would play the games, and if he won a prize, he would give it to the kids who were hanging around," says Carl Jr.

Although "Heartbreak Hotel" was the Number One record in America, Elvis was not the headliner at the Cotton Carnival that year. Movie actor and singer Eddie Fisher was the main attraction. He had married actress Debbie Reynolds the year before, and it was probably Debbie's strong ties to Memphis that made him the most attractive headliner. The following year Debbie Reynolds made history by becoming the first female to knock Elvis off the top of the charts. She did it with her one and only hit song, "Tammy."

The controversy over Elvis's perceived onstage sexuality was becoming the focal point of his performances, at least with reporters who knew a good hook when they saw one. All the press on that subject began to concern Elvis. The last thing in the world he wanted was for his mother to think he was traveling around the country performing some kind of hoochie-coochie show. According to Scotty, Elvis never understood the sexual references. He just did his thing on stage, moving with the music in whatever direction his body told him to go.

After his swing through Minnesota and Wisconsin, an editor at the *La Crosse Register*, the official newspaper of the Catholic diocese, wrote a letter to FBI Director J. Edgar Hoover in which he proclaimed Elvis to be a "definite danger to the security of the United States." Although the editor admitted he himself had not attended the performances, he said he had sent two reporters to cover Elvis's second show.

"From eyewitness reports about Presley, I would judge that he may possibly be both a drug addict and a sexual pervert," wrote the editor. "In any case I am sure he bears close watch—especially in the face of growing juvenile crime nearly everywhere in the United States. He is surrounded by a group of high-pressure agents who seem to control him, the hotel manager reported."

Later that summer, a newspaper reporter in Jackson, Mississippi, labeled the entertainer "Elvis the Pelvis."[30] Asked about the nickname by a *TV Guide* writer, Elvis bristled, saying it was one of "the most child-ish expressions I've ever heard, coming from an adult." To a reporter for the International News Service, he said, "I'm not trying to be sexy. It's just my way of expressing how I feel when I move around."

Exactly how much of the Elvis "sex-teria" sweeping the nation was the result of enterprising reporters and how much was due to Parker's off-the-record comments to reporters may never be known. Certainly, Parker used the press to his boy's advantage. He had a fairly simple gauge of success: if a news story brought in money, it was good; if it did not bring in money, it was a scandalous, libelous outrage that threatened democracy itself.

The controversy over Elvis's sexuality was the best of all, for it brought in money-packed envelopes by the thousands to Parker's Madison office, all requesting photographs of his boy Elvis. "Sometimes they ask me what is the secret of Elvis Presley's success," Parker told a reporter for *TV Guide*. "Well, I don't know the answer, and I don't want to find out, either. Business is too good already."

By the end of the summer, Elvis had made his first appearance on *The Ed Sullivan Show* and received his first death threat on a post-card mailed in Buffalo, New York. The anonymous message said: "If you don't stop this shit, we're going to kill you." The FBI took the threat seriously and sent it to the FBI lab for analysis, but when agents spoke to Richard Moot, the U.S. Attorney for Buffalo, about the case, he advised them that he would decline prosecution in the event the letter writer was identified. Apparently, not everyone was an Elvis Presley fan.

That was made even clearer when the entertainer went to Louisville, Kentucky, for an appearance in November. The police chief announced that he would not permit "any lewd, lascivious con-tortions that would excite a crowd." When asked about the ban by re-porters, the police chief said, "As you can surmise, I just don't hap-pen to be one of his admirers."

Most of the initial hostility directed toward Elvis came from males. Women seemed to think his onstage gyrations were cool. And there was no age limitation on the adoration. Bill Black's wife, Evelyn, said that even her mother loved Elvis. "He called her his antique sweet-heart," she says. "Elvis was a good boy, as sweet as he could be."

☆   ☆   ☆

Love Me Tender was more than a movie to Tom Parker. It was an entire carnival midway, a cornucopia of opportunities and investments, all wrapped into a neat package. When production on the movie began in August, Parker was right there at his boy's side.

Originally titled *The Reno Brothers*, it was a pretty straightforward story with lots of action and no music, other than what normally would be applied to the soundtrack. Co-starring with Elvis were Richard Egan and Debra Paget. Although Elvis's movie contract was with Hal Wallis at Paramount, Parker had exercised the loan-out clause of the contract to do this motion picture, Elvis's first, for Twentieth Century-Fox.

When Elvis first read the script, there was no mention of him performing any songs. The band went with him to Hollywood, however, because Steve Sholes thought he would use the opportunity to record a new slate of songs for RCA. It was a way to kill two birds with one stone.

As usual, Colonel Tom Parker had a covey of birds in his sights. If songs were added to the script, that meant tie-ins with his recordings and that meant more money, especially if the songs were written by tunesmiths at Hill and Range. That was basically how Parker perceived the movies, as an opportunity to maximize his investment.

In the case of *Love Me Tender*, he saw an opportunity to drive yet another wedge between Elvis and the band. When the decision was made for Elvis to perform songs in the movie, the band naturally assumed they would be working on the soundtrack. To their surprise, they had to audition for Twentieth Century-Fox. "No one told us it was going to be a western movie with hillbilly songs," says Scotty. "Elvis didn't know either. So we did our regular act."

After the audition, the music director for the movie said it wasn't what he was looking for. He wanted something with more of a country edge to it. Twentieth Century-Fox decided to use someone else to back Elvis in the movie.

Scotty, Bill, and D. J. were astonished. They could play country music as well as the next guy, but they had naturally assumed the music director wanted them to play the type of music Elvis had been recording. Elvis told them not to worry about it, that he would make sure they were used in the next movie.

The incident left Parker beaming. The sooner he got rid of the band, the better. Now Elvis would realize that he was the star and could get by just fine without Scotty, Bill, and D. J.

The only time Elvis left Los Angeles during the filming of *Love Me Tender* was to fly to Tupelo, Mississippi, in September for "Elvis Presley Day." As part of the festivities, Elvis and the band performed at the Mississippi–Alabama Fair and Dairy Show. Joining Elvis on stage was Mississippi Governor J. P. Coleman, who presented Elvis with a "scroll of honor" and then proclaimed that day "Elvis Presley Day."[31]

The King of Rock 'n' Roll, wearing a blue velvet shirt and white buck shoes, accepted the honor with great humility. Whether Elvis knew it or not is unclear, but J. P. Coleman was the founder of the Mississippi Sovereignty commission, the man who made the appointments to the newly created commission and the one who set the initial agenda for the secret agency's covert operations. Coleman and Elvis were photographed together, and Colonel Parker made certain the photographs were widely disseminated among the southern news media.

Elvis gave two performances that day, one at noon and the other in the evening, singing for the first time on stage the title song from *Love Me Tender*. It was also the first time the band had ever been asked to play a song Elvis had recorded without them. Whether the band members realized it or not (Parker certainly knew what he was doing), that performance in Tupelo planted a seed of discontent that would fester for an entire year and then erupt on the same battleground with nearly disastrous results. Much has been made of Parker's genius as a promoter, but not nearly enough has been said about his abilities as an amateur psychologist.

4

THE KING ROCKS HIS WAY
TO THE TOP

On the surface, the Memphis draft board was no different from any of the others in the country. The board itself was comprised of men appointed by the president on the recommendations of local senators and congressmen. It was the board's job to determine who would be drafted into the armed forces.

During wartime, board members made life-and-death decisions on a daily basis that affected the lives of thousands of Memphians. However, during peacetime those decisions were done in a fairly low-keyed and relaxed manner, and the pressure felt by board members was more indirect and less passionate.

The Memphis draft board shared a common history with other boards in the South. The politics of race was always a major consideration. Unless advised by wealthy white planters that there was a dangerous shortage of young black laborers to work in the fields, local boards across the South tended to give a higher priority to drafting black males.[1]

From the 1940s, when Congress enacted the draft, until the mid-1950s, the Crump machine controlled Memphis draft board appointments. The positions were much sought after because of the almost unlimited power they afforded board members to manipulate business contracts, court decisions, and a host of other financial transactions.

Desperate men and women would agree to almost anything to keep their sons out of the service, especially if the family businesses depended on the sons in question.

E. H. "Boss" Crump never served in the military. Generally speaking, white males of political or social influence in the city were seldom asked to serve, unless, of course, they were publicly patriotic or wanted to receive specialized experience in the military—and there were more men in that category than you might imagine, for the city has long been imbued with a deep-running spirit of patriotism.

Early on, Elvis Presley's Selective Service record was routine. He registered on January 19, 1953, shortly after his eighteenth birthday, at the Selective Service System office on South Main Street. He listed his address as 698 Saffarans and stated that the person who would always know his address was his uncle Ed Smith, who lived at 1534 Mississippi Street in Memphis. Elvis said he was 5 feet 11-1/2 inches tall and weighed 150 pounds.

On March 1 the draft board mailed him a questionnaire and, based on the information received from him classified Elvis as 1-ANF. No one knows for sure what that classification meant: 1-A defined him as available for military service (NF was probably the local board's shorthand to indicate he was not finished attending high school).[2]

It was a bad time to be classified as 1-A. The Korean War was still being fought, although peace talks were underway. More than 25,000 American soldiers had been killed in the conflict, most of them draftees. Unless fate intervened, Elvis was a sure bet to go to war. Gladys was grief stricken to think that her only living son might be placed in harm's way.

A few weeks before Elvis's high school graduation, a truce was signed in Korea, thus allowing Elvis to escape the threat of wartime service. Ordinarily, he could have been expected to receive a draft notice during the year after graduation, but the armed forces had a surplus of men following the Korean truce and none of the thirty-two men registered by the Memphis draft board between January 1 and January 13, 1953, were sent notices until January 1957.[3]

During the summer of 1956, Elvis was often asked questions about the draft from reporters who wondered why he wasn't in uniform. That August he told a reporter for the International News Service that he hadn't heard a word from the draft board in three years, then added, "and I hope I never do."

Shortly after making those statements, he received a questionnaire from the draft board asking for updated information on his health and marital status. Tipped off that Elvis had received the document, a United Press International reporter asked the draft board if it was close to sending the entertainer an induction notice. "The new papers were sent to bring Presley's status up to date," said a draft board spokesman. "Lots of boys don't report address changes, marital status, and other facts, so we mail out a selective service dependency questionnaire."

"I honestly don't know what the questionnaire meant," Elvis told the reporter. "I haven't heard anything about . . . a physical. When they want me, I'm ready."[4]

Colonel Tom Parker faced a dilemma. The last people on earth he wanted trouble from were the U.S. Army. If he were to ask for special privileges for Elvis from a civilian draft board—and he knew that all it would take to keep Elvis out of the army was a telephone call to the local board—there could be trouble that might lead to his deportation.

By the same token, a two-year stint in the army could destroy Elvis's career. Rock 'n' roll was just two years old. What would be the new music two years hence? Newspaper writers were saying that rock 'n' roll would not last much longer, and while Parker never believed anything he read in newspapers, he had to at least allow for the possibility that they could be right from time to time.

Elvis could go into the army for two years and come home to find America in the throes of a new music fad. Complicating everything else was Parker's personal life, which, for the first time, was interfering with his business decisions. In the years since his first visit to Las Vegas to arrange Eddy Arnold's engagement, the Colonel had returned time and time again, not for the glitzy entertainment for which the city is famous but for the slot machines and gaming tables.

Gambling was the one passion in his life. There is no record of his losses in the late 1950s, but by the 1960s they were running at one million dollars a year in one casino alone, according to court records.[5]

By 1957, his gambling losses must have been substantial. When the *Nashville Banner* ran a story alluding to his gambling debts, Parker was so distressed he did something he had decided early on that he would never do: he threatened to file a lawsuit.

To sue or to be sued could open the door to revelations about his illegal immigrant status. *Banner* editors responded that they would be delighted to defend a lawsuit against the Colonel. They reminded him that he would have to bring all of his gambling receipts to court with him. Not surprisingly, Parker never pursued the lawsuit.

One theory has it that Parker owed so much money that the cabal that ran the city called in his markers and demanded a piece of Elvis's contract. His contacts with organized crime figures in Louisiana would have helped soften that squeeze, since Las Vegas and New Orleans were linked by the same Cosa Nostra network, but friendship will get you just so far when money is involved.

Earlier that year, *Billboard* published an article, based on confidential sources, that predicted that Elvis would be drafted in December. The article said he would go into the Special Services and be allowed to perform for the duration of his military service. Parker had three options with the military: he could telephone the draft board and keep his boy out of the army; he could do nothing and allow Elvis to be drafted; or he could arrange for Elvis to enlist in the army and receive a plum assignment.

As far as Parker's gambling debts were concerned, he had only two choices: he could hand over whatever portion of Elvis's contract his creditors asked for, sit back, and watch his projected fortune go down the drain; or he could stall for enough time to pay off his debts, thus keeping his boy out of the grasp of his creditors.

What Parker needed was a place to put Elvis on ice until he could pay off his debts. Someplace where he would be safe and his creditors couldn't get to him. Someplace where it wouldn't look like he was going into hiding.

To accommodate Parker, the Memphis draft board arranged for Elvis to receive a private pre-induction physical. Parker didn't want

Elvis to go through what he himself had gone through. He didn't want a roomful of rowdy Memphis draftees seeing his star-spangled boy buck naked. He didn't want a doctor groping his boy's private parts in view of other men (in those days doctors didn't wear rubber gloves).

From the beginning, Parker had been jealous of those who got close to Elvis. He was jealous of Scotty and Bill for traveling with Presley and for sleeping in the same room with him. He was jealous of the women Elvis dated, and it was always a source of contention. June Juanico, a Mississippi girl Elvis dated during the summer, said in later years that Parker always got angry, door-slamming angry, when he caught them together. She wasn't the only one to feel hostility from Parker. He always reacted that way toward the women in Elvis's life.

As ordered, Elvis reported for his private pre-induction physical on January 4, 1957. Accompanying him to the Kennedy Veterans Hospital in Memphis, where he had once performed to promote his first record, was a Las Vegas dancer named Dotty Harmony, who was spending the Christmas holiday with him and one of his Memphis friends, Cliff Gleaves.[6]

As they pulled up outside the hospital in Elvis's cream-colored Cadillac, an army of reporters and photographers greeted them. Elvis was wearing a red jacket and black trousers. Intimidated by the crowd, Dotty decided to wait in the car. Before Elvis could enter the building, photographers asked him to pose on the steps with an army sergeant and an air force officer. The navy had not sent a representative.

One of the photographers, eager to snap a cheesecake photo, asked Elvis to invite Dotty inside.

"No, sir, I'd rather not," he said. "She has nothing to do with this."

Inside, Dr. Leonard Glick greeted the singer and said that he would be conducting the examination. Right behind Elvis shuffled a mob of photographers. Visibly disturbed by the motley crew, he told the physician that he had understood there would be no photographers present during his examination.

"That's up to you," said Glick.

Elvis told the photographers he would be happy to pose for them after he completed the examination.

"Hey, how 'bout a shot with your shirt off?" shouted one photographer.

Suddenly, as Elvis headed toward the examination room, a crowd of about twenty teenagers dashed toward him from a side corridor, but before they could get to Elvis, they were pushed aside by military personnel.

When he emerged from the examination room, he told reporters it had gone about the way he expected. After answering their questions—they were particularly interested in how he thought he did on the intelligence test—he agreed to sign autographs and pose for pictures. It was at that point that he invited Dotty inside the building.

For one photographer, Dotty, Cliff, and the army sergeant toasted Elvis with two cups and a soft drink bottle. Asked what kind of shape Elvis was in, Dotty gave the reporters what they wanted. "He's a fine physical specimen," she cooed.

What seemed to interest the reporters most was what Elvis thought the army would do about his trademark sideburns. Elvis sidestepped the issue, but Memphis writer Robert Johnson, who edited a magazine named *16: The Magazine for Smart Girls*, said he didn't think keeping the sideburns would be an issue with Elvis: "He once indicated that he isn't as fond of his sideburns as he once was." One of the Special Forces officers present told Johnson that the army "wouldn't take a chance of messing it up" by trimming his sideburns.

Elvis gave the reporters and photographers all the time they wanted. As he was leaving the hospital, a nurse dashed past him and touched his jacket to the delight of her squealing female friends who had formed a starchy-white gauntlet along the corridor.

After the physical, Dotty returned to Las Vegas and Elvis boarded a train to New York with Scotty, Bill, and D. J. for their third, and final, appearance on *The Ed Sullivan Show*. Elvis found it hard to believe that the Colonel would ever allow him to be drafted. All it would take to get him out of that jam was a telephone call. It was no big deal.

The idea that the Colonel would let his boy go into the army was so farfetched that Scotty didn't waste any time thinking about it. No one believed it would happen. After doing *The Ed Sullivan Show*, Elvis and the band returned to Memphis for a week before heading to Hollywood to start work on Elvis's next movie, *Loving You*. To everyone's surprise, the draft board held a press conference to announce that Elvis had passed his pre-induction physical.

In the early years of his career Elvis often seemed troubled by his relationship with the Colonel. Says Scotty: "We'd be traveling together in the same car, and Elvis would bring up something the Colonel said, and I'd say, 'Elvis, you have to stand up and speak your mind. There's nothing wrong with you all arguing about something.' He'd say, 'Oh, well, I made a deal with him. I'd do the singing and he'd take care of the business.' He'd mumble and grumble about it for a day or two and that'd be it. He'd go ahead and do whatever it was he didn't want to do."

To Colonel Tom Parker, motion pictures were a vehicle by which he could make more money from Elvis's music. He never believed Elvis could make it as an actor. When some critics panned *Love Me Tender*, Parker decided that future movies would have to have more singing and less talking.

Elvis's acting in his first movie had a certain raw energy to it that could have been developed into something special for the screen. When the movie was released, neither Elvis nor Parker considered the existing cultural bias among reviewers against southerners. If you peruse those early reviews, it is apparent that what most of the critics who wrote negative reviews about the movie had against Elvis was not that his acting skills needed work, but that he was a southerner. They didn't like his accent.

Perhaps with that in mind, producer Hal Wallis chose a southerner to direct the next movie, *Loving You*. Hal Kanter, a native of Savannah, Georgia, had written the screenplay for Tennessee Williams's *Rose Tattoo* and had directed one movie, *I Married A Woman*.

Scotty, Bill, and D. J. had asked Elvis to stand up for them with the Colonel to make certain they were included in the movie, and he promised to do so, but that did not happen. The only reason they ended up in the movie, according to Kanter, was because he insisted that they be included. Says Kanter: "Elvis may or may not have been responsible for their inclusion on the sound track."

Before work began on *Loving You*, Parker and Wallis reached an understanding that Elvis's acting ambitions would have to take a backseat to the music. Wallis had produced most of the Dean Martin and Jerry Lewis musical comedies, and he knew a little something about packaging.

Parker would get no argument from him. Wallis once said that he thought Parker was a "genius" at squeezing every drop he could from Elvis. Wallis would know because Parker also squeezed the movie mogul for every drop he could get. Each time Wallis thought he had him figured out, the old Colonel came up with something new. For example, when negotiating the contract, Parker suggested that Elvis should be paid extra if he wore his own clothing.

Wallis agreed because the studio had a wardrobe department and he knew there wouldn't be much chance of Elvis wearing anything of his own. Once Wallis agreed, Parker said they should set a figure, a dollar amount, for how much his boy would get in such a situation. By then, Wallis was growing tired of talking about it.

"So, let's say you pay $25,000 each time that happens," said the Colonel.

"$25,000!"

Parker held firm and Wallis agreed to the dollar amount. He would make damned sure that Elvis wore only what was in wardrobe. Like most people in the movie and music business Wallis believed that small details are not as important to the success of a project as is the overall vision. Parker was just the opposite: small details were damned near everything.

Hal Kanter recalls the Colonel confining his visits to the set of *Loving You* to brief conversations with Elvis. "I had a feeling that Elvis was a little bit in awe of him and deep down didn't care about him," says Kanter. "But that may be because it was my feeling and I was transferring it to Elvis. Colonel Parker was the most accomplished con man since Barnum. He was about as reliable as a hurricane. You never knew when he would strike."[7]

Whatever his talents in the music industry arena, Kanter considered Parker a hindrance to Elvis's career as an actor. "He wasn't really interested in the script. He was more interested in how many songs he could get onto the screen."

When Parker found out that Kanter had written the script for *Loving You*, he asked him if he would be interested in writing his autobiography with him. Said Parker: "If you write it, I have the title—*How Much Does It Cost If It's Free?*"

"Needless to say, I never did write the book," says Kanter.

Once, Parker arrived on the set with a handful of homemade sausages. Kanter watched him give away some of the sausages to people on the set, but when he approached Kanter with sausages in hand, he didn't offer to share the country delicacies. "He offered to sell me some," recalls Kanter with a laugh. "Incredible! Other people got angry at him. But I was amused by him." For years after *Loving You*, Kanter received Christmas cards signed Elvis and the Colonel. "He always tied himself in with Elvis," says Kanter. "I had the feeling that the Christmas cards were paid for by other people."

Once, when they were shooting one of Elvis's later movies, Parker came onto the set to watch. He stayed out of the way, blending into the shadows, and they didn't even know he was there.

Suddenly, Parker spotted something from across the room and dashed across the soundstage, walking right in front of the camera. Everything came to an abrupt halt. "The boy's wearing his own watch," Parker said, shifting his cigar from one side of his mouth to the other. "See—he's got his watch on. That'll cost you another $25,000."

The Colonel and the boys in the band shared a common disregard for each other, but it was Parker, the king maker, not the boys in the band, the myth makers, who had the power to express it. When the owner of a Los Angeles Chrysler dealership offered to provide the boys with new cars if he would be allowed to advertise that Elvis Presley's band members drove cars from his lot, Parker said no. Same thing with RCA, which offered to provide the boys' families with appliances in exchange for the right to exploit their use of RCA products. Parker wouldn't hear of it: No, no, no.[8]

There was no way Parker was ever going to give an inch for the boys in the band. They were $200-a-week employees, nothing more. No matter how many records Elvis sold, no matter how many movies he made, no matter how many concerts he played, the boys in the band received a salary of $200 a week, unless, of course, they were not in the studio, helping record songs for the movies, or performing on the road, in which case they were paid only $100 a week. It was a source of great delight to Parker that the boys in the band made less than Elvis's valets and groomsmen, later called the Memphis Mafia.

"Oh, yeah, you had to watch him," says D. J. "He didn't want us as the band. He'd say, 'Don't pay the boys, they'll just want more money. We'll get more guys.' If it hadn't been for Elvis, we'd have been gone at Heartbreak Hotel time. The Colonel just didn't care."

"He kept the people he was dealing with always looking over their shoulder: what's he going to do next?" says Scotty. "He wasn't dumb; he was double street smart. He could look at all the angles. He'd spend $100 to beat you out of a dollar to have a joke about it. He liked to win. There were instances where he'd make a deal and they'd give him a price and he'd say, that's fine for me, now how about my boy?"

While in Los Angeles filming *Jailhouse Rock*, Elvis and the band went into the studio to record new singles and a Christmas album for RCA. For more than a year Scotty, Bill, and D. J. had been talking to Elvis about recording an album of instrumentals. Elvis would play piano on the tracks and they would call themselves the Continentals. Elvis was excited about doing something fresh, especially since he would get to play the part of the anonymous piano player. It would be like being a secret agent.

On the final day of the RCA sessions, they stayed in the studio to start work on the instrumentals. They already knew what they wanted to do and had been rehearsing the songs for several weeks. However, before they started that day, Parker sent word that they could not do the session. He had not approved it and Elvis simply did not work on projects that did not have his approval.

Scotty, Bill, and D. J. were stunned. They looked to Elvis for support, but he said nothing and stepped behind the protective wall of his entourage. Bill slammed his electric bass into its carrying case. Anger wasn't the first emotion that hit Scotty. He felt disappointment that someone he cared about and trusted would not back him up at a critical moment. Elvis left the studio without ever really apologizing or offering an explanation. Whatever Parker said was law. Nothing was open to negotiation.

On the way back to Memphis, Scotty and Bill discussed the reality of their situation. They were $200-a-week sidemen and that was all they would ever be. They would never receive any royalties from their work on Elvis's recordings and Parker would never allow them to record anything with Elvis that did not involve him.

If they had not started out as partners with Elvis, they might have had a different perspective. The music they had created in Memphis Recording Service, the music that had catapulted Elvis to fame, had been a joint effort. Elvis didn't arrive in the studio with a pocketful of music. He didn't say, "Boys, I'm gonna invent rock 'n' roll, and here's what I want you to do." On the contrary, the magic that had occurred in the studio was the result of three men working together, each contributing his own part. The voice belonged to Elvis, and Elvis alone, but the music . . . well, that was a different story.

Scotty and Bill had a long talk with their wives. They had all made sacrifices to make Elvis a success. Bobbie had loaned him her car and had even gone out on the road to promote the early releases with radio stations. Bobbie and Evelyn had suffered through the long absences while their men were out on the road with the expectation that the uncertainties, the lack of money, and the hardships would someday come to an end.

Scotty and Bill had the unenviable task of informing their wives that the dream was just that—an apparition of hope that had no basis in reality. All of them blamed their situation on the Colonel. Everything had been fine until he came into the picture. After several days of soul-searching, they decided to confront Elvis with the reality of their desperate situation. Both families were in debt, and the further up the road they went with Elvis, the more their debts increased.

Scotty and Bill decided to send Elvis letters of resignation. They talked to D. J. about making the resignations a threesome, but D. J. pointed out that, unlike the two of them, he had been hired as a salaried sideman and really didn't have the same cause for complaint that they did. He told them he wouldn't blame them if they did resign.

When Elvis received their special-delivery letters, he was still in Los Angeles. Their resignations came as a total shock. He passed the letters around for everyone in his entourage to see. As the initial shock wore off, he became angry, accusing Scotty and Bill of being disloyal.

When Elvis tried to talk to Parker about it, he wisely said it was none of his business. Steve Sholes told him to just hire another band. He had never liked Scotty and Bill anyway. He could find Elvis some top-ranked New York or Los Angeles musicians who didn't speak with a southern drawl.

Elvis didn't know what to think. When he returned to Memphis, he called Scotty and asked what it would take to get him and Bill back on the job. Scotty told him they didn't want to quit, but needed something to show for their efforts. Their first concern, said Scotty, was that they were able to pay off their debts. If Elvis would give them $10,000 each to pay off the debts they had incurred out on the road with him, plus a raise of $50 a week, they would be happy to return to work. Elvis said he would think about it.

In the interim, Scotty and Bill talked to newspaper reporters about their situation. They thought they were in the right and wanted to tell their story because they didn't want any of the fans thinking Scotty and Bill were abandoning Elvis. That may have been a good move so far as the fans were concerned, but it only aggravated their rapidly deteriorating relationship with Elvis. Seeing his private business aired in the press only embarrassed him further and drove him into the waiting arms of the Colonel, who told him not to worry about it; he would help Elvis find new boys twice as good as Scotty and Bill.

Instead of calling Scotty back to discuss it further, Elvis met with *Memphis Press-Scimitar* reporter Bill Burk and sent his answer to Scotty and Bill in an "open letter" that was published in the newspaper. In effect, he told his sidemen good luck and good-bye. "If you had come to me, we would have worked things out," Elvis said, addressing his comments to Scotty. "I would have always taken care of you. But you went to the papers and tried to make me look bad, instead of coming to me so we could work things out."

"I knew later, when Parker got involved in it, there was no way it was going to work out," says Scotty. "Every time I saw something in print, Elvis said we quit because we wanted more money and recognition. We didn't want any recognition. We just wanted some perks, I guess, so we could stick a few bucks in the bank."

When he read Elvis's comments in the newspaper, Scotty knew there were only two conclusions to draw: either Elvis was lying and attempting to make himself look good in the press, or Colonel Parker had not told him about their many requests over the years for a needed raise. Scotty knew Elvis too well to think he would lie in a situation like that. While he, Bill, and D. J. had long been aware of Parker's enmity toward them, they had never wanted to believe that he would actually keep things from Elvis. Now they knew Parker was playing hard ball.

With an upcoming appearance scheduled for the Tupelo Fair the following month, Elvis began auditioning guitarists and bassists to replace Scotty and Bill. Any hope that Scotty and Bill had that the situation could be salvaged was dashed by letters Vernon sent to them accepting their resignations. Scotty's letter included a check for $86.25, payment "in full" for his services as Elvis's guitarist.

Now that they knew where they stood, Scotty and Bill wasted no time finding a new gig. The first offer that came their way was a sixteen-day engagement at the Texas State Fair in Dallas. The contract called for them to do four shows a day from October 5 through October 20. They were paid $1,600 and all their expenses were paid by fair officials. It was more than twice what they had earned working for Elvis.

To replace Scotty and Bill, Elvis hired two Nashville musicians, Hank Garland on guitar and Chuck Wiginton on bass. When the Jordanaires showed up for the Tupelo engagement, they had heard nothing about the squabble and were shocked to find that Scotty and Bill had been replaced.

Jordanaire Gordon Stoker noticed that Elvis was very upset that day. Once he heard the story about Scotty and Bill's leaving, it didn't take Stoker long to figure out what had happened. "The Colonel kept Elvis in the dark about a lot of things," he says. "Didn't tell him things he should have told him."[9] After the Tupelo concert Elvis told D. J. that it just wasn't the same without Scotty and Bill.

With a big concert tour already in place for Los Angeles and San Francisco, Elvis took a rare stand with the Colonel, telling Parker that he wanted Scotty and Bill back for the tour. Parker passed the buck to his assistant Tom Diskin, who called Scotty and Bill when they returned from Texas and asked them to rejoin the band. He agreed to pay them $1,000 each for four shows. Scotty and Bill accepted on the condition that all future performances would be handled on a per-diem basis. That was agreeable to the Colonel.

The next time they saw Elvis was at the San Francisco Civic Auditorium. He acted as if nothing unpleasant had happened between them. He was so elated that he gave one of the great performances of his career. When they closed with "Hound Dog," as they always did, Elvis got down on the floor to rock and roll with a plaster dog as nine thousand cheering fans shook the foundation of the building.

In December 1957, only a week before Christmas, Elvis received an unexpected visitor at Graceland, his newly purchased home in Memphis. The visitor was Milton Bowers, the chairman of the local draft board. An appointee of the Crump era, Bowers had been on the job since 1943. He told Elvis, as *Billboard* had predicted, that his number was coming up and he soon would be ordered to report for a pre-induction physical.

For a draft board member to visit the home of a potential inductee was unprecedented, but it was just the first of several preferential gestures the draft board and the military extended to the entertainer. Nothing about Elvis's military experience would be according to regulations.

After Bowers's pre-Christmas visit, Parker knew he had run out of time. Various branches of the military, each offering a special deal if Elvis were to enlist, had contacted the Colonel. The military already had decided that it could use Presley's services more as an entertainer than as a grunt soldier. That didn't appeal to Parker. He didn't want the army to profit from his boy's musical talents.

In the author's view, Parker decided to allow Elvis to enlist, but to ease the pressure on himself with his creditors, it had to look like Presley was drafted and there was nothing he could do to prevent it. Parker didn't want it to look like he was trying to get Elvis out of the country. That could be very bad for his health.

To make that ploy work, Parker needed the cooperation of the Memphis draft board. Of the thirty-two Memphis men who registered with Elvis between January 1 and January 13, 1953, nine were ordered to report for pre-induction physicals (Elvis's name was not among them). Of those, five were drafted and four were rejected for service. Of the group of thirty-two men, fourteen, including Elvis, went into the armed forces, which means that nine men enlisted.

Selective Service records pertaining to Elvis contain a handwritten notation that could be read as either "Enl" (for enlisted) or "Ind" (for inducted), but Elvis's record is consistent with those men who enlisted and there is no notation at all under the heading that shows when registrants were called in for pre-induction physicals. In the author's opinion, Elvis's Selective Service record shows that the entertainer enlisted and was never drafted.[10] Apparently, his much-publicized private examination at the veterans hospital was arranged to accommodate his entry into the armed forces as an enlistee.

By that point in Presley's career, the Colonel was taking care of everything for Elvis. Exercising what must be the ultimate power ever wielded by a manager, Parker apparently enrolled his boy in the U.S. Army—and told him about it later, the way he would tell Elvis about a booking or a new movie deal. "You're doing a tour in the Northeast . . . then you'll finish up that movie . . . then, oh, yeah, I almost forgot, then you're going into the army for two years. Make the old Colonel proud, you hear?"

Rather than risk losing his interest in Elvis's contract to his creditors, Parker allowed Elvis to risk losing his career. If he couldn't be involved in Elvis's career, what was the point in Elvis even having a career? For Parker, it was all or nothing.

To accommodate Parker, the Memphis draft board drew up an induction letter for Elvis. Board members said they would prefer not to mail it to him and asked if he would mind stopping by the office to pick it up in person. That was fine with Elvis.

After getting the letter, he stopped by Memphis Recording Service. Sam Phillips wasn't there, but Jack Clement, who was running the studio at that point, was present. Elvis announced that he had been drafted and showed the letter. Clement got the distinct impression that the young singer was happy about going into the army.

"Well, might as well have fun," Elvis said.[11]

Elvis expressed a different attitude around his family and friends. He really did not want to go into the army, and was often despondent when discussing it. Vernon didn't have much to say about it, but Gladys thought it was a fate worse than death. Elvis hadn't had a face-to-face talk with the Colonel in a while, so he drove over to Nashville to give Parker his Christmas present in person—a tiny red Isetta sports car. He loaded the car into a truck and drove it himself, with two members of his entourage following behind in a Lincoln.

When he arrived at the Colonel's house, there was a mob of reporters and photographers waiting for him. It's not clear whether Parker invited them because he wanted to publicize Elvis's "draft" notice or because he wanted other people around in case Elvis became emotional.

"Now, isn't he a sweet kid?" Parker asked the reporters. He even managed to make his eyes look teary. "He could have just sent something in the mail."

At Parker's request, Elvis changed into a suit of army surplus fatigues for the photographers. He tried his best to be his usual upbeat self, but as photo ops go, it was pretty much a borderline success. His heart just wasn't in it.

Gordon Stoker of the Jordanaires arrived during the photo op and told Elvis they were going to perform at the "Grand Ole Opry" that night and why didn't he come along? When Elvis said he didn't have any clothes to wear, Gordon offered to take him to a local men's store, where Elvis purchased a tuxedo and dressy black shoes.

As was always the case with Parker, he had an ulterior motive for asking Stoker to stop by that day. The Colonel wanted him to invite Elvis to the "Opry" because one of his cronies, Dub Albritten, had signed a little girl from Georgia who was going to be there. She was tiny, but showed lots of promise.

That night, Elvis posed for photographs with Albritten's child prodigy, thirteen-year-old Brenda Lee. It was just the shot in the arm Albritten needed to help launch his new star. Brenda recalls Parker working behind the scenes, helping Albritten with her career. She credits Parker for helping her to land her first movie role.

"I found [Parker] to be a nice guy—I liked him," says Brenda. "He was his own person. He dressed like he wanted to and he didn't care what anyone thought. I guess he had enough self-esteem to be who he wanted to and he didn't much care whether you agreed or not. He was a genius at marketing. Dub was a genius, too, but he was more quiet about it."[12]

Elvis left Nashville without ever knowing that Parker had used him to boost Brenda Lee's career and without obtaining any satisfaction from the Colonel over his situation with the draft. The Colonel had made up his mind and that was all there was to it. Enlisting Elvis into the army was a dirty thing to do, but there were even worse things to come.

Three days after Christmas, Parker announced that the Memphis draft board had given Elvis a sixty-day deferment so that he could finish work on *King Creole*. Both Elvis and Paramount had requested the delay. Parker assured reporters that the deferment would not be extended.

"I know of nothing that would prevent his induction when his deferment is up," Parker said. "And don't think Elvis would consider making another request because I know he feels personally about it." He went on to explain to reporters that Elvis planned to continue making records while in the army. "We'll set up some recording dates with RCA for weekends," he told Richard Allen of *The Commercial Appeal*. "This deferment will let him complete the Paramount picture and there are a number of songs in that that will keep him before the public for some time."

With Elvis when he received news of the deferment were two Las Vegas showgirls who had stopped by to visit him on their way to New York, where they planned to audition as showgirls at the Copacabana. Elvis and the two women, nineteen-year-old Kathy Gabriel of Cleveland, Ohio, and twenty-year-old Hannerl Melcher of Austria, posed for a photograph that the wire services used to accompany a news article about the singer's deferment. Gabriel was identified as "Miss Ohio" and Melcher as "Miss Austria."[13]

The FBI was very interested in the photograph. The agency opened a file on the women and their relationship with Elvis. Agents reported that Elvis had met the women at the Tropicana while in Las Vegas. Melcher became the object of an FBI investigation at the request of the Department of Immigration and Naturalization. Exactly why she was targeted for investigation has never been explained.

FBI agents tracked the women's movements from Nevada to Memphis and then on to New York, but neither the women, Elvis, nor Colonel Parker were ever notified of the investigation. One can only imagine the Colonel's reaction had he known the Department of Immigration and Naturalization was snooping around the fringes of his secret world.

In January 1958, Elvis and the band went to Hollywood to work on the soundtrack for *King Creole.* By that point, Parker had arranged for Hill and Range songwriters Jerry Lieber and Mike Stoller to receive advance copies of the script so that they could write songs to accompany individual scenes.

Elvis had virtually no say in the musical content of the movie. While they were filming the movie, Parker sent Lieber a new "contract." When Lieber opened the envelope, he thought there had been a mistake. There was just a blank piece of paper that had a place for him to sign his name. He called Parker to notify him, but the Colonel told him it was no mistake.

"There's nothing on the paper," Lieber protested.

"Don't worry, we'll fill it in later," said Parker.

That was all it took for Lieber and Stoller. They never worked with Parker again; they never even bothered to speak to him again.

After completing work on the movie, Elvis and the band took the train back to Memphis, though Elvis grew restless and he got off in Dallas and rented a fleet of Cadillacs so that they could drive back. When he arrived at Graceland, a reporter was waiting for him. Elvis said that he had just finished the best movie of his career and planned to stay in Memphis until the time came to enter the army. "Would his popularity go on the skids while he was in the army?" the reporter asked.

"I wish I knew," said Elvis.

In his final days as a civilian, he called old friends and said goodbye. He often broke down in tears, crying out, "Why me?" Oddly, he bought a new car for his girlfriend and did favors for other friends, but he failed to make any provisions for his band in his absence, although he did call them before he left. For all practical purposes, Scotty, Bill, and D. J. had joined the ranks of the unemployed.

When the time came for Elvis to report to the induction station, Parker drove over from Nashville to give his boy a proper send-off. A telegram from Tennessee Governor Frank Clement arrived, praising Elvis as a "young man willing to serve his country when called upon to do so." Parker wanted him to read the telegram to the crowd gathered outside, but he didn't want to do it and stuck it deep into his pocket.

As Vernon and Gladys openly wept, the Colonel paraded among the wellwishers with balloons that advertised Elvis Presley's soon-to-be-released movie, *King Creole*. Whatever he owed the U.S. Army was now paid in full.

☆   ☆   ☆

When Elvis shipped off to basic training at Fort Chaffee, Arkansas, Colonel Parker went with him, leading a procession of news reporters, photographers, and a hundred or so civilian fans. Parker continued to nudge Elvis out before the cameras. At one point, he suggested that Elvis wear a western-style string tie with his uniform.

No sir, Elvis responded, politely pointing out that wearing a string tie would get him in trouble. Why didn't the Colonel wear the string tie? Parker ignored the suggestion and, always the master of misdirection, snapped at the photographers to quit taking pictures of each other.

Elvis wasn't at Fort Chaffee long before he was told that he would be assigned to the Second Armored Division at Fort Hood, near Killeen, Texas. Parker didn't want to have any more dealings with the army than absolutely necessary, but until Elvis was safely out of the country, he knew he would need to do a certain amount of troubleshooting. When he discovered a loophole in army regulations that allowed recruits with dependents to live off base, he arranged for Elvis to have a private residence large enough to house him, his father, and mother.

Gladys was not too happy about moving to Texas. Relocating only compounded the grief she felt over her son entering the army. She was not feeling well and her bouts with alcoholism were recurring with increased frequency. She had all the symptoms of liver disease, but everyone was so absorbed with Elvis's departure, herself included, no one noticed the alarming rate at which her health was deteriorating.

The Colonel followed him to Fort Hood, but then returned to Nashville after he was set straight by a real Colonel—and a woman at that. It wasn't as if he had nothing to do with his time. He was a busy man. Managing Elvis's money was a full-time job. He bragged to Nashville reporters that he would make just as much money with Elvis gone. With a new movie coming out and continuing record sales, Elvis didn't have to worry about the well going dry—and neither did he.

Serving in the army was pretty much a nine-to-five job for Elvis, who put in his time at the base—he earned a marksman rating with a .30-caliber carbine—but at day's end went home to Vernon and Gladys, and lived much as he had in Memphis. A few of the other soldiers resented his special treatment and sometimes yelled insults at him. Most, however, seemed to understand the pressure under which he existed.

The Colonel visited him a few times, often with contracts in hand, but it was obvious he wanted to keep his distance from the base. Elvis was usually polite to Parker when he was there, but once he left, Presley cursed and stomped about the house, clearly angry at something the Colonel had told him.

By June, Elvis had completed his basic training and was eligible for a fourteen-day furlough. He returned to Memphis with his parents and then went to Nashville, where the Colonel had arranged for a recording session. For the first time since they had started out together in Sam Phillips's studio, Scotty and Bill were not invited to the session. D. J. was invited, but he was not used as the main drummer.

The slight stung Scotty and Bill. They both needed the money. Since January, Scotty's only income for the year had come from his work on the *King Creole* soundtrack—and that amounted to just a little over $2,000.[14]

When his furlough ended, Elvis and his parents returned to Fort Hood. He already had been told he would be stationed in Germany and Gladys was distraught at the thought of moving to a foreign country. As his training was nearing an end, Elvis put Vernon and Gladys on a train to Memphis. He planned to get another furlough and spend time with them at Graceland before going overseas.

On the day after Vernon and Gladys returned to Memphis, she was admitted to a hospital with an advanced case of hepatitis. The doctors saw that it was serious and called Elvis and told him that he needed to come home. At first, his request for leave was denied. Elvis called the hospital every hour to get an update on his mother's condition. He said that if his leave did not come through soon, he would leave anyway.

After hearing that Elvis was talking about going AWOL, Gladys's physician called the commanding officer and pleaded with him to release Elvis. The officer took a hard line and told the physician that he couldn't do anything that would make the media think he was showing Elvis special treatment.

The physician, who had himself spent five and a half years in the army, told the officer that if he *didn't* give Elvis leave, he was going to talk to the media and "burn his ass good." The officer granted Elvis leave in quick order.

When he arrived in Memphis, he went straight to the hospital, where he found his mother looking better than he had expected. After visiting for several hours, he left Vernon at the hospital and went to Graceland to spend the night. The next morning he returned to the hospital and stayed several hours. On the third day, he received an early morning telephone call at Graceland, informing him that his mother had died.

Elvis responded to Gladys's death as everyone had expected—with overwhelming grief. When reporters arrived at Graceland, they found Elvis and Vernon sitting on the front steps, their arms wrapped around each other, oblivious to the presence of other people. When Parker got word of Gladys's death, he rushed over from Nashville and took charge of the funeral preparations. Elvis and Vernon wanted to have the funeral at Graceland, but Parker overruled him and insisted that it be held in a chapel.

Elvis wanted to add a Star of David and a cross to her footstone, but that, too, fell to the wayside. Some time later, Elvis asked Marty Lacker to have the footstone made. When it was finished, Lacker drove Elvis out to the monument maker to give his approval. Tears flooded Elvis's eyes when he saw the stone. He asked Lacker to call a Jewish jeweler with whom he had done business and tell him what he had done for his mother. Unfortunately for Elvis, the footstone was never placed at his mother's grave. When last seen, it was stored in the garage at Graceland.[15]

More than four hundred people crowded into the tiny chapel to hear the services, and more than six thousand mourners filed past to view the casket; outside the chapel, sixty-five police officers provided crowd control. Everyone, it seemed, was there to comfort Elvis in his time of need. Everyone except the two men with whom he had embarked on the long road to glory—Scotty and Bill.[16]

The final weeks at Fort Hood before Elvis's departure overseas were a blur to all involved. The anguish that had been building all year was kicked into overdrive with the death of his mother. The Colonel visited Elvis at his rented home in Killeen several times to talk to him about future releases from RCA, but stayed no longer than was absolutely necessary.

For the first time, Parker really had work to do at his garage office in Madison. He had been telling reporters for the past year or two that he had a staff of twenty or thirty people in his office to handle all the letters coming in. That was a lie, but now, with Elvis leaving the country, the tiny office was being inundated with cards and letters. He didn't like to ignore those letters since, at best, they might contain cash money, and, at worst, they would provide him with addresses for his merchandise mailing lists.

Since it was customary for the army to use trains to transport large numbers of troops across the country, the plan called for Elvis to board a train near Fort Hood and travel to the Brooklyn Army Terminal in New York. Colonel Parker rode on the train with Elvis, glad-handing the army brass with the same enthusiasm he had shown midway goers nearly thirty years ago. The biggest problem the army had, Parker concluded, was that it just didn't think big enough.

When Parker learned the train would not be going through Memphis, he convinced the army that it should detour through the city to reap the full benefits of the publicity just waiting out there ripe for the picking. As a result, the army changed routes and arranged for a one-hour refueling stopover in Memphis. Waiting for Elvis and the Colonel (by this point the two were inseparable whenever a photographer was present) were Elvis's friends and more newspaper reporters.

By the time the train finally made it to New York, more than one hundred reporters and photographers had gathered, along with RCA executives, Vernon, Anita Wood (the girl he had been seeing on a steady basis), and various army officers, all of whom seemed overwhelmed by the commotion.

Before Elvis was allowed to speak to reporters, an army spokesman laid down the ground rules. For the first fifteen minutes photographers would be allowed to take photographs. Then Elvis would respond to questions. He would board the ship with eight friends selected from the troops he rode with on the train. They would all pause on the gangplank for photographs. Finally, a handful of reporters would be allowed on board the ship for a few minutes.

Throughout it all, Colonel Parker beamed. It was better than anything he had ever seen on the midway. Those army boys could flatout pull a hustle when they wanted to.

When Elvis emerged, he kissed a WAC the army had provided for the occasion, and, after posing for photographers, sat down to field their questions.

"Is your family going to Germany with you?"

"What does the 'A' stand for in your name?"

"What was the train ride like?"

"Are you going to sell Graceland?"

"What are those medals for?"

"When was the last time you were in love?"

"Is there anything you'd like to say about your mother?"

The Colonel must have winced at that question. He had been able to shield Elvis from questions about Gladys, and wasn't sure what the reaction would be. It would be horrible if he broke down and cried while in uniform. Good soldiers don't cry.

To Parker's relief, Elvis handled the question well. "I mean, everyone loves their mother, but I was an only child, and Mother was always right with me all my life. And it wasn't only like losing a mother, it was like losing a friend, a companion, someone to talk to."[17]

The absurdity of it all must have hit Parker like a load of bricks. When he had come to America, rock 'n' roll didn't exist. Now it was dominating the news. He couldn't figure it out. What Elvis did on stage didn't really sound like music to him. When they were out on the road, his off-the-cuff comments about Elvis's fans, especially the female ones, showed outright contempt for them. P. T. Barnum was right: there *was* a sucker born every minute (and most of them wore skirts).

The press conference lasted almost an hour. When it was over, Elvis shouldered a borrowed duffel bag and trudged up the gangplank as the U.S. Army band broke out into a rousing rendition of "Tutti Frutti." Actually, he did it eight times so that the photographers and newsreel cameramen could get everything they needed.

Following Elvis aboard ship was Colonel Parker. They huddled in the ship's library, where the entertainer cum soldier recorded a Christmas message for his fans. Another press conference followed in which Elvis gave the media messages for his fans.

After the last of the reporters left, Elvis and the Colonel had a few minutes alone together. He wouldn't see Elvis for one and a half years, but there was no need to tell him that now. The boy had enough to worry about.

As the ship pulled out, Parker, his face beaming, stood on the dock with more than two thousand screaming relatives of other GIs and waved. Elvis stood on deck and waved back, growing smaller by the minute. The army band played "Hound Dog," "Don't Be Cruel," and "All Shook Up." It was one hell of a show, as good as anything ever presented by Royal American out on the carnival circuit. It made the Colonel proud to be an almost-American.

Back in Madison, once he cleared away the mail, Parker held a press conference, at which he announced that Elvis would earn one million dollars by the end of 1958 and probably just as much the following year. Presley was a moneymaking machine, he told reporters, and with the Colonel there to look after his boy's business affairs everything was going to be just fine.

With each passing year, Parker's wife, Marie, seemed to play a smaller role in his life. They had an untraditional marriage, to say the least. Their private life will probably always remain a mystery, but to those who worked with Parker she was his invisible partner. He was never affectionate toward her in public, and, with the absence of children in their marriage, there is no certainty they ever had a sexual relationship. The few photographs of Marie that exist show a kindly, intelligent face. In her later years, she could have been a poster model for grandmother of the year.

With Elvis on ice, the Colonel had his work cut out for him. He took care of what he could, then hit the road, leaving Tom Diskin behind to man the phones. With Elvis in the army, Parker needed to be seen in public. The last thing in the world he wanted was for people to think he was hiding.

One of the first things Diskin did, at Parker's suggestion, was to call reporters and tell them that Elvis had signed a deal to do a series of television specials for ABC-TV. The story wasn't true, but it was picked up by the wire services and got Elvis's name in newspapers across the country. Parker knew most newspapers wouldn't see a need to call ABC-TV for verification. The press was in the business of telling readers what people said; whether what they said was true or not was beside the point.

The Colonel went down to Louisiana, where being a Colonel counted for something, and where his buddy Jimmie Davis was getting ready to run for governor again. Passions were running high all across the South because of efforts by the federal government to speed up racial integration in the schools. It was a time of great violence and real-life conspiracies; who you knew was more important than what you knew, although what you knew could be dangerous to your health.[18]

Jimmie Davis and his friend Leander Perez were at the center of the storm, with the squall line radiating out to Carlos Marcello and the Dixie Mafia, the Mississippi Sovereignty Commission, and the all-white Citizen's Councils. In New Orleans, Aaron Kohn, a New

Orleans prosecutor who had built a case against Marcello, by then known as the Dixie Godfather, was making news. Unable to secure the FBI's cooperation in targeting Marcello, Kohn approached it from the other direction by getting indictments against public officials he accused of taking payoffs from the Dixie Mafia.[19]

From Louisiana, Parker made his way to Tampa, where he visited with old friends and rested before going to Los Angeles to do a little business with Abe Lastfogel, Elvis's personal representative at the William Morris Agency. At the Colonel's request, Lastfogel escorted him around town and introduced him to all the right people.

As usual, Parker had a scheme afoot. One of the favors the Colonel asked of Lastfogel was that he set up something with Frank Sinatra, a heartthrob crooner in the 1940s. Sinatra's career had cooled somewhat with the arrival of rock 'n' roll. His public comments about Elvis had all been negative, but Parker had a hunch that Sinatra wouldn't snub a business deal that would benefit both of them.

Sinatra was reputed to have mob connections in Las Vegas. The Colonel may have had specific knowledge of those connections, or he may have just been guided by what he had heard. If Parker owed a large amount of money to mob-controlled casinos—and that seems to be the case, especially since the Frontier, where Elvis had last been booked in Vegas, was subsequently among those found by the FBI to have mob connections—a deal with Sinatra for a televised special would not only be the perfect homecoming vehicle for Elvis, it would help divert the heat from the casinos.

Parker had reason to be concerned. The public perception of organized crime, supported by movie versions of submachine-gun rampages by beefy guys with broken noses, and the reality of it were miles apart. Usually, the only time Vegas mobsters used violence was against each other and against those who didn't pay their bills.

After doing what he could in Los Angeles, Parker circled by Las Vegas for a little rest and relaxation—and to be seen walking about like a man able and willing to pay his bills. Then he returned to Madison, where he geared up to promote Elvis's new RCA releases.

"I Got Stung" and "One Night" were the first singles released after Elvis went into the army. They went out in November, with "I Got Stung" peaking at Number Nine in December, then quickly dropping from sight. "One Night" fared better, peaking at Number Three in December.

With Elvis's records sinking on the charts, the Colonel must have had misgivings about sending him off to Germany, especially with news that "The Chipmunk Song" was the Number One record in America. He called his friend Al Dvorin and asked if he had any ideas about how to keep Elvis's name before the public.

Dvorin had just the thing—the Elvis Presley Midget Fan Club.

"I had put together a midget group for Continental Airlines for the introduction of their new jet fleet," recalls Dvorin. "The Colonel asked me if I could do the same thing for the Elvis Presley Midget Fan Club. I took Bobby Powers and, oh, I don't know, ten or twelve midgets, and created the [fan club] out of my office. We set them up at a hotel in Chicago for RCA and marched them all over the hotel, then marched them down Dearborn over to Madison. It was just beautiful. We had the nicest midgets in the world working for us!"[20]

Even with a team of paid midgets as allies, the Colonel must have spent some restless nights over the Christmas holidays. He had held on to Elvis's contract—and prevented it from falling into the wrong hands—but at what ultimate cost? It was either the cruelest thing a manager had ever done to a recording artist, or it was the smartest.

5

BACK FROM THE BRINK
AND INTO THE SPOTLIGHT

Elvis had to worry about a lot of things, but being treated like a regular GI was not one of them. In its own way, the U.S. Army assumed the role—and even the personality—of a surrogate Colonel Tom Parker. When Elvis's transport ship, the USS *General Randall*, arrived, the docks were lined with hundreds of screaming fans who wanted a glimpse of the King of Rock 'n' Roll. As was customary, he gave blood, along with many other soldiers, and then was transported to Bad Nauheim, the home of the U.S. Seventh Army.

With him were his father, grandmother Minnie Mae Presley, and several members of his Memphis entourage. The day after his arrival, the army arranged a press conference for Elvis, thus giving new meaning to the phrase "Selective Service." The army made it clear from the onset that Elvis would receive special treatment while in the service.

Within ten days, he was allowed to move off-base into a rented, three-bedroom house in Bad Nauheim that he shared with Vernon, Minnie Mae, and an alternating corps of his Memphis buddies. He stocked the house with a piano and several televisions, and he filled the refrigerator with plenty of hamburger, pork bacon, and homemade southern rolls.

The U.S. Army was doing a fine job of managing Elvis.

Meanwhile, back in Tennessee, the *real* manager did what he could to further his boy's career. If anyone was going to assume his public relations responsibilities with Elvis, it might as well be the U.S. Army. The Colonel was sure they would make him proud. In February 1959, RCA released a new Elvis album entitled *For LP Fans Only*, consisting of ten recordings, all of which were at least a year old. One of them, "Playing for Keeps," had been on the flip side of "Too Much." Sun Records had originally released four of the songs.

When Elvis went into the army, the one thing that the Colonel and RCA agreed on was the salability of the entertainer's old material. Parker argued that *anything* they released would rise to the top of the charts. He was wrong. *For LP Fans Only* quickly sank into oblivion, and for the first time since RCA had taken over his contract, Elvis had no songs on the charts. Parker called a press conference to tell reporters that he was planning a "blockbuster" homecoming for Elvis next year that would be carried over closed-circuit television in one hundred cities across the country. As he knew they would, the media dutifully published his comments without bothering to verify their accuracy.

Toward the end of March, someone in RCA's legal department telephoned Parker and told him RCA had received a disturbing letter with a Canton, Ohio, postmark. The anonymous letter stated that a Red Army soldier stationed in East Germany had plans to kill Elvis Presley.

"He has been given orders to kill him, even if he has to blow up the hotel or home where he and his father live," said the letter writer. "Please, please don't take this as a crank letter because as God is my witness every word is true."[1]

Apprised of the contents of the letter, Parker told RCA not to worry about it. He said it sounded like letters he had received from an Ohio woman who the FBI subsequently investigated. "She's nuts," said Parker, who made it clear that he really didn't want to get involved. Nonetheless, RCA contacted the New York office of the FBI, which proceeded to conduct a handwriting analysis of the letter.

The woman to whom Parker had referred had voluntarily entered a mental institution after being questioned by the FBI on previous occasions. The agency had turned the results of that investigation over to the U.S. Attorney in Cleveland, who had declined to prosecute the woman because of her emotional condition.

When the FBI compared the handwriting of that woman with the handwriting on the latest letter, they did not get a match. The case was referred to the Memphis bureau, which showed no interest in pursuing it; but FBI Director J. Edgar Hoover took the threat seriously enough to refer it to the army assistant chief of staff for intelligence. Wrote Hoover in a memo: "The above is being forwarded to you for your information and no further investigation will be conducted by this Bureau."[2]

Colonel Parker had a curious attitude toward the death threats that arrived with increasing regularity. He had spent his entire life avoiding contact with the FBI or other law enforcement officers. He didn't notify the FBI of any threats he received, and was reluctant to talk to bureau agents about any threats they received. If someone killed Elvis, then they killed him. It wasn't any of his business—or so he seemed to reason.

Taking care of business was Parker's business, and what really grated against his nerves that month was not the death threats, but what he saw when he looked at the charts. In March, the Number Eight record in the country was Thomas Wayne's "Tragedy," a song that Scotty Moore had produced for his new record label, Fernwood Records.

Thomas Wayne was really Thomas Wayne Perkins, the brother of Johnny Cash's bass player, Luther Perkins. With his breathless baritone, Wayne was being heralded by disc jockeys as the "new" Elvis Presley. Also playing on the record was Bill Black, who would soon garner headlines as the front man for the Bill Black Combo.[3]

"Tragedy" was quite a coup for Scotty. Only three singles recorded in Memphis had ever scored higher on the pop charts: Carl Perkins's "Blue Suede Shoes," and Jerry Lee Lewis's "Great Balls of Fire" and "Whole Lot of Shakin' Going On." None of the records Scotty made with Elvis for Sun Records had ever charted that high.

Perhaps to rub it in just a little bit, Scotty sent a copy of "Tragedy" to Colonel Parker, along with a nice note that he signed "Scotty Moore, Vice President, Fernwood Records." The Colonel responded with a letter of his own addressed to "Scotty Moore, Vice President," in which he wrote that it was "only proper" to congratulate him on his success. Scotty liked that letter so much, he saved it.[4]

Throughout his tour of duty in Germany, Elvis lived off base in the rented house in Bad Nauheim. Each morning he put on his uniform and one of his bodyguards drove him to the base. He happily did whatever the army asked him to do. Mostly they asked him to just wear his uniform and ride around in a Jeep.

Whatever plans the army originally had for Elvis were changed after the death-threat letter arrived. It didn't matter whether the letter was written by a crazed fan or not. It made the army realize that some people viewed Elvis as a symbol of American capitalism. If someone with a political agenda killed Elvis, the action could have international implications and destabilize the fragile Cold War truce in Europe.

From that point on, Elvis was viewed somewhat differently. The top brass made sure that his fellow soldiers kept an eye out for him. Alive, he was a public relations bonanza for the army. Dead, he was a potential military and political disaster.

Once Elvis realized the army was not going to ask him to do anything dangerous like the soldiers did in the movies, or like what Scotty did while serving in the navy in China during the Communist revolution, he relaxed and adjusted to military life. Certainly, the mind-numbing protocol was no problem for him: he had been saying "yes sir" and "no sir" to strangers his entire life.

There was a constant stream of visitors from the States, and he went out with his friends in the evenings and on the weekends when he had leave. He attended a Bill Haley and the Comets concert in Frankfurt and posed for photographers with Haley in the dressing room. With the Colonel not there to disapprove, he let his hair down for the first time since becoming a star.

One thing Elvis did not have to worry about was finding a date for Saturday night. Women were constantly going in and out of his house. Those his age or older didn't stand much of a chance. He preferred younger women—well, actually, young girls in their teens. He dated a sixteen-year-old German girl for a while, then was seen with a string of young girls. Ever since his mother's death, he had been obsessed with having female companionship around him at all times.

Anita Wood, whom he had been dating on a steady basis before going overseas, obtained a passport and got all of the required shots so that she could visit him, but when the Colonel learned of her plans, he vetoed the trip. He said it would be bad publicity because the foreign press would make it appear that they were going to get married.

When word of Elvis's off-base activities got back to the Colonel, it made him uneasy, for it was during his down period, when he was beginning to have doubts. He had maintained a "hands off" attitude thus far toward Elvis's play time, but in June when he learned that Elvis and the Memphis boys had chartered a plane to Paris, he sent Hill and Range attorney Ben Starr to Germany to keep them out of trouble.

In Elvis's absence, the Colonel busied himself booking events for his old client Eddy Arnold, but he never told Elvis about it. During this time the Colonel's friendship with Texas Senator Lyndon B. Johnson blossomed.[5] How they met remains a mystery. The most likely scenario is that Johnson's assistant, Walter Jenkins, encountered Parker in the course of Jenkins's close associations with Texas vending machine operators. Later, Jenkins would narrowly escape a full congressional inquiry only through the behind-the-scenes legal wrangling of Memphian Abe Fortas.

By late 1959, the Colonel's relationship with Lyndon Johnson was strong enough for him to receive an invitation for himself and Eddy Arnold to attend a barbecue at Johnson's Texas ranch. The barbecue was given in honor of Mexican President Adolfo Lopez Mateos.

Several weeks later, the Colonel wrote to Walter Jenkins to request one of the group photographs taken at the party. Jenkins responded that he did not have the photograph the Colonel wanted, but would try to locate it. The following month, Johnson wrote a personal note to the Colonel.

"Lady Bird and I will always be grateful to you and Eddy for making President Lopez Mateos' visit a memorable one," said Johnson. "I hope our paths will cross again in the days ahead and that you will always feel free to call on me as your friend at any time for anything."[6]

Colonel Parker was not leading a double life, he was leading a *triple* life. He was a married man with no proof of either marriage or citizenship. He was an "aw-shucks" manager with friends in high and low places. Now he was linked to the president of the United States. For the next several years, he would correspond with Lyndon Johnson and Jenkins on a regular basis, sometimes as regularly as once a month. Often he sent gifts or records, and occasionally advice, as when he advised Johnson on a design for his campaign calling cards.[7]

What troubled the Colonel most about Elvis was not the wild parties, the drinking, and the childish pranks, but his appetite for young girls. He knew it could destroy his boy's career if it got out of hand. The Colonel was accused of many things over the years, but chasing women was not one of them.

Toward the end of his stay in Germany, Elvis met the young girl who would cause the Colonel the most grief. Priscilla Beaulieu was the fourteen-year-old stepdaughter of Joseph Beaulieu, an air force captain. Beaulieu thought the twenty-four-year-old entertainer was too old for his daughter, but didn't prohibit her from dating him. Elvis saw Priscilla throughout the Christmas holidays, but did not stop dating other young girls. During this time he began to wonder about his looks, about whether he was beginning to show his age. He still had acne marks on his face from his teenage years and the pockmarks seemed to grow more noticeable each year.

At the end of November, Elvis began skin treatments with a man named Johannes, who had written earlier in the year from his home in South Africa. Claiming that he was a skin-care specialist and masseur, he offered to cancel all his appointments and fly to Germany to administer his treatments to Elvis.

Under the impression that Johannes was a medical doctor, a specialist in dermatology, Elvis agreed to undergo the treatments. "I feel honored and very privileged in having been chosen for this important task," Johannes wrote before leaving South Africa. "In fact, I am greatly enthused in my mission and assure you, as you are soon to see, that I am going to work wonders with your skin."

The treatments were administered at Elvis's home and, according to a report that the Army's Provost Marshal Division prepared for J. Edgar Hoover, were directed toward his face and shoulders.[8] Apparently, Johannes administered treatments on a nightly basis. Presley spent so much time with him that Priscilla, who had only been seeing Elvis for a month or so, complained he was neglecting her, and Vernon, who wrote the checks for the treatment, complained that it was costing too much. The bills for one month's treatments amounted to $15,000— roughly equivalent to the total salary Scotty and Bill had received for the first three years they worked for Elvis.

The sight of two men going upstairs and disappearing behind closed doors every evening was beginning to make everyone in the household uncomfortable. The treatments continued for almost a month, then abruptly ended when Elvis learned from his entourage that Johannes had made homosexual advances toward some of them.

Elvis angrily told Johannes to leave his house.

Johannes erupted into a fit of rage, ripping apart a photo album that contained pictures of Elvis. He threatened to ruin the singer's career and to expose his relationship with fourteen-year-old Priscilla Beaulieu. He told Elvis he had incriminating photographs and tape recordings that showed him in "compromising situations."

FBI records don't indicate if Elvis consulted with the Colonel about the incident, but almost certainly he did. Parker was very open-minded about homosexuality. He had encouraged Elvis's friendship with actor Nick Adams, who, at the time, was rumored to be homosexual. During the two weeks Elvis was booked at the Las Vegas Frontier, Parker had nudged Elvis into a friendship with pianist Liberace, a flamboyant Las Vegas entertainer. In fact, Liberace had an influence on the way Elvis dressed in the years after their Las Vegas meeting, according to Scotty Moore, who didn't know Liberace was homosexual. "I thought it was all an act," he says. "That's how naive I was."

Rather than worry about what Johannes would do to him, Elvis went on the offensive and filed a report with the Army Provost Marshal. He told investigators his version of events and repeated Johannes's threats to expose him for his involvement in "compromising situations."[9]

"Presley assures us that this is impossible since he never was in any compromising situations," reported Major Warren Metzner, chief of the army's investigative branch. "Presley contends that [Johannes] is mentally disturbed. This is based upon the fits [he] has had and on his statements concerning the shock treatments he has been taking."

Johannes was never prosecuted, and the army ended up acting as an arbitrator between Elvis and the masseur. In his report to the FBI director, an army spokesman said he wanted to avoid any publicity in the matter since Elvis had been a "first-rate soldier and had caused the army no trouble during his term of service."[10]

Elvis agreed to pay Johannes $200 for the last treatment he received and another $315 for airfare to London. He accepted the money, but did not leave as promised. Instead, he demanded an additional $250, which Elvis paid. According to the FBI report, Johannes left for London on January 6 on British European Airways Flight 491.

Before leaving, Johannes sent Elvis a handwritten letter in which he wished him "every success and happiness" for the future. He said he had decided not to press charges against him upon the advice of a German lawyer. "You have lost a mother and since this is your second year in the army and since you had to go through so much in life, I sympathize with you and forgive you," he wrote in the letter. When last seen, Johannes was seeking entry into the United States.

On March 1, 1960, the day before Elvis was to leave Germany, the army held a press conference for him in a Bad Nauheim gymnasium.[11] The Colonel had arranged for him to use the occasion to announce that work on his next movie, *GI Blues*, would begin upon his return to civilian life.

To Elvis's surprise, one of the first people he saw when he walked into the gymnasium was an old friend, Marion Keisker. She had joined the air force in 1957 after having a falling out with Sam Phillips and had made a new life for herself in the military. The music business, in her estimation, was one of the "filthiest, dirtiest, back-stabbingest" endeavors in which she had ever been involved.

Now she was Captain Marion Keisker.

"Hi, hon," she said.

Elvis turned when he heard her voice. "Marion!" he said, not believing his own eyes. "In Germany! And an officer! Do I kiss you or salute you?"

"In that order," she answered, then flung herself into his arms.

Outraged, the army public relations officer chastised Marion, threatening to have her court-martialed. "I certainly expected this sort of thing from some of the magazines, but not from a member of the armed forces," he said.

Marion explained that she was there to cover the press conference for the armed forces television station, but that explanation did not satisfy the army officer. He demanded that she leave, but, hardheaded Memphis belle that she was, she steadfastly refused. At that point Elvis intervened, politely explaining to the officer that they would not be gathered there today if it had not been for Marion's eye for talent.

For Elvis, it was the perfect send-off.[12]

Since the first of the year, Colonel Parker had been in overdrive. Elvis had not had a Top Twenty record on the charts since "Big Hunk O'Love" went to Number One in August 1959. The biggest thing on the charts was the Bill Black Combo, whose gritty, jukebox-destined "Smokie–Part 2" had entered the Top Twenty in January.

Music had changed greatly during Elvis's absence. New heartthrobs like Frankie Avalon, Paul Anka, and Bobby Darin had taken over the pop charts. The raw, down-and-dirty rock 'n' roll that had originated with Sun Records had fallen to disfavor with the public. Jerry Lee Lewis had self-destructed in the wake of his marriage to his teenage cousin and the ensuing public backlash. Sun Records hadn't had a Top Twenty hit on the pop charts since July 1958, when Johnny Cash's "Guess Things Happen That Way" charted.

Several weeks before Elvis's discharge, stories circulated that Colonel Parker planned to reproduce copies of the discharge papers and sell them to fans. To end the rumors, Parker called Malcolm Adams at the *Commercial Appeal* in Memphis to debunk what he called a "screwball story." Said Parker: "That's ridiculous! We wouldn't think of such a thing even if we could." When asked by the reporter if Elvis planned to change his singing style, Parker said he had no reason to think he would. "Of course, he may as he becomes more mature. Elvis is a talented artist. I never try to tell him how to sing or what songs to pick." Of course, that was not true, but Parker knew the reporter would never be able to prove otherwise.

The following week, Charles Holmes, a reporter for the *Commercial Appeal* who was apparently not satisfied with the Colonel's response, wrote a story about the "exiled" entertainer's return to show business. At the conclusion of his article, the reporter asked "Will he recapture his prominence in the fickle world of singing or movie making? We will know soon."

From Parker's perspective, old-fashioned rock 'n' roll had run its course. What he saw happening on the charts were pretty boys singing slick, New York–style arrangements that transferred with unctuous ease to television and the movies. He didn't know much about music, but he had an instinctive feeling about what suckers wanted to spend their money on—and he had as a client the most famous pretty boy of all time. The Colonel knew what he had to do.

There was a blizzard on March 2 when Elvis and seventy-nine other soldiers arrived at McGuire Air Force Base in Fort Dix, New Jersey, aboard a military air transport DC-7. Some said it was the worst snowstorm of the year. Waiting for him were singer Nancy Sinatra and reporters and photographers. Actress Tina Louise was there to cover his homecoming for the Mutual Broadcast Network.

Directing media traffic was Colonel Tom Parker, who told reporters that the entertainer had television and movie guarantees totaling more than $850,000 for the remainder of the year and expected to make "millions more before the year was over."[13] With his cigar rolling about in his mouth, Parker said Elvis had earned $1.6 million while in the army. Then, thinking better of what he said, he told reporters, "Please state carefully the government gets ninety-one percent in tax. Elvis is no millionaire."

When it was disclosed that Elvis's final check from the army would be for $109.54, Parker pointed out that the government would claim ninety-one percent of that as well, which meant that Elvis would actually take home $9.86 from his last army paycheck. That may or may

not have been true. Parker always overpaid his and Elvis's taxes so as
not to attract attention from federal authorities.

At a two-hour press conference, which the army was becoming
adept at arranging—too adept, some would say—Elvis answered the
reporters' questions with his usual good-natured honesty:[14]

"How do German girls compare with American girls?"

"They're both females," he answered.

"Do you drink or smoke yet?"

"No, and I don't chew tobacco."

"What about these new rival singers in the field?"

"When I started out, I was lucky to get a break. If other young fel-
lows do, too, more power to them."

"It's been said rock 'n' roll is disappearing. What do you think?"

"I would never abandon it as long as people appreciate it. People
will let you know—then it's time to change. I could never take it on
for myself [to change it]."

"Ever been in love?"

"I thought I was. A time or two."

After the press conference, Parker met with Elvis and explained
what he had lined up for him thus far. He also told his client what
they were up against, as far as the competition was concerned. To be
competitive, Elvis would have to smooth some of the rough edges and
appeal to an older crowd.

"I just can't get it in my mind that I'm here," Elvis told a crowd of
about fifty reporters and one hundred and fifty fans, when his train
pulled into the Memphis station.[15] It was early in the morning, before
most of the city had had breakfast, and snow was falling. Later that
afternoon, during a press conference at Graceland, Elvis said he had
been unable to sleep on the twenty-four-hour train ride because he
was so excited about coming home. He said he was hungry, but
couldn't stop walking around the house long enough to eat.

One of the reporters asked if he would pose for a photograph with
one of the teddy bears from his collection. Elvis politely declined, saying
it wouldn't look right for a man just home from the army to cuddle up
with a teddy bear. Elvis didn't really have a teddy bear collection anyway.

There had been several stories about his alleged teddy bear collection, but they were all concocted by Colonel Parker, who saw it as a

merchandising ploy. Once he even went so far as to buy Elvis a teddy bear and place it in his bedroom for photographers to see. The Colonel thought the teddy bear hoax was a hoot; Elvis was embarrassed and avoided the subject whenever possible.

The Colonel allowed his boy two weeks off before putting him back to work. An article in the March 14 issue of *Life* magazine painted a gloomy picture of Elvis's prospects of recapturing his crown as the King of Rock 'n' Roll. The magazine quoted Elvis as saying, "I want to become a good actor, because you can't build a whole career on just singing. Look at Frank Sinatra. Until he added acting to singing he found himself slipping downhill." The Colonel could not have said it better himself.

Elvis called Scotty, Bill, and D. J. and asked if they would join him for an upcoming recording session in Nashville and for his first public appearance since his return, a television special with Frank Sinatra. Scotty and D. J. agreed, but Bill, still bitter over the way Elvis had handled things, said that he would be too busy performing with the Bill Black Combo.[16]

Elvis arrived at the Nashville session wearing his army uniform and using the name Sivle Yelserp (Elvis Presley spelled backward). With advance orders for his first post-army release already over the one-million mark, the Colonel wasn't too concerned about the session. He could put dead fish in the record sleeves and sell a million.

What the Colonel *was* worried about was Elvis's post-army image and the upcoming television special with Frank Sinatra. Elvis didn't know it, but he was at a pivotal point in his career. The Colonel, always a shadowy figure, had become even more inscrutable during Elvis's absence, immersing himself even deeper into the subterranean currents of the Las Vegas gambling world.

Since Parker did not suggest any changes in his manager's contract, it may be assumed that he was able to use the singer's two-year exile to extricate himself from his gambling difficulties. What he needed was time. Some may criticize him for putting his client on ice at a crucial moment in his client's career, but in doing so Parker may have actually extended the life of his career. The Colonel lived in the present, but it was the future that dazzled him.

One of the things that impressed him about Americans was their seemingly inherent capacity for showmanship. He had been mightily impressed by Harry Truman's presidential campaign for his willingness to use trains as a joystick to lure potential voters to his speeches. Parker's friend Jimmie Davis had used the same device in his gubernatorial campaign.

When Elvis, Scotty, D. J., and the Jordanaires left Memphis on a Miami-bound train to videotape the Sinatra television special, the Colonel borrowed a page from Harry "Give 'em Hell" Truman's campaign book and Jimmie Davis's rabble-rousing "Let's Party" media blitz.

The Colonel called ahead to every village, town, and city along the route, and told reporters when the train would be passing through. The result was an almost constant line of waving fans along the route. Each time the train stopped, the Colonel took Elvis to the platform of the observation car to wave to the wellwishers. You would think he was running for political office the way he catered to their goodwill.

When they arrived in Miami, they checked into the Hotel Fontainebleu. The Colonel's first order of business was to meet with the members of the fan clubs who had followed them to Miami. He thanked them for staying loyal to Elvis during his stint in the service, and then sold them publicity packages of the King. The last time he and Elvis had been in Miami was for a performance at the Olympics in 1957. On that occasion, he had worn an apron and hawked photographs of Elvis in the lobby. This time he took a more sophisticated approach and did it without the apron.

The television special was scheduled to be taped in the hotel ballroom and then aired at a later date. Also appearing in the show were Nancy Sinatra, Joey Bishop, Peter Lawford, and Sammy Davis. Backing everyone, including Elvis, was Nelson Riddle and his forty-two piece orchestra.

Musically, the show marked the end of Elvis's experiment with rock 'n' roll. The Colonel had decided that Elvis's future was with heavily orchestrated music, the lush, big-band-with-strings sound that Sinatra had made famous. Rock 'n' roll really didn't translate well to the movie screen and, as he already had witnessed, was not compatible with the Las Vegas sound.

The Colonel also had political reasons for the Miami booking. He was in deep with Las Vegas power brokers and the Sinatra connection was an integral ingredient. He had worked hard to connect with Sinatra and he was sure the association would pay off. Shortly before the show aired on May 13, Sammy Cahn, who co-produced the television special, mistakenly told *New York Times* reporter Murray Schumach that adding Elvis to the show had been Sinatra's idea. "We were sitting around one day, wondering about the next show," said Cahn. "Suddenly out of left field, Frank asked, 'What about Elvis Presley?' That's Sinatra. He wants to do what he wants to do."

Reviews of the show were not complimentary of Elvis. *New York Times* critic John Shanley wrote: "Although Elvis became a sergeant in the Army, as a singer he has never left the awkward squad. There was nothing morally reprehensible about his performance; it was merely awful." Even so, Shanley acknowledged, however reluctantly, that the ballroom crowd had reserved its greatest applause for the King.

Whatever the musical merits of the show, Elvis had been inducted into the glittery Las Vegas Hall of Shame. It was the second time the Colonel had volunteered his client for service beyond the call of duty.

☆   ☆   ☆

Elvis was a changed man after returning to Memphis. That became apparent when he, Scotty, and D. J. went to Nashville to record the soundtrack for *G.I. Blues*. The theme of the movie was that serving in the armed forces was a blast. MGM publicity executives designed a campaign around the new image they had created for Elvis as the all-American boy every mom and dad would be happy to see their daughter bring home.

That was in direct conflict with the bad-boy, rock 'n' roll image he had fostered before going into the army. There is no question that Colonel Parker was the driving force behind Elvis's makeover, but it is obvious that Elvis did not object. That may have had something to do with his mother's death—a desire to do something he thought would please her—or it may have been what he had in mind all along.

When they went into the studio to do the soundtrack, Scotty realized that the *new* Elvis was not going to be a temporary phase. That observation was confirmed when he learned that the Colonel had scheduled no concert tours for Elvis. The absence of a concert tour was a surprise to Scotty—and a bad one at that, since his Fernwood Records had gone under, and he was struggling to make a living—but the new image was not unexpected.

Scotty had always thought that their music was more pop-oriented than rock 'n' roll. If Elvis were to wear a crown, he thought it should be as the "King of Pop," not the King of Rock 'n' Roll. History would prove Scotty correct, but, at the time, it was all very confusing to anyone trying to label Elvis's music. None of that mattered to RCA, which already had 1,430,000 pre-sold orders for his next release.

G.I. Blues would be the last movie in which Scotty and D. J. appeared. They were allowed to play the part of the band members in the film, but they were given no lines and asked to wear Bavarian-style short pants and leg makeup.

Elvis didn't like the music in the film, but he sang what he was told to sing. The Colonel had convinced him that if he really wanted to become a top-ranked movie actor, then he had to play ball with the studio. During filming Elvis received a number of unexpected visitors, all lined up by the Colonel, including the king and queen of Nepal and the king and queen of Thailand. Enthused by his induction into the inner circle of the world's royalty, Elvis telephoned Liberace to share the news.

By the time Elvis returned to Memphis that summer, magazines were attacking him for abandoning rock 'n' roll. Leaping out from the cover of *Movie Mirror* was the headline "The King of Rock 'n' Roll Is Dead!" Of more concern to Elvis than attacks from the media was Vernon's impending marriage to Dee Stanley, a younger woman he had met in Germany. Elvis was appalled that Vernon would remarry so soon after Gladys's death and he refused to go to the wedding.

In the years leading up to Elvis's enlistment in the army, the Colonel's problems had been mostly of a logistical and financial nature. Gladys was the only member of the family who was skeptical of his intentions, and, with her death, he thought a major obstacle had been overcome.

Elvis's return brought a whole new set of problems that the Colonel had not anticipated. Vernon was in the Colonel's back pocket and would do anything he asked, probably because Parker had learned that Elvis's father had served three years in Mississippi's Parchman Penitentiary for forgery. The Colonel used information the way a street fighter uses a razor: more as a fearsome threat than as an actual weapon. But the value of that alliance would be significantly decreased if Vernon alienated Elvis by remarrying so soon.

Then there was Priscilla. When Parker learned that Elvis had been dating a fourteen-year-old in Germany, he hit the roof, holding up Jerry Lee Lewis's ruined career as an example of what can happen when young girls enter the picture. Of equal concern to the Colonel was Elvis's new friendship with soul singer James Brown. They met at the Continental Hotel in Hollywood, where they sat around and sang together at the piano. Elvis wanted to record with James Brown's band, but the Colonel told him it was out of the question to do any projects with African Americans.

Parker was no hardcore racist, at least not openly, but his extended power base was built on a solid foundation of racism. His friend Jimmie Davis had again been elected governor of Louisiana, and the talk coming out of Louisiana, Mississippi, and Tennessee had grown increasingly violent. Davis spoke of calling out the state militia to deal with what were being called "nigger lovers."[17]

Davis's inauguration coincided with Elvis's return. One of the governor's first acts was to put his chief backer, Leander Perez, in charge of forming a secret commission based on the Mississippi model. While this was happening, New Orleans prosecutor Aaron Kohn was continuing his investigation of Marcello's links to government.

Throughout it all, yet another key figure was emerging. Several months before Davis's inauguration, Kohn went to Washington to talk to Robert F. Kennedy, the chief counsel on the Senate's committee to investigate corruption in labor and management. Kohn gave him a rundown of what was happening in the South, especially in the particulars of Marcello's influence. Kennedy took notes, then thanked the prosecutor for making the trip. "I can assure you that, sooner or later, we will do something about Mr. Marcello," Kennedy said.[18]

Colonel Parker understood the seriousness of the situation. To his horror, Tennessee Senator Estes Kefauver—the sworn enemy of his Louisiana friends—had welcomed Elvis home by paying tribute to him in the *Congressional Record*. The Colonel could not afford mixed signals going out to the wrong people.

Elvis would have to be careful with whom he was seen and photographed. African Americans were out of the question. How much of that he explained to Elvis may never be known, though when people recall when the entertainer first started showing symptoms of the paralyzing fear that would torment him later in life, they usually associate it with his return from the army.

No sooner did Elvis finish *G.I. Blues* than he jumped right back into another movie, *Flaming Star*. It is the story of a mixed-race man, the son of a white father and Indian mother, who becomes involved in the Indian wars of the 1870s. Elvis's character attempts to become the peacemaker, but dies in the end (after singing four songs).

The Colonel tried to get Elvis to sing on horseback, a ploy that Roy Rogers and Gene Autry once used to their cinematic advantage, but Elvis refused and attempted to play the role relatively straight. To his delight, while he was still filming *Flaming Star*, *G.I. Blues* was released and quickly proved to be the biggest box office draw of the decade. The *G.I. Blues* album sold over 3,000,000 copies and stayed at the top of the charts for nearly three months.

After completing work on the film in October, Elvis went to Nashville to record a gospel album, *His Hand in Mine*, then returned to Hollywood to start work on his third film of the year, *Wild in the Country*, co-starring Hope Lange and Tuesday Weld. All summer and into the fall, he experienced manic-depressive episodes during which he was abusive toward his staff and himself. He gorged on food, especially the junk variety, and went for days at a time without bathing.

Women were a constant source of comfort, however temporary, and he slept with as many wannabes, actresses, and wardrobe assistants as he possibly could, sharing the spillover with the staff, who already had circulated the word that the best way to get to Elvis was through their bedrooms. He had always used eye makeup, even in the early days with Sun Records, but now he was dyeing his hair coal-black, a look he associated with the matinee idols of his childhood.

By Christmas, Elvis desperately needed to trust someone, a person from whom he could receive unquestioning approval. That person was Priscilla Beaulieu. He persuaded her parents to allow her to fly to Los Angeles to visit him while he worked on *Wild in the Country*. During the Christmas break he took her to Memphis and put her up in the east wing of Graceland, where she stayed with Vernon and Dee. She returned to Germany on January 2, after staying up all night with Elvis to celebrate the New Year.

When Elvis returned to Los Angeles to resume work on the movie, he had words with the Colonel, first over Priscilla, who frightened Parker to death because of her tender age, then over what he would sing in the movie. Elvis had been told he would not sing, and when songs were added, he refused to sing them.

The Colonel didn't mince words: he told Elvis that songs meant more money for the movie package, and his boy had no choice but to do it. Elvis sang the songs, but then struck back at the Colonel by telephoning Priscilla's parents to ask if they would allow her to move to Memphis and live in Graceland with him. Pointing out that she was only fifteen, they said no.

After wrapping up work on the movie, Elvis returned to Memphis for a few weeks of relaxation. He had been out of the army for over a year and during that time he had not played a single concert. His only public performance in three years had been the taping of the Sinatra television special. He called the Colonel and told him he needed to get out before a live audience again, for sanity's sake if nothing else. He begged his manager to line up a gig for him. Elvis said he would get in touch with the boys in the band.

As always, Scotty told him to count him in. About six months earlier, he had taken a day job as the head of production at Sam Phillips's Recording Service. After supervising several sessions with the explosive Jerry Lee Lewis, he was more than ready to play before a live audience.[19]

D. J. and the Jordanaires were equally enthusiastic. Saying no, again, was Bill Black, who was too busy with his combo. He had enjoyed a monster hit in 1960 with an instrumental version of "Don't Be Cruel," and his gritty, down-in-the-groove music was enormously successful with party-oriented college students.

The Colonel really did not want Elvis to perform live again, but since he could not prohibit his client from doing it, he made the most of what he saw as a bad situation by setting up a charity concert at Memphis's Ellis Auditorium. He arranged for Elvis to play two concerts and make an appearance at a $100-per-plate luncheon, with all the proceeds going to an assortment of charities, including a milk fund for needy children and a day nursery. Elvis paid the overhead for the concerts from his own pocket.

The Colonel made sure he received credit for his good works—tossing pennies to needy children has always been good for business, *any business*—but he had an ulterior motive for setting up the concert the way he did. The message was clear: Elvis could perform live any time he wanted to, if that was what he just had to do, but the entertainer would not be allowed to make money from the performances. On the contrary, he would have to pay money from his own pocket for the pleasure of performing before a live audience.

Elvis was so despondent he really didn't care. He needed to perform, even if he had to pay for it himself. The show ended up being the social event of the year. Tennessee Governor Buford Ellington declared "Elvis Presley Day" and attended the concerts, along with Memphis Mayor Henry Loeb.

RCA sent an emissary to honor the entertainer for selling 75,000,000 records. At a forty-five-minute press conference Elvis was apologetic about his recent lack of musical performances, pointing out that moviemaking was consuming all his time.

"I have not been on stage in three years," he said. "I've almost forgotten the words to one of my songs." When asked if he was nervous about performing again, Elvis said he was, but that it didn't compare to his recent performance with Frank Sinatra. "I wasn't just nervous—I was petrified."[20]

Reporters asked a variety of questions, ranging from observations that he appeared to be getting more conservative—"I'm a little older, you know"—to inquiries about his sideburns—"They were OK for a while, but you outgrow them"—but they always seemed to return to his lack of live performances. When asked if he would be doing any more "barnstorming" like he did in the old days, Elvis's response revealed just how far apart the two had grown on his long-term career goals. Said Elvis: "Colonel Parker could answer that better. Eventually I'll have to do a European tour."

Obviously, Elvis had already talked to Parker about a European tour. Just as obviously, he was perplexed over the Colonel's standoffish reaction. His comment at the press conference seemed to be directed more at Parker than to any reporter present.

It was a comment that psychologists recognize as symptomatic of strife in a relationship. Elvis knew the answer to the reporter's question, but he didn't want to be the one to say it since it was a taboo subject with the Colonel. It was also an opportunity to tell Parker in public that he fully intended to do a European tour.

Scotty recalls the performances that day as being vintage Elvis. They played the old songs, the ones that had put Memphis on the map, and they did so with the old energy, that knack they had of communicating without words, even when engulfed in the midst of a veritable hurricane of musical sounds. At times, Elvis seemed unsure of himself, approaching Scotty between songs to consult about the next number, but clearly the excitement of being on stage again energized him.

For the final song, they performed "Hound Dog," their favorite closer. Elvis dropped to his knees and gave the audience everything he had. Scotty said the audience "went to pieces." Agreeing with Scotty was *Memphis Press-Scimitar* reporter Bill Burk, who wrote the next day that "When the King closed with 'Hound Dog,' as hot a number as he has ever sung, they went wild."

Everything went exactly as the Colonel had planned, except to his surprise—and displeasure—the Tennessee Assembly invited Elvis to Nashville the following week to accept an award. He was made an honorary Tennessee Colonel. Wearing a black suit, and looking slightly incredulous, he stood at the speaker's platform in the House of Representatives and accepted the award with his customary humility.

Mixed in with the lawmakers were dozens of women—the sisters, daughters, mothers, and friends of friends of the lawmakers, who had pulled strings to see the King in person. When he left the room, there was sheer bedlam as a mob of screaming young women pursued him from the chamber and into the hallway. Alone with their thoughts in the sobering stillness of the august chamber, the Tennessee lawmakers pondered the real meaning of power.

"Now I'm a Colonel, too," Elvis told Parker, jabbing him to the quick.[21]

The Colonel's plan called for Elvis to do three films a year. That provided Parker with a guaranteed income of $750,000 a year from the movies alone. When you added the income from record royalties and publishing, that amount was doubled, even tripled.

If Elvis did what he wanted to do and went out on tour, Parker's income would have been significantly reduced. Concert tours required costly logistical support and those expenses would have been deducted before he could take his commission. Movie commissions and record royalties were dependable, delivered in lump sums without deductions, arriving with the regularity of a roulette wheel that travels in the same circle regardless of who is winning or losing.

However, the Colonel had learned a lesson from the Memphis concert. Charity concerts were worth millions in free publicity and goodwill, and they were a convenient and legal tax shelter for expenses incurred in the name of charity. With Elvis's next movie, *Blue Hawaii*, scheduled to be filmed on location, the Colonel decided to organize another charitable concert, with the proceeds going to the proposed memorial for the USS *Arizona*, the battleship sunk in Pearl Harbor by the Japanese.

That news was music to Elvis's ears. He called the boys in the band, and to a man, with the exception of Bill, they signed on for the trip. Elvis would pay them from his own pocket, but it would be worth it to perform in front of a live audience again.

For Scotty, who had spent time in Pearl Harbor in the navy, it represented an opportunity for a homecoming. Marie's presence on the trip surprised everyone. Parker was not in the habit of including his wife in his activities. Why he took her on this particular trip, while excluding her from so many others, is not clear. Perhaps it was because the trip would be the closest he ever came to leaving the country and he wanted Marie's moral support.

Parker was a gamesman. Every action he took was camouflaged with layers of misdirection and self-aggrandizement. When he was engaged in business negotiations, it was never enough to deal with his adversary in a straightforward manner. There was always an angle. Once he negotiated a multi-million-dollar movie deal for his client, but would not accept the hard-fought final offer until his adversary threw in a nearby ashtray as an added incentive.

One of his business associates, who declined to be interviewed on the record, said that Parker had a system of under-the-table signals they used while negotiating business deals. Parker would set the associate up as the deal maker and sit next to him or directly across the table from him, saying nothing in front of the adversary, allowing the associate to do the talking, but always calling the shots under the table by stepping on his toes—one tap for no, two taps for yes, and three to break for a conference.[22]

When the Colonel and Marie arrived in Honolulu aboard the ocean liner *Matsonia*, the city's official greeter, Duke Kanamoku, a part-time movie actor and champion swimmer, welcomed them. Parker was chin deep in floral leis, but he allowed Kanamoku to plant a floral hat atop his head.

Parker made a big deal about raising money for the USS *Arizona*. He told reporters that he expected to raise $200,000 of the million dollars needed for the project. Grateful admirals and generals clustered around Parker, eager to hear more about what he was going to do for them. He told them that they were the guardians of the free world and deserved the gratitude of every mama and papa on the mainland. The admirals and generals slapped him on the back and lapped up his platitudes like milk in a dish. Then Parker told them that he had a little something for each of them.

The Colonel swung open the top of a trunk he had shipped over from Los Angeles. The admirals and generals watched with anticipation as the Colonel reached into the trunk and rummaged about with great ceremony, lifting, moving things about, huffing and puffing, finally finding what he was looking for. He gave each of the men a small

Royal American Shows midway in Tampa (circa 1940s). (Tampa-Hillsborough Public Library System)

Royal American Shows midway as it prepares to open in Memphis. (Mississippi Valley Collection)

Tom Parker with actor Gig Young, during the filming of *Air Force* at Tampa's Drew Field (1942). *(The Tampa Tribune)*

Early public relations photo of Eddy Arnold. (Archive Photos)

Louisiana Governor Jimmie Davis, center, with his band during a campaign stop. (Mississippi Valley Collection)

Colonel Parker, far left, with Eddy Arnold, left of poster, in Tampa in 1946. (Country Music Foundation)

Elvis, Bill Black, and Scotty Moore with Sam Phillips, right, in Sun Records studio. (James R. Reid)

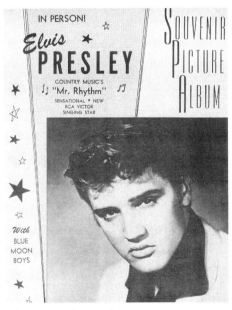

The cover of an early souvenir picture album (circa 1957).

Elvis with Brenda Lee backstage at the Grand Ole Opry. (James L. Dickerson)

Colonel Parker counts complimentary tickets for concert. (James R. Reid)

Colonel Parker in Memphis (circa late 1950s). (James R. Reid)

Elvis and Colonel Parker returning to Memphis after Elvis's discharge from the army. (James R. Reid)

Elvis Presley's Memphis homecoming after discharge from army.
Parker can be seen to the left saying good-bye to army officers.
(Archive Photos)

Tom Parker with movie producer Hal Wallis, left, and Wallis associate,
Joseph Hazen, right, at Paramount Studios (January 18, 1961).
(Mississippi Valley Collection)

Tom Parker with his wife, Marie, and Duke Kanamoku upon their arrival in Hawaii. (Mississippi Valley Collection)

Colonel Parker congratulates Elvis at a birthday part on the set of *Wild in the Country* (1961). (James R. Reid)

Tom Parker with Vernon Presley, center, and Mark King, left (circa 1961). (Mississippi Valley Collection)

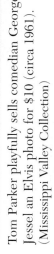

Tom Parker playfully sells comedian George Jessel an Elvis photo for $10 (circa 1961). (Mississippi Valley Collection)

Colonel Parker out on the road selling souvenirs.   (James R. Reid)

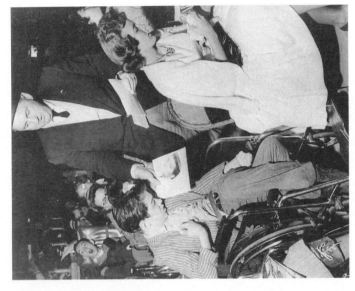

Colonel Parker works the audience at an Elvis concert. (James R. Reid)

Tom Parker meets with Elvis fans: Mrs. Bertha Smith, grandmother of Carol Smith, 17, and Susan Comer, 16. (Mississippi Valley Collection)

Publicity photo of Elvis for his movie *Harum Scarum*. (MGM Publicity Photo)

Colonel Parker all dressed up with nowhere to go. (Country Music Foundation)

Record producer Chips Moman in 1968, about five months before he went into the studio with Elvis to record his celebrated Memphis album. (Mississippi Valley Collection)

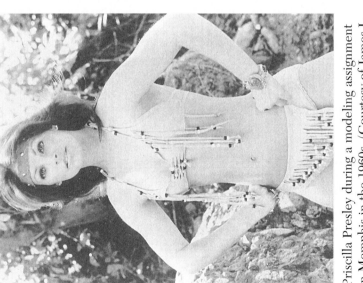

Priscilla Presley during a modeling assignment in Memphis in the 1960s. (Courtesy of James L. Dickerson; photographer unknown)

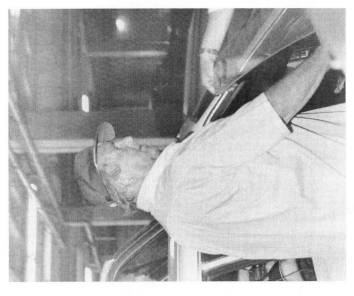

Colonel Parker in Memphis in 1981. (James R. Reid)

Fans tour Elvis's jet, the Lisa Marie, at Graceland. (James L. Dickerson)

Scotty Moore on the steps of a Nashville
business (1995). (James L. Dickerson)

Scotty Moore with the Jordanaires at his home in Nashville. (James L.
Dickerson)

pocket calendar and thanked them for the sacrifices they were making for their country.[23]

When they asked if they could have complimentary tickets to the concert, Parker said that was out of the question. Since it was for charity, everyone had to pay. Even Elvis paid for his own ticket, he said, which was true, for the Colonel had convinced the entertainer that civic duty required him to pay his own way. There would be a special section set aside for the army and navy top brass, though, and it wouldn't cost them a penny above the standard $100-a-ticket price.

After the admirals and generals left the room, the Colonel raised the lid on his trunk to show a local disc jockey his treasure. The trunk was filled with eight-by-ten color photographs of Elvis—bright, glossy, *expensive* souvenirs. He had given the admirals and generals the trinkets he thought they deserved, and kept the good stuff to sell at the concert.

With the disc jockey looking on, Parker counted out two tickets and handed them to the black chauffeur who had been assigned to him. The complimentary tickets placed the chauffeur right in the middle of the top brass. He would be the only black man there. What a hoot that was going to be!

Since Elvis was paying for everything, the Colonel beefed up the show with one of his former clients, country comedian Minnie Pearl (and probably took a commission on what Elvis paid her). Parker had not been joking when he said that if Elvis wanted to play live, he would have to pay for it himself.

Joined by Scotty and D. J., the Jordanaires, Boots Randolf on sax, and Floyd Cramer on piano, Elvis gave the crowd of four thousand one of his best performances ever, according to Scotty, who was surprised to see him perform for nearly an hour. He strutted across the stage, dropping to his knees, playing the crowd like he and they were still teenagers. It would be Elvis's last performance for eight years.

At the end of the concert, the Colonel settled up with the memorial committee. Different sources give different totals for the amount paid to the committee—author Jerry Hopkins says the committee received $47,000, plus another $10,000 from Elvis and the Colonel; another source says the Colonel gave only $5,000 to the committee—but, whichever total is used, it was considerably smaller than the

$200,000 the Colonel promised to reporters and far less than the sum brought in by the $100-per-ticket, 4,000-seat, sold-out concert.

After the benefit performance, the band returned to the mainland, but Elvis and the Colonel stayed in Honolulu to film *Blue Hawaii.* It was the story of a man who returned from the service to take a job, against his parents' wishes, with a travel agency. It co-starred Angela Lansbury as his mother and Joan Blackman as his love interest. Juliet Prowse was scheduled to play opposite Elvis, but was replaced at the last minute, to the great displeasure of her fiancé, Frank Sinatra, who felt she was mistreated.

At age fifty-two, Colonel Parker was experiencing his second childhood. He made a pest of himself on location, frequently interrupting filming with inane questions. According to Jerry Hopkins, he also made a fool of himself at the hotel, where he made a dummy microphone from an aluminum cigar tube and roamed about the lobby interviewing people for what he said was the Pineapple Network.

Parker talked two of the local disc jockeys into wearing oversized snowman suits in the hotel lobby. He told them that they had to do it to become members of the Snowmen's League. He said they would receive official Snowmen's League memberships, but waited five years to send them the cards.

A snowman, of course, was a carny who stuck the poker into the sucker and extracted the cash. In Parker's case, the word snow was a misnomer, for his "snow" was invariably as black as the coal from his fictitious home of West Virginia. "He's so weird," said Ron Jacobs, one of the disc jockeys. "I love that weird sonofabitch."

After finishing *Blue Hawaii,* Elvis returned to Memphis for a few weeks, then went to Florida to film *Follow That Dream.* He was now a full-time movie actor. When Parker and Presley arrived in Florida, they set up headquarters at the Paradise Motel near Crystal River, a small town about fifty miles north of Tampa.

Most of the film was scheduled to be shot in and around Crystal River and nearby Port Paradise, but some scenes were booked for Tampa, which delighted Parker because it gave him an opportunity to visit old friends. One of Parker's Tampa friends was Frank Connors, a former vocalist with Abe Lyman's band and an announcer on NBC radio.

When Parker learned that Frank's twenty-three-year-old daughter, Sharon, who had graduated Phi Beta Kappa from the University of Chicago, wanted to be an actress, he arranged for her to get the role of a secretary in *Follow That Dream*. When Tampa reporters tracked down Sharon and talked to her about her big break, she was optimistic about her future as an actress: "I like variety in acting . . . [and] would love to do Lady Macbeth."[24]

Throughout filming, the working title was *What a Wonderful Life*. Only after work was completed was the title changed to *Follow That Dream*. The screenplay, based on the Richard Powell novel, *Pioneer Go Home*, was a take on the country bumpkin *Li'l Abner* theme and had Elvis's character besieged by young women and not sure what to do about it as he fights for the rights of a squatter who refuses to vacate his land.

Mirisch Brothers, in association with United Artists, produced the movie. Mirisch Brothers already had two substantial hits under its belt with *Some Like It Hot* and *The Apartment*, and Florida officials went out of their way to facilitate production of the movie. As it turned out, some Floridians felt the state went *too far*.

In August, newspapers across the state carried an Associated Press story that reported that the Florida Development Commission had paid $8,000 in state funds to Mirisch Brothers to assist in the production of the movie. Typical of headlines across the state was the one in the *Tampa Tribune*—"Florida Pays $8,000 for Elvis Movie."

Reacting to the headlines, Parker lashed out at the newspapers. "If the state is paying Presley $8,000 to come here, we haven't seen any of the money," he told a reporter for the *Tampa Tribune*. "I know the newspapers can't help how the subscribers read their stories, but one lady went up to Elvis in Inverness today and said she didn't know the state had to pay his expenses. The funny part of it is—the state isn't paying Presley anything. It's the studio that's supposed to get the money. We get a salary, no more, no less, for coming here."

It was Colonel Tom at his best playing the role of a W. C. Fields character, raising his voice, rolling his cigar, showing outrage at the folly of mere mortals intent on hindering the advancement of art.

The criticism stunned the state. Florida Governor Farris Bryant defended the agency's actions by saying it was a worthwhile investment and would promote tourism. Coming to the governor's aid was the *Tampa Tribune*, which said in an editorial: "True, there may be a few of us whose opinions of Elvis Presley's worth as a singer or movie actor fall somewhat below the $8,000 mark. But that has no more to do with it than a houn' dawg."

The newspaper pointed out that Mirisch Brothers spent half a million dollars making the film and that the commission's main job was to promote new business, ". . . [and] anytime the Development Commission can bring in half a million dollars of new money by spending $8,000 it's a good deal."

Parker admitted that the whole thing puzzled him. "I tell you one thing," he told reporters. "After all this stink spreads around a little more, the movie producers in Hollywood will take a second look before they come to Florida again for a picture. Nobody likes to get caught in the middle of a political football game, like this thing seems to be."[25] The Colonel had the last word and the uproar dissipated almost as quickly as it had arisen.

Of course, there was more to the uproar than met the eye. The Colonel never ventured into the media snakepit without good reason or a sense of control. The entire episode—at least Parker's involvement in it—was apparently devised as a smokescreen for what he really wanted from the state of Florida: legal protection.

The script for *Follow That Dream* called for a scene in which pretend mobsters conducted illegal gaming operations with real roulette wheels and blackjack tables. To film the scene, Mirisch Brothers needed gaming equipment. Since gambling was illegal in Florida at that time, the moviemakers asked Parker to help. Obtaining the roulette wheels and blackjack tables was no problem for Parker. No one knows for sure where the equipment came from, but the most likely sources were Tampa warehouses owned by the Trafficantes or from his Las Vegas friend Bill Miller, then president of the Dunes Hotel.

Parker did not want the set to be raided by local or state police, who would then demand to know from where the illegal devices came. The uproar over the state's $8,000 investment in the movie, which Mirisch Brothers never needed, linked the governor and the state to the project in a way that guaranteed there would be no raids on the set and nothing said about the gaming equipment. Whether the Colonel devised the scheme or simply took advantage of it matters less than the fact that he was able to use state officials and the media to his advantage.

One interesting development was Elvis's decision to cancel a visit to Tampa for scenes scheduled for filming on the causeway. Doubles were used instead. Elvis wanted no part of his manager's hometown. Most of the press coverage for the past several weeks had focused on the entertainer's relationship with Parker, leading Art Sarnow, the movie's publicist, to tell reporters, "It's true Presley relies heavily on Tom Parker, but the boy's no dumb-bunny. He shows pretty good judgment himself."[26] Staying away from Tampa was Elvis's way of displaying that good judgment.

The following April, *Follow That Dream* premiered at a movie theater in Ocala, Florida, leading the enthusiastic director of the Development Commission to proclaim that the movie would "sell Florida around the world."

No one said a word about the gaming equipment.

By 1962, the plot lines of Elvis's films were all beginning to run together, and the music was taking on a sameness that horrified his earlier fans. *Kid Galahad* was about boxing and girls, and *Girls! Girls! Girls!* was about girls and girls. And so it went. Paramount's Hal Wallis never pretended the films were anything other than hormone candy for America's female moviegoing audience. He and the Colonel were in perfect agreement about what they were doing, and while he often told people he would just as soon make a deal with the devil himself, he confessed respect for the Colonel, a man he described as a "big, rough kind of guy."

"We would make a deal on a handshake and the papers would come through four or five months later," he told archivists at Southern Methodist University before his death in 1986. "We would be making pictures under a handshake deal. And he always kept his word. He made sure Elvis was always there."

Of all the things about which the Colonel and Wallis agreed, the most important was their assessment of Elvis's acting potential. Neither thought he had a chance of becoming a real actor. To them, he was a singing cartoon character who could pack the movie theaters as well as Daffy Duck or Snow White.

That is one reason Wallis kept changing directors for Elvis's films. The good directors, such as Hal Kanter, would see potential in Elvis and want to develop it, only to run into a brick wall. Unlike some of the other directors who worked with Elvis, Kanter saw a spark of intellectual curiosity that only needed a little work.

"Elvis seemed to be a student of the cinema," says Kanter. "He was a movie fan. He wanted to do a good job in anything he attempted. I had the impression that if he was a truck driver, he would want to be the best truck driver around."[27]

Elvis was offered meatier opportunities on a consistent basis, such as the role of Chance Wayne in Tennessee Williams's *Sweet Bird of Youth*, the part opposite Barbra Streisand in *A Star Is Born*, and a role in *West Side Story*, but the Colonel would not allow him to accept them.

"He could have been a great actor, and might still be here today," says Scotty Moore. "That was something he could have done, even when he got fat. Look at Marlon Brando. He's still a great actor. If Elvis had been given a chance in the movies, that would have given him another avenue."

When it came to Elvis's career, the Colonel had a one-track mind. He would allow no deviation from the tried-and-true formula musicals. The reason for the Colonel's opposition to concerts is understandable—his percentage from live performances involved too much overhead—but his reasons for decisions in other areas remain a mystery.

Frances Preston, head of Broadcast Music, Inc., one of the country's mammoth music licensing organizations, tried for years to get Parker to sign Elvis with BMI so that he would receive royalties from the song titles that bore his name. The Colonel would have no part of that. To Preston's consternation, he steadfastly refused to do it.

"You would write him letters, and he would toss them aside, and you would go talk to him about it and it was like he didn't need the money," Preston says. "It was not until after Elvis's death that Priscilla did that."

☆   ☆   ☆

With the movies being cranked out on schedule, and all that low-overhead money rolling in, the only problem the Colonel had was in managing Elvis's personal life. Against his advice, Elvis called Priscilla's parents and arranged for her to move to the United States to live with him. He promised that he would take good care of her, and he asked his grandmother and his stepmother, Dee, to explain to Priscilla's parents how they would supervise her and enroll her in one of the Memphis Catholic high schools.

Priscilla arrived in Los Angeles while Elvis was still filming *Girls! Girls! Girls!* He arranged for her to stay with a local Cadillac dealer and his wife, but later moved Priscilla out in a huff when he discovered that the dealer was providing Liberace with higher-quality automobiles.

By fall, Priscilla was safely installed at Graceland and enrolled in high school, a great relief to the Colonel who felt that Elvis's relationship with the young girl could be better managed in Memphis. Parker knew that if the Los Angeles media discovered that Elvis was living with Priscilla, they would have a field day. As destructive as the press was toward Jerry Lee Lewis over his marriage to a teenager, it would have been ten times worse if they had not been *married*.

Priscilla was a ticking time bomb.

In Parker's eyes, Elvis's preference for young girls was a weakness—and he despised all weaknesses in others. It is an attitude not uncommon among people who themselves have addictive personalities.

As 1962 drew to an end, the Colonel learned that his friend Lyndon Johnson, who had been elected vice president, planned a trip to Los Angeles. He offered the vice president the use of his home in Palm Springs.

As it worked out, Johnson did not have time to go to Palm Springs; but when he returned to Washington, he dropped the Colonel a line, thanking him for offering the use of his home: "I do appreciate it and perhaps another opportunity will come up—I hope so."[28]

6

TARRED AND FEATHERED WITH HOLLYWOOD GLITTER

Colonel Parker, who increasingly viewed music as a major hindrance to his client's movie career, by 1963 had bargained the creative soul of Elvis Presley to Hollywood. To his way of thinking, the value of Elvis's music lay in its adaptability as a promotional tool for his movies.

If Elvis's future was in Hollywood as an actor, so was Parker's as a manager. He and Marie left their home in Nashville—they held onto it with plans of someday converting it into a museum of the Colonel's treasures and artifacts—and moved into homes in Bel Air and Palm Springs, California.

In need of a substitute for his dingy garage office, Parker talked Paramount into providing him with a five-room suite on its lot. He covered the walls with photographs of Elvis and posters from his movies. One office was devoted entirely to autographed pictures of entertainment and political celebrities. In his private office were dozens of miniature elephants and snowmen of varying sizes, and on the walls were certificates of merit he had received over the years. His desk was covered with tiny statues of elephants and nearby was an elephant's foot trash can.

The Colonel had a low threshold for boredom. His suite of offices quickly became more of a playground than an actual business location. Always a sucker for gadgets, Parker had a public address system installed in his office that allowed him to sit at his desk and bark commands into a microphone that transmitted his words to speakers in all the other offices.

The Colonel seldom used verbal commands to mobilize his staff, according to actor Jon Hartman, who worked in his office for a short time in the 1960s. Instead, he placed a bulb horn, the type used by circus clowns, next to the microphone and squeezed it whenever he wanted to summon his staff. *Honk! Honk! Honk!* In an interview with author Jerry Hopkins, Hartman said the office staff were always tense when Parker was present. "He would call us by squeaking the horn and we'd all have to come running," he said. "He'd squeak the horn into the PA or just squeak until everybody was in there at attention. It was just a game we were playing. It was the Elvis Presley Game."

With the exception of his longtime assistant, Trude Forsher, most people who worked for Parker over the years were male.[1] He didn't seem to have much use for women employees. The male employees were all either related by marriage or by prior association, with the exception of the young men he recruited from the William Morris Agency to work as office interns. Most only stayed a short time.

Elvis's first motion picture of 1963 was *Fun in Acapulco*, which co-starred Ursula Andress, a Swiss-born actress who had co-starred with Sean Connery in *Dr. No*, the first of the James Bond films. Some of the scenes in the movie were filmed in Acapulco, but none included Elvis, who did all of his scenes at Paramount. There were rumors that Elvis had an affair with Andress during the filming, but if that was the case, the affair did not continue after the movie's completion.

Fun in Acapulco concerned a former trapeze artist, played by Elvis, who takes a job as a lifeguard in Acapulco following an accident on the high wire. Of the movies he had made since his discharge from the Army, it had the strongest storyline to date. He sang about a dozen songs in the movie, but there were no singles released from the film and he had to content himself with yet another soundtrack album certified gold. It gave him something to hang on the wall at Graceland, but not very much satisfaction.

Elvis had not forsaken his dreams of becoming a serious actor, but unknown to him, Parker and Hal Wallis had no intention of ever offering him that opportunity. Parker concluded a new deal with Wallis that kept Elvis under contract to Paramount for another three years, through 1966. The Elvis formula was lucrative, and Parker saw no reason to risk a sure thing with a gamble that had no payoff.

Unlike Hal Kanter, who felt Elvis's acting skills could have been cultivated, Wallis never thought his star had the talent to become a serious actor. In later years, after Elvis's death, Wallis told interviewers that he had pushed the entertainer to his limit as an actor. The producer never had any intention of employing him as a serious actor, at least not in the traditional sense. Elvis's value, said Wallis, was in his identity as a rock 'n' roll star and in his charismatic screen presence. The key to a successful Elvis Presley movie, he said, was to have a storyline that would allow him to sing a few songs, to have a fling with a pretty girl, and then to live happily ever after.[2] The idea was to send moviegoers out of the theater with a smile and a fuzzy-wuzzy glow that left them feeling good about themselves.

Unfortunately, it did not allow Elvis to feel good about *himself*. He was being passed over by rock 'n' roll, that bastard child that he, Scotty, and Bill had birthed on a hot night in Memphis and sent out into the world to fend for itself. By 1963, Bobby Vee, Steve Lawrence, the Beach Boys, and Jan and Dean had bumped him off the top of the charts, and while his soundtrack albums invariably went gold, it wasn't the same. It just wasn't.

Scotty accompanied him faithfully into the studio to play on the soundtrack sessions, but it was hardly ever as the lead guitarist and the music they recorded bore little resemblance to what they had done in the early days. Scotty knew they weren't recording great music, but it was a paycheck—a hundred dollars here and there—and that counted for something.

It became a habit as much as anything else.[3] It was mind-numbing work, both in the studio and on the movie lot, and Elvis retreated from the reality of it by bingeing on food, sex, and drugs. In her book, *Elvis and Me*, Priscilla said Elvis started using drugs before entering the army. He took sleeping pills to get him through the night. While stationed in Germany, he started taking amphetamines to keep him alert during the day.

In June, Priscilla graduated from the Catholic all-girls high school, Immaculate Conception. Elvis gave her a Corvair for a graduation present. Out of school, she wasn't sure what she was supposed to do with her life. She did what many young girls do who find themselves in that position: she enrolled in ballet class.

At about that same time, Elvis made a rare visit to Parker's home in Bel Air. The reason for the visit is unclear, but the timing suggests that it was to discuss his relationship with Priscilla. The Colonel was becoming increasingly concerned about what he saw as a potential public relations nightmare. Whatever the nature of their discussion that day, the issue was apparently left unresolved, because Priscilla's status at Graceland remained as it was. For all her attempts at growing up as quickly as possible and assuming a legitimate role in Elvis's public life, she remained a movie star's child-toy.

For his next movie, *Viva Las Vegas*, Elvis went on location. Despite the somewhat subdued reception he had there earlier in his career, the city fascinated him, and he possessed a childlike wonder at the variety of Bible-belt "sins" that were paraded about in broad daylight with apparent immunity. Parker was delighted. He had never stopped going to Vegas; the movie gave him yet another excuse to feed his mushrooming gambling addiction.

Viva Las Vegas, the story of a race car driver on a quest to raise money for a new engine, co-starred Ann-Margret, a striking redhead who had made a splash in the movie *Bye-Bye Birdie* (a take-off on a southern rock 'n' roll star drafted into the army). While on location, Elvis was asked about that by reporters. He said he hadn't seen *Bye-Bye Birdie*, at least not all the way through, and didn't know enough about the movie to comment.

Scenes for Elvis's latest movie were shot in a variety of locations in and around Las Vegas, but the hotel scenes were shot at the Tropicana Hotel and the Flamingo Hotel. Throughout the filming Parker was noticeably unhappy, although no one was ever sure why. He had several run-ins with the picture's producer, Jack Cummings—once over Cummings's refusal to allow him to select the security force used for the movie—but the Colonel didn't win many of those confrontations because Cummings was Louis B. Mayer's son-in-law and was used to getting his own way.

The first verification Priscilla had that Elvis was dating other women came while he was in Las Vegas making the movie. Elvis and Ann-Margret were obviously having an affair, most notably in the President's Suite at the Sahara Hotel, but those involved with the movie company were discreet, as always, and protected Elvis's privacy.

Tearing apart that protective veil was Associated Press movie writer Bob Thomas, who wrote a story about the romance. "This is news to make the younger set flip—Elvis Presley and Ann-Margret are having a romance," wrote Thomas. "They hold hands. They disappear into his dressing room between shots. They lunch together in seclusion." When Thomas asked Ann-Margret about the romance, she said, "That's something I won't talk about."

Thomas's story was printed in the *Memphis Press-Scimitar*, where Priscilla read it. The story crushed her. She may have suspected that he was seeing other women, but she never knew for certain. Reading it in the newspaper made the betrayal even more painful.

The article also shocked Elvis, who had always counted on the press to keep details of his extracurricular activities vague. Thomas's story was an eye-opener. Elvis had always felt that the relative isolation of Memphis somehow protected his relationship with Priscilla. Now he knew that information about his relationships flowed both ways, both in and out of Memphis, and for the first time he began to understand the reasons for Parker's concern.

In November the Colonel was stunned, along with the rest of the nation, by the assassination of President John F. Kennedy. The good news, in Parker's view, was that his friend Lyndon had moved into the Oval Office. Now he was in tight with the *president*! Less than a week after Johnson changed residences, the Colonel sent him a housewarming gift—his trademark covered wagon—to commemorate that very special occasion.[4]

As production began on *Kissin' Cousins*, Elvis's tenth movie since returning from Germany, a new MGM producer entered the picture—Sam Katzman, a penny-pinching administrator known as the "King of the Quickies" because of his penchant for turning out movies in two weeks or less. His most recent film was *Hootenanny Hoot*, a musical revue, and he was working on *Your Cheatin' Heart*, the story of Hank Williams's life, when work began on *Kissin' Cousins*.

The Colonel thought he was a godsend, because the faster a movie was made, the less money was spent on production. Under the terms of Parker's profit-sharing plan with the studio, that meant more money went into his own pocket (he and Elvis received fifty percent of the profits).[5] For example, *Kissin' Cousins* was given a budget of 1.3 million dollars. The picture was made for $600,000, which meant that Elvis and Parker received the difference of $700,000. Once the picture was released, they received fifty percent of the profits from theater receipts.

Gene Nelson, the director Katzman chose for the movie, said that every studio in Hollywood was submitting scripts to Elvis. "In fact, some of us had to wait in line," he told authors Rose Clayton and Dick Heard in *Elvis Up Close*. "Someone would come up with a project and submit it to Colonel Parker. The Colonel always said, 'I don't care what the script is. If you can pay the money up front and twenty-five percent [or whatever], we'll do it.'"[6]

Because he saw Elvis as a country boy, Katzman hired screenwriter Gerald Adams to write an original story for him that would poke fun at what Katzman felt was Elvis's country's roots. In truth, Elvis knew nothing about "country life," having lived in cities his entire life. Katzman's characterization reflected more than a little cultural prejudice against southerners, and was not uncommon for that era. Nobel Prize–winning author William Faulkner, born and raised not far from Elvis's hometown of Tupelo, underwent the same sort of abuse during his career.

Nelson didn't like Adams's script and told Parker that he wanted to make changes. Parker replied that he knew where to find a talking camel that would be perfect for the movie—and at a decent price. Nelson balked at putting the talking camel in the movie, but spent a lot of time rewriting the script. When it was finished, he sent a copy to Parker, perhaps thinking it would be a good idea to have a southerner's opinion, since the Colonel had always claimed West Virginia roots. With the script was a note from Nelson requesting that the Colonel read the script before forwarding it to Elvis.

Parker responded with a note of his own: if Nelson wanted him to evaluate the script, it would cost an additional $25,000. Later, when Nelson asked him about it, Parker said that he and Elvis didn't know anything about making motion pictures.[7] All they were interested in, he said, was getting enough songs into the movie to comprise an album.

Parker was being honest. He wanted a movie that would make money. How that was accomplished depended on the movie companies. The director's job was to use scripts that utilized the "Elvis, girls, fun, and singing" theme that had proved profitable and to work enough songs into the movie to provide RCA with material for an album.

Nelson did what most of the directors that preceded him did—and what all the directors that came after him did. He sent a copy of the script to Freddie Bienstock at Hill and Range in New York. Bienstock's job was to peruse the areas where the director wanted songs and then to assign the songs to writers in the Hill and Range stable.

The writers would create several songs for each suggested scene, make demos, and send them to the director, who would then pick the songs he liked best. The material that Elvis recorded grew worse every year, but the singer felt helpless to do anything about it.

Elvis was so despondent about his career that he refused to celebrate his twenty-ninth birthday. In another year he would be *thirty*. His worst fears about his career were realized less than a week after his birthday when the *Memphis Press-Scimitar* ran a story that criticized him for forsaking rock 'n' roll and chastised him for making so many substandard movies.[8]

Elvis had always rationalized his departure from music as an upward career move that would elevate him to a higher level of stardom, but now he knew it was all just self-deception. To make matters worse, whenever he turned on the radio, he heard a style of rock 'n' roll that was foreign to him. The most played song on the radio that month was the Beatles' "I Want to Hold Your Hand." By the end of the month, it would be the Number One song in America. Elvis had abdicated the rock 'n' roll throne to a bunch of post-teen foreigners. He knew it, and it caused him unbearable pain.

From a business standpoint Colonel Parker's decisions usually were profitable, but there were times when he seemed to be off his game. Early in 1964, he advised Elvis to purchase the *Potomac*, the presidential yacht once used by President Franklin D. Roosevelt, for $55,000 and then to donate it to St. Jude Hospital in Memphis.[9]

The *Potomac* was owned by Hydro Capital of Newport Beach, California, which had invested $250,000 in the ship, and had moved it to Long Beach Harbor at Los Angeles. Why a company that had invested a quarter of a million dollars in refurbishing a ship would sell it for $55,000—and the nature of the company's relationship with Colonel Parker—remains a mystery to this day. Both Parker and company officials declined to discuss with reporters the nature of the relationship. Once he purchased the ship, Elvis turned it over to entertainer Danny Thomas, chief benefactor of St. Jude Hospital, who told reporters he felt like he was "playing ping pong" with a historical artifact.

Pushed by reporters for a statement on what the hospital would do with the ship, Thomas said it would probably be sold as scrap—and at a price less than what Elvis paid for it. Not helping Elvis's self-image was an article in the *Memphis Press-Scimitar* that referred to the ship as a "white elephant."[10]

Exactly what Parker had in mind is uncertain and may never come to light, but whatever it was he had up his sleeve almost certainly involved a second- and third-level payoff, artfully disguised and designed to benefit someone other than Elvis. That was just the way the Colonel operated. Never was that more evident than in his machinations to distribute Elvis's earnings from the songs registered in the singer's name under the Hill and Range umbrella and from various merchandising schemes. For example, Elvis owned fifteen percent of Songman Music, but Parker owned forty percent; Bienstock owned fifteen percent, George Parkhill at RCA owned fifteen percent, and Tom Diskin owned fifteen percent.

Basically, Parker's motivation for cutting so many people into Elvis's profits was to save money for himself. When he needed something done, instead of paying the individual, he would create a new publishing company and give the individual a percentage of the company. That way, it was Elvis, ultimately, who paid for everything.

Adding to Elvis's concerns and self-doubts were a series of events and misfortunes involving his friends and new threats against his personal safety. In January Elvis received a postcard with a Huntsville, Alabama, postmark that was addressed to "President Elvis Presley." The card said, "You will be next on my list." Beneath that warning was a list of five names that began with Elvis and included Johnny Cash, Alabama Governor George Wallace, and a "President JBJ [sic]."[11]

Vernon took the postcard to the Memphis FBI office, but when FBI agents showed the postcard to the U.S. Attorney, he said he didn't consider it prosecutable within the federal extortion statute. He really didn't want to get involved. What seemed to bother the FBI more than the threat against Elvis was the reference to a "President JBJ."

The initials were close enough to those of President Lyndon B. Johnson that the FBI considered the postcard a potential threat against the president and handled it accordingly. The postcard was examined by the FBI lab, which was unable to match it with other anonymous letters on file. Nor were there any identifying watermarks on the card or indented writing features that would be useful in identifying the letter writer. The case was turned over to the Secret Service and the threat, insofar as Elvis was concerned, was ignored by authorities.[12] As always, Parker kept his distance.

As all that was going on, Elvis's guitarist and friend, Scotty Moore, was having problems of his own. While overseeing operation of Sam's studio in Nashville, he was asked by producer Billy Sherrill, who worked with him in the studio, to do an album of instrumentals. Scotty had been talking to Sam about that for a long time, but Sam had always put him off. When Sherrill offered to produce the album and then obtained a contract from Epic Records, Scotty jumped at the chance. The album was entitled *The Guitar That Changed the World* and featured many of the early hits Scotty had recorded with Elvis, all recorded as instrumentals.

Scotty told Sam about the album, but Sam's reaction was unexpected—he fired him. Scotty moved to Nashville, yet another indication to Elvis that his world was slowly coming apart. Hopeful that Colonel Parker would help him out with the album, Scotty sent an acetate of the recording to him, along with a note saying that he would "deem it an honor" if Parker wrote the liner notes.[13]

Parker asked Tom Diskin to respond. In a letter Diskin informed Scotty that the Colonel would be unable to contribute liner notes since there were "restrictions that do not permit the use of Elvis's name in conjunction with another commercial record." Diskin returned the acetate to Scotty and promised to purchase the record when it was released. Said Diskin: "You have to admit that is the best kind of endorsement."

It was a slap in the face, one the Colonel didn't have the guts to deliver himself, but Scotty was not the least bit surprised. When he asked the Colonel to write the liner notes, he had omitted the critical ingredient: he had not included cash, check, or money order.

Each year the movies seemed to get worse.

The first movie of 1965 was *Harum Scarum*, a nonsensical piece of fluff directed by Gene Nelson and produced by Sam Katzman. Elvis's co-star was Mary Ann Mobley, the former Miss America from Mississippi. No sooner did he finish it than he started work on *Frankie and Johnny*, a bigger budget film for MGM that was produced by Edward Small and directed by Frederick de Cordova, who later was best known as the producer of Johnny Carson's *Tonight Show*.

Then followed another film for Paramount, *Paradise, Hawaiian Style*, produced by Hal Wallis and directed by Michael Moore. Although some scenes were shot at the Paramount lot, most were filmed in Hawaii during the first couple of weeks in August, thereby giving Elvis a break from the stifling heat in Memphis and the isolation of his Hollywood lifestyle.

Unfortunately, Hawaii didn't have the soothing effect on Elvis that everyone thought it would. He displayed sudden mood swings and outbursts of temper, and didn't show up on the set for two days because of what his aides described as "stomach cramps." His actions on the set were so out of line that newspaper columnist Hedda Hopper was prompted to write a critical story about him; it was the first time anyone had pointed out his increasingly erratic nature.

Elvis's exotic and unpredictable behavior on the set of *Paradise, Hawaiian Style* was subsequently attributed to the uppers and downers he was taking regularly, and to the slump in his career as a recording artist. Both factors may have played a role, but the most likely instigator of his behavior was probably the news that Bill Black had been diagnosed with a brain tumor, the very mention of which strikes fear in the hearts of creative people. Recording artists, writers, painters—anyone who makes a living using their creative talents—know it is the very worst way to die. For that to happen to one of the original Blue Moon Boys, someone with whom he had begun his career, devastated Elvis.

Even if Elvis had not maintained affection for Bill—and there is every indication he did, despite Bill's refusal to continue working for him—the diagnosis hit too close to home to be dismissed as one of those unfortunate things that happen in life. The recovery rate for brain surgery was not high in 1965 and the diagnosis of brain cancer was usually considered a death sentence. When Elvis learned of Bill's illness, he visited him at his home. Before Elvis left, he took Bill's wife, Evelyn, aside and asked her not to be offended if he did not attend the funeral, for he felt his presence would make a sideshow out of the solemn service. Evelyn said she understood.[14]

By the time Elvis returned from Hawaii, the Colonel was growing concerned about his boy's emotional well-being, and decided to start a public relations campaign designed to stroke Presley's fragile ego by focusing media attention on him as a superstar. The first thing Parker did was to arrange a meeting between his client and the Beatles.

The Beatles' manager, Brian Epstein, had been in contact with Parker for more than a year in an effort to set up a meeting. Elvis had not been interested. Watching the popularity of the Beatles eclipse his own had depressed him; he wanted nothing to do with them. Whenever the Colonel had to say no to Epstein, he always followed up with gifts from "Elvis and the Colonel." Once he sent cowboy suits and real six-shooters.

As Elvis wrapped up *Paradise, Hawaiian Style*, the Beatles began their second American tour by performing at Shea Stadium in New York before 55,000 fans. It was the largest rock concert crowd in history and the media were inundated with stories about the antics of Paul, John, George, and Ringo. As they had done during their 1964 American tour, they again performed at the Hollywood Bowl.

Epstein contacted the Colonel about arranging a meeting. The Beatles idolized Elvis and had no idea that he was bitter about their success. They simply wanted to meet the King of Rock 'n' Roll. This time Parker persuaded Elvis that it was in his best interests to meet with them. When the Beatles arrived at his house, Elvis greeted them at the door. Whatever his personal feelings about their music and their un-American lifestyles, he played the role of the gracious host. In the background a jukebox alternated Elvis songs with Beatles songs.

The Colonel was there as well, gleefully yanking the cover from a roulette wheel to show the Beatles his favorite toy. After an awkward beginning (for what seemed like an eternity the Fab Four and Elvis sat and stared at each other without anyone saying a word), everyone loosened up. Before the four-hour visit ended, they jammed on several songs, including the Beatles' "I Feel Fine," on which Elvis played bass.

As the Beatles were leaving, they invited Elvis to visit them the following night (he said he would, but didn't). They also received tokens of appreciation from "Elvis and the Colonel": small covered wagons that lit up whenever the battery-powered bulbs were activated. The gifts were not as spectacular as the cowboy outfits they had earlier received, but it was the thought that counted.

Witnessing the public's reaction to the Beatles made the Colonel even more determined to get his boy back in the spotlight. Shortly after the Beatles left, Parker helped *Variety* and the *Saturday Evening Post* put together stories that proclaimed Elvis to be the biggest star in show business. The publications based their assessment on his estimated 1965 income. *Variety* put Elvis's income from all sources for the year at between $4 and $5 million, with his movie salaries alone amounting to $2.7 million.

For the first time, Parker allowed numbers to be tossed about that revealed income from specific projects. For *Harum Scarum*, Elvis received $1 million, plus forty percent of the net. For *Frankie and Johnny*, he received $650,000, plus fifty percent of the net. *Variety* said that Elvis's royalties for the year would amount to $300,000, not including publishing royalties and money received from performance fees.

Towing the Parker-inspired line was *Memphis Press-Scimitar* entertainment writer Edwin Howard. "I don't believe that anybody in show business, except possibly the Beatles, will be in that $5 million bracket with Elvis this year," wrote Howard. "And don't forget—everything they make is subject to a four-way split. Elvis, like the rest of us, can be thankful there are not four of him."

That was exactly the message Parker wanted the public—and, most of all, Elvis—to hear. Elvis wasn't making hit records like the Beatles were doing, but he had been there, done that. He had moved on to a higher level of stardom, one measured by the size of a paycheck and not by the size of the crowd.

At first, it looked as if Parker's plan might work. Then, early in October, Bill Black went into a coma. Memphis newspapers reported the news, writing retrospective stories about the success the thirty-nine-year-old bassist and Elvis had enjoyed in the 1950s. It must have come as a cold shot to Elvis, who not only had to deal with the impending death of a friend, but the impending death of his career as a recording artist. The way they wrote about Bill's success with Elvis made it sound as if it had all happened so long ago.

After regaining consciousness for a short time, Bill died on October 22. Evelyn and other family members had maintained a constant vigil at his bedside, but when the end came, Bill was alone in his room. Everyone had gone to the cafeteria to get something to eat, largely at the insistence of the nurses who wanted them to keep up their strength.[15]

Elvis did not attend the funeral, but he invited Scotty and D. J. and their wives to Graceland immediately after the service so that they could commiserate together. Later, Elvis went by to pay his respects to Evelyn. At his side was Priscilla, who alone seemed to truly understand what Elvis was going through.

Feeling the benefits of his publicity blitz slipping away, Parker revved up his public relations engine yet again by giving Hollywood writer Dick Kleiner a story that was syndicated in newspapers across the country. This time, Parker released information about the money Elvis donated to charity ($35,000 to Memphis charities alone), the salaries he paid his twelve aides and bodyguards ($10,000 a year, according to the story), the number of cars and motorcycles he owned, and the luxuriant dressing room provided to him by Paramount (two refrigerators, one used exclusively for ice cream).

Kleiner's story also focused on the adoration Elvis received from his fans. He told of the time Elvis was in New Orleans and was held hostage for an hour on a stalled elevator by six young girls who gagged and bound the elevator operator. The Colonel seemed to be saying, Let's see the Beatles top that! As with any Parker anecdote about Elvis, the reader is advised to consider the source.

What Parker wanted to prove to Elvis and to a world seemingly gone mad over the Beatles and other emerging British groups like the Rolling Stones was that there existed a larger, more significant legend sitting on the throne of American music. The publicity blitz didn't work. Not with the public: not even with Elvis, who was becoming increasingly morose about his career and surprisingly unresponsive to the Colonel.

Commercial Appeal reporter James Kingsley heard rumors that the Colonel was going to retire and that Elvis was looking for another manager. He called the Colonel and asked if the rumors were true. "Not on your life," the Colonel sputtered. Retirement was the last thing on his mind. He said that Elvis also had called him about the rumors. According to the newspaper, the Colonel told Elvis, "It's the usual rumor, son. If I ever decide to retire, you will be the first to know. You can bet on that."

In March 1966, while filming *Spinout*, Elvis received visitors on the movie set—Lynda Bird Johnson, daughter of President Lyndon Johnson, and Lynda Bird's date, actor George Hamilton.

Elvis was cocky about the visit, according to reports, and made certain that everyone around him could see how important he had become. He was gracious to his visitors, but not so endearing to those working on the movie. Some described him as obnoxious.

Johnson's primary behind-the-scenes advisor was Memphis-born Abe Fortas, whom he had appointed to the Supreme Court the previous year. Fortas was to Johnson what Diskin was to Parker—a trusted confidant, the one individual he could count on to get the job done, whatever was involved. Since a Supreme Court justice advising a sitting president on sensitive political issues violated the separation-of-powers doctrine, Johnson and Fortas kept their working relationship a secret.

Just as Parker had a secret connection to Johnson, Fortas had a secret connection to Elvis. Fortas's link to Elvis began in Memphis, where the Supreme Court justice had grown up amid the wicked and violent nightlife that thrived on Beale Street, and from there it extended into Elvis's inner circle.[16] At Humes High in Memphis, Elvis went to school with a heavyset boy named Alan Fortas. Growing up, Alan excelled at football, probably because of his size, and had a reputation as a tough guy. Elvis hired him as a bodyguard and traveling companion in 1958, and provided him with several pistols that he was expected to keep on his person or close by in the event he was called upon to defend the King. Alan Fortas was Abe Fortas's nephew.

The Johnson-Fortas-Parker connection was significant. By the time Lynda Bird showed up on the set of *Spinout*, Abe Fortas had formed ties with a company that was involved with various Las Vegas casino operations. The Great American was a Nevada company that had ties to the Thunderbird Hotel, whose license had been revoked in 1955 because of the hotel's links to organized crime. Fortas served on the Great American's board of directors. FBI investigators also were interested in his suspected involvement, through Justice William Douglas, with the Parvin Foundation, which held stock in a Las Vegas casino associated with Florida crime boss Meyer Lansky.[17] The Colonel had always enjoyed walking the darker side of American life. It had been a cheap thrill in the early days, before his gambling obsession had gotten out of hand, but now the stakes were much higher.

☆   ☆   ☆

Elvis returned to Memphis after wrapping up work on *Spinout* and once again was inundated by another public relations campaign orchestrated by Parker. There was talk of building an Elvis Presley monument in Memphis. Said one city commissioner: "Elvis Presley . . . has brought much good publicity to our area. I think the city and county should dig in and do something for him."[18]

The extent of the Colonel's concern about Elvis's future—and the future of their relationship—can be seen in his decision to have Memphis radio stations air a Mother's Day tribute to Gladys Presley. A Memphis newspaper reporter was the first to inform Elvis of the Colonel's plans with a story that said twelve area stations would be airing the tribute, with additional stations in Tampa, San Francisco, Los Angeles, and Palm Springs also carrying the half-hour show. Wrote the reporter: "Your mother, who raised you through the hard days of youth, lived to see you famous and wealthy. She did not live to see the respect you earned as a person in your public conduct."

News that the 1966 Cotton Carnival would feature wax dummies of the Beatles erased whatever good effects had accrued from the Mother's Day show. Elvis always had a soft spot in his heart for the Cotton Carnival, for it had been one of his early supporters and the site of good times on the midway, but it was a definite downer for the Beatles—and wax ones at that—to be proclaimed the stars of the show.

Royal American had no idea how strongly Elvis felt about the Beatles. Carl Sedlmayr had died since the previous Cotton Carnival and his son, Carl Jr., had taken over operation of the midway. Royal American's last two visits to Memphis had not been without controversy. One year, the girlie show was not allowed to open. Another year, a disabled veteran, who complained that midway officials had charged him ten dollars to peddle his wares, publicly criticized Royal American. The 1966 Memphis Cotton Carnival was Carl Jr.'s first as the new boss and he wanted to put a contemporary face on the midway. To him, the Beatles were perfect.[19]

Coming on the heels of that indignity was a review of Elvis's new movie, *Paradise, Hawaiian Style*. John Knott, the *Commercial Appeal*'s movie critic, savaged Elvis in a review that bore the headline: "Elvis'

Acting Still Limps After 10 Years, 12 Movies." Knott pointed out that there was a line of people waiting outside the theater when he arrived, a rarity for an afternoon showing, but then he downplayed the importance of the movie and called its star "a little bit jowly." Wrote Knott: "His movies haven't changed: Not much acting, not much plot."

In some respects the Colonel was himself fraying at the seams. The frequency of his trips to Las Vegas had increased, as had his losses at the tables. By 1966, gambling was a full-blown addiction with him. The only aspect of his personal life that was under control was his marriage and that probably played a major role in the level of stability he was able to maintain in the face of Elvis's erratic behavior.

Toward the end of the year, the Colonel went to Memphis to have a heart-to-heart with Elvis. The King had not had a record on the charts in quite some time. The movies were still turning profits, but no one knew how much longer that would last. What really worried Parker was Elvis's five-year relationship with Priscilla. Elvis's popularity was too fragile, too uncertain for the long haul, for the entertainer to risk his history with a minor coming to light and its successive exploitation by news-hungry reporters. The press would destroy him, just as it had destroyed Jerry Lee Lewis.

The Colonel was blunt: Elvis needed to get rid of the girl, send her back to live with mama and daddy, or he needed to marry her. According to some reports, Parker leaned toward marriage. He probably thought it would settle Elvis down, providing him with the grounding Parker had received from his own marriage. Love or sex was not a consideration. It was a business decision.

After the Colonel returned to California, Elvis resolved to propose to Priscilla. He had invested too much time and emotion into the relationship to turn it loose. A day or so before Christmas, Priscilla was alone in her room when she heard a light tapping at her door. Then she heard the voice, his voice, saying that he needed to talk to her about something.

At first, she teased him, requiring that he use the childish password they had devised. Finally, he gave in. "Fire Eyes," he said. Once inside the room, he told her to close her eyes. When she opened them, he was on his knees with a small velvet box in his hand. He showed her the ring inside the box, then told her that they were going to be married.

Priscilla couldn't believe her own eyes. "Our love would no longer be a secret," she wrote in her autobiography, *Elvis and Me.* "I'd be free to travel openly as Mrs. Elvis Presley without the fear of inspiring some scandalous headline. Best of all, the years of heartaches and fears of losing him to one of the many girls who were always auditioning for my role were over."

Elvis and Priscilla agreed on a spring wedding. Colonel Parker, that most unlikely of nuptial experts, was in charge of all the arrangements.

Informing Elvis of his upcoming wedding was not the only news the Colonel had for his client when he made his pre-Christmas visit to Graceland. Beginning January 2, 1967, the Colonel's management percentage would increase from twenty-five percent to fifty percent, except from publishing, which would remain at twenty-five percent. In two years, all other "music firm" percentages also would increase to fifty percent.[20]

There was no witness to the conversation when the Colonel informed him of the change, and no letters were exchanged or clarifying documents drawn up. The Colonel's explanation for the change and Elvis's reaction to it may never be known. Certainly, he could not have been very happy about it.

The industry standard for a manager's commission was ten to fifteen percent, with isolated examples of twenty-five percent commissions. Fifty percent commissions were not unheard of in the entertainment industry, but in those rare instances when they occurred, they always represented true partnerships between the client and the manager. In those cases, the manager also provided the client with fifty percent of his or her income. The most famous example was the agreement between manager Ken Greenspan and entertainers Steve Lawrence and Edie Gorme. Greenspan took half of their income; Steve and Edie took half of his income. Unusual, but fair.

The Colonel offered Elvis no such deal. Under the Colonel's plan he kept everything he earned, and he took half of what Elvis earned. It was unprecedented. Why would Elvis agree to such a deal?

Some explain it by saying that his career was in such bad shape he felt he had no choice. They point to his lack of hit records. If he wanted to keep earning a living, so the argument goes, he would have to give the Colonel whatever he asked for. That rationale simply does not hold up.

Elvis's income for 1965, according to newspaper reports that the Colonel himself orchestrated, was $4 to $5 million, including nearly $3 million from his movie salaries. Elvis was hardly desperate. He did three films that year—*Harum Scarum, Frankie and Johnny*, and *Paradise, Hawaiian Style*. In 1966, he did three films—*Spinout, Double Trouble*, and *Easy Come, Easy Go*. The following year, the year his new contract went into effect, he did three films—*Clambake, Speedway*, and *Stay Away, Joe*.

So, what was the Colonel thinking?

By 1967, his gambling losses in Las Vegas were staggering. Within a couple of years, Alex Shoofey, general manager of the International Hotel, would say publicly that the Colonel's losses at his hotel amounted to $1 million a year.[21] That was just at one hotel. With Elvis's yearly income averaging $4 to $5 million at that point, the Colonel's twenty-five percent commission would have given him $1 to $1.25 million a year in income, hardly enough to cover his losses at one hotel.

One possibility for the Colonel's explanation to Elvis for a change in the contract could have been that he owed more money than he could raise and needed a greater percentage of Elvis's earnings so that he would have enough money to live on. Perhaps he was honest with Elvis and told him that he was in trouble. The second possibility—and the more likely one, according to the available facts—is that the Colonel lost his twenty-five percent commission, either outright in a wager or as the result of his accumulative gambling debts, to whomever held his Las Vegas markers.

It is doubtful that Parker told Elvis that was the reason he put him into the army in 1958, for his client would not have understood at his age; but now Elvis was older and had time to see how the world really operated. This time he would have explained to Elvis that someone else owned twenty-five percent of his contract and unless he received an additional twenty-five percent he would be unable to continue working as his manager.

If Elvis had protested, the Colonel could have said, "I lost you fair and square." If Elvis had suggested they contact the authorities, the Colonel could have said, "Where you gonna go? They brought the president's daughter by to see you, that's how powerful they are. You can't go no higher than the president." If Elvis had expressed fears about his own personal safety, the Colonel could have told him that he was right to be afraid. He would point out that his most trusted bodyguard, Alan Fortas, was Abe Fortas's nephew: "In a showdown, who's he gonna take orders from—you or Las Vegas?"

We now know that the December–January period was when Elvis first started suffering from prolonged periods of depression. He never talked to his entourage about his new contract with the Colonel, but he told Marty Lacker, according to authors Rose Clayton and Dick Heard, that he was being pressured to marry Priscilla.

Of all the places for Elvis and Priscilla to be married, Las Vegas was the most inappropriate, but with Parker in charge of the ceremony, what would you expect? Obviously, Las Vegas was where the Colonel was most comfortable. With the wedding set for May 1, 1967, Elvis and Priscilla went to Los Angeles several days prior to that date to peruse the schedule the Colonel had arranged for them. Since he was worried about the press getting wind of the impending marriage, the Colonel arranged for them to use a house in Palm Springs.

The day before the wedding, he had them drive to Palm Springs and spend the night (it was a ruse to throw reporters off the track). The next morning Elvis and Priscilla rose before dawn, flew to Las Vegas in a Lear jet borrowed from Frank Sinatra, and arrived at the city clerk's office shortly after it opened to obtain a marriage license. From there, they rushed to the Aladdin Hotel, where a Jewish judge married them in hotel owner Milton Prell's private suite. Parker could not have used a rabbi without attracting attention, but a judge was different.

Also attending Elvis and Priscilla's wedding were the Colonel and Marie; Vernon and Dee; Priscilla's stepfather and mother, Major and

Mrs. Beaulieu; the two best men, Joe Esposito and Marty Lacker (and their wives); his old friend George Klein; and a handful of other people. Not invited were Alan Fortas and the other members of the so-called Memphis Mafia.

Immediately after the wedding, the Colonel escorted Elvis and Priscilla to a press conference, during which Elvis answered questions about his private life. From there they went to a reception, where the guest list was composed mostly of the Colonel's friends and business associates. "I wish I'd had the strength then to say, 'Wait a minute, this is our wedding, fans or no fans, press or no press. Let us invite whomever we want, and have it wherever we want,'" Priscilla wrote in her autobiography. "It seemed that as soon as the ceremony began, it was over."

After a brief honeymoon Elvis returned to work, completing three films in 1967—*Speedway*, *Clambake*, and *Stay Away, Joe*. He made it clear to Priscilla that he would be living alone much of the time in Los Angeles and she would be expected to keep the home fires burning at Graceland.

Priscilla had mixed feelings when she learned of her pregnancy. She had waited *so long* to become his wife, and the realization that she would be pregnant for much of their first year together as husband and wife filled her with dread. Once, without ever actually using the word abortion, she discussed that possibility with Elvis. He told her that it was her decision to make, and that he would support her decision.

Priscilla decided to have the baby. After Lisa Marie's birth—Lisa's middle name was taken from the Colonel's wife, Marie—she was horrified to discover that Elvis had lost interest in her sexually. When she confronted him about his lack of interest in having sex with her, Elvis told her that he was afraid of hurting her and wanted to wait until her system returned to normal. It was months before he made love to her again.[22]

In November 1967, Mary Ann Mobley, who had co-starred in two of Elvis's motion pictures, *Girl Happy* and *Harum Scarum*, and had become close friends with Colonel Parker, received high-powered visitors from Mississippi: Erle Johnston, head of the Mississippi Sovereignty Commission, Mississippi Governor Paul B. Johnson, and a state highway patrol officer. Commission Director Johnston had written to the Mississippi native several weeks in advance of their visit and asked her to be their escort while they were in Los Angeles. She readily agreed. She and her future husband, actor Gary Collins, had dinner with them and showed them around town.[23]

The commission was particularly concerned about the stance some movie and television actors had taken in favor of racial integration. When three members of the television show *Bonanza* canceled appearances in Mississippi, citing the racial issue, the commission undertook a secret campaign against the television show. The commission may have just wanted to make its presence known, or it may have wanted to get a message to the Colonel about Elvis's associations with black entertainers. It was not an organization to take lightly.

A little over four months after the commission's Los Angeles visit, civil rights leader Martin Luther King Jr. was assassinated in Memphis at the Lorraine Motel, just a couple of blocks from Abe Fortas's birthplace. Riots erupted in Memphis and in seventy-nine other cities. By the time the National Guard was able to restore order, twenty-nine people were dead and over two thousand were injured.

Lyndon Johnson had recently announced that he would not seek a second term as president. With King's influence in the black community and his opposition to the Vietnam War, he had become a potential power broker in the upcoming election. For such a powerful public figure to be gunned down only a few minutes' drive from Graceland made Elvis fully aware of just how vulnerable he himself was to his enemies.

Elvis told the Colonel that he needed to do something, that he needed to speak out against injustice—that he needed to get involved. The Colonel told him to keep his mouth shut. Martin Luther King Jr. had been instrumental in causing Johnson not to run for reelection. The preacher-activist was upsetting the apple cart. He was making the Teamsters Union nervous because they had invested their pension fund with the mobsters who ran Las Vegas casinos and their fortunes were tied to Democratic Party control of the White House. King had been a loose cannon and had made enemies in the wrong places, and he had paid a stiff price for meddling in the affairs of others.

Actually, King's assassination worked to the Colonel's advantage in that it affirmed his warnings to Elvis that no one was so powerful or popular that he couldn't be taken down. Besides the politics involved, the Colonel was not known for his high regard of African Americans. He never hired them, never worked with them, and was never involved in any causes that could benefit their struggle for equal rights. The Colonel did everything possible to prevent Elvis from being associated with African Americans. In Parker's view, they were bad for business.

Earlier in the year, Colonel Parker announced that Elvis would do a television special for NBC-TV, his first since his appearance on the 1960 Sinatra special. It would be taped in June and aired during the Christmas holidays. When NBC first approached the Colonel about the special, it was presented to him as a traditional Christmas show that would contain holiday songs; but Steve Binder, hired as the producer and director, had other ideas. He wanted to do a show that had a gritty, rock 'n' roll edge to it, one that would recapture the "old" Elvis.

The Colonel exploded when he learned Binder wanted to deviate from the tried-and-true Christmas concept. "At first NBC and the Colonel held the line: 'He's gonna do twenty-four Christmas songs and say Merry Christmas, everybody,'" said Bones Howe, the show's music director, in an interview with *Musician* magazine. "Finally at one of the meetings we started talking to Elvis. And it was a lot of trouble, but the wheels began to grind. The Colonel was no dummy."

Parker finally gave in and allowed Binder to do the show his way, but demanded that the special contain at least one Christmas song. Binder agreed, then later removed the Christmas song at the last minute without telling the Colonel.

After talking to Binder and the others involved in the show's production, Elvis became excited about the special. At Binder's suggestion, he called Scotty Moore and D. J. Fontana and asked them to back him up in the show. Both agreed. Elvis saw it as an opportunity to regain the fans he had lost to the Beatles and the Rolling Stones. The prospect of going head-to-head with the new titans of rock 'n' roll terrified him, but he knew it was now or never. As depressed as he had been in recent months, he was not so far down that he didn't want to come back up.

When Scotty and D. J. arrived at the Burbank studio, they were surprised at how healthy Elvis looked. He had slimmed down and firmed up, and he seemed to have that old spark for which he had been famous in the early days. They visited in the dressing room, going over songs that they would play on the "live" part of the show. Binder explained to Scotty and D. J. that they would be performing on a small stage before an audience that would be seated along three sides of a fifteen-foot-by-fifteen-foot stage.

Late that night, Elvis invited everyone to his house for dinner. He showed off Lisa Marie, although he didn't hold her and seemed awkward around her. Priscilla arrived home late, well after midnight, and everyone could see and feel the tension between them.

When Scotty's wife, Emily, asked one of the bodyguards what was going on, he told her that Priscilla had been with Mike Stone, a karate instructor whom Elvis had met in Hawaii the previous month and asked to give karate lessons to Priscilla.[24]

After dinner, Elvis told Scotty and D. J. that he wanted to talk to them in private. They went into a bedroom, away from his entourage. Elvis trusted the Memphis boys in his entourage, but knew that some of them reported back to the Colonel.

Elvis asked Scotty and D. J. if they wanted to join him on a European tour. They had wanted Elvis to tour Europe for years, but the Colonel had steadfastly blocked it. Obviously, Elvis was planning an end run around the Colonel on this one. That was why he wanted to talk to them in private, so the Colonel would not know about the tour until it was too late to stop it. Scotty and D. J. said they would be delighted to perform with Elvis across the Atlantic.

Elvis asked if Scotty still had the studio in Nashville. When Scotty said yes, Elvis asked what he thought about their going into the studio for a couple of weeks and locking the doors, just to see what they could create. Again, Scotty agreed, realizing that his friend was serious about returning to his musical roots.[25]

Elvis rehearsed with Scotty, D. J., and Charlie Hodge for about a week, practicing the songs they might play. Binder, who wanted it to have a sense of spontaneity, told them to go out and play whatever they wanted to play. During rehearsals Parker kept a low profile, but made his presence felt nonetheless.

Outside his dressing room door, he placed two guards garbed in red jackets and furry hats. The two men had been sent over from the William Morris Agency at Parker's request, according to Bones Howe, and were meant to resemble Buckingham Palace guards. Outside Elvis's dressing room a single guard sat in a chair.

Binder wanted to do two shows, bringing in a new audience for the second one. Before the first show began, the Colonel surveyed the crowd. He had some of his people there—Tom Diskin, for example. When the setup didn't look right to him, Parker suggested that the young girls in the audience, especially the pretty ones, be moved down next to the stage. He thought it would be a good idea if some of them actually sat on the edge of the stage.

Sitting in the audience was twenty-five-year-old Paul Lichter, manager of a Philadelphia-based blue-eyed soul band named the Soul Survivors. Lichter was in the process of organizing a multigroup package show with promoter-manager Sid Bernstein, representing at that time one of the hottest new acts in the country, the Young Rascals.

Since Bernstein was a close friend of the Colonel's, Lichter received several tickets to the show, but when he tried to give them away to his associates, he couldn't. "At that time, it wasn't that cool to be an Elvis fan," recalls Lichter. "The rest of the guys politely declined, but I jumped at the opportunity."[26]

For the show Elvis wore a black leather suit, something he had never before done, though many people associated him with the black-leather look. Perhaps other icons of the 1950s, James Dean and Marlon Brando, influenced him. Before going on stage, Elvis confessed to feeling nervous. "What if they don't like me?" he asked.

Moments before Elvis went on stage, the Colonel breezed into the dressing room and told everyone to leave him and Elvis alone. After a few minutes, the two men emerged from the dressing room. Elvis, up on his toes like a prize fighter, had lost his jitters. Whatever the Colonel had said transformed him.

Accompanying Elvis onto the small stage were Scotty on electric guitar, Charlie Hodge on acoustic guitar, and D. J., who placed a guitar case across his lap and played it with drum sticks. Offstage and out of sight of the television cameras was someone playing an electric bass. Later, Elvis asked Scotty to switch guitars with him, an exchange that made D. J. wince, knowing how particular Scotty was about his expensive Gibson guitar.

Also on stage with Elvis was Alan Fortas. Dressed in the same burgundy-colored suits as the musicians, he had no purpose other than to sit there with his back to the camera. No one seems to know why Fortas was chosen to sit on the stage. It may have been to send a message to Elvis's new investors or it may have been at their request. Or Fortas might have been present at Elvis's request to protect him from following in Martin Luther King's footsteps.

Elvis's performance, during both sets, was one of the best of his career. When the show aired later in the year, critics lavished praise on him and renamed the show his "Comeback Special." *New York Times* writer Jon Landau wrote that there was something "magical" about seeing a man who has been lost "find his way home."

Most of America agreed: Elvis had regained his crown.

After the show, Paul Lichter went backstage with Bernstein to meet the Colonel and Elvis. His encounter with Presley was brief—"I've enjoyed your music for a lot of years," countered by a "Thank you very much" from Elvis—but, while Lichter spent only a little more time talking to Parker, the conversation impressed him significantly.

"He was extremely intimidating and a very, very powerful presence," says Lichter. "He had those steely gray eyes that seemed to stare right through you. There was no question about it that he was the most important person in the room. Everyone looked at him before they made a move. There was no question in my mind that he ran the ship."

After work on the television special was completed, the Colonel felt it would be a hit, but didn't know for sure until its airing. Almost immediately, Elvis began work on a new motion picture, *Live a Little, Love a Little.* His relationship with Priscilla was strained and, according to some reports, he began seeing other women.

To Elvis, the world was neither a friendly nor a particularly loving place. His only true ally, Priscilla, was slowly drifting away from him. Half of his income went to someone other than himself, and God only knew who was receiving that second twenty-five percent commission that the Colonel demanded.

Elvis genuinely felt his life was in danger, especially after the second assassination of the year, the one that removed Robert Kennedy from the presidential campaign. It didn't matter that the police had charged a lone gunman in the murder. Elvis knew that Robert Kennedy had been Frank Sinatra's enemy ever since the attorney general had expanded the Justice Department's organized crime division to sixty members and ordered a report documenting Frank's alleged mob connections. The nineteen-page report listed Sinatra's connections with ten Mafiosi leaders. Bobby's complaints about Sinatra persuaded Jack Kennedy to pull back from his friendship with the entertainer.

By summer's end, Elvis had finished filming *Charro!,* for which he had grown a beard to play the role of a gunfighter. Vernon Scott, for United Press International, interviewed him on the set. Scott noted that Elvis's "self-conscious slouch" was gone and voiced surprise at how fit the thirty-three-year-old singer looked. He also noticed that Colonel Parker was nowhere visible on the set. "[Parker] is rarely seen in public with Elvis," wrote Scott. "Both men go their separate ways."

Elvis was in Los Angeles preparing for his third film of the year, *The Trouble with Girls,* when his aunt received a telephone call at Graceland from a caller who told her that Elvis had been killed in an airplane crash. The caller said that Elvis's body was at Manning-Dunn Funeral Home in Louisville, Kentucky.

When his aunt called the funeral home, neither the owner nor the employees knew what she was talking about. They didn't know anything about a plane crash, and certainly Elvis Presley's body was not in their possession. One can only imagine Elvis's reaction when his aunt phoned him in Los Angeles: "Honey, they said you were dead."[27]

The FBI office in Louisville got involved in the case and learned that a telephone operator had become suspicious when the caller had given her an inappropriate number. The operator traced the call while it was in progress, tracking it to a phone booth outside a food mart in West Louisville.

The FBI report described Elvis's aunt as "extremely distraught" over the incident. Both the Louisville police department and the FBI attempted to locate the caller, even to the point of staking out one address where they had identified a suspect, but the caller was never apprehended.

People could say what they wanted—that he was paranoid or overreacting to turbulent times—but Elvis was getting harassing phone calls and death threats. He had seen twice that year what could happen to public figures who challenged the status quo. It's not paranoia if they're really trying to get you.

The November election, in which Republican presidential candidate Richard M. Nixon defeated the Democratic contender, Hubert Humphrey, must have confused Elvis, for he had no way of knowing how the election would affect him. The Colonel's man, Lyndon B. Johnson, was on his way out, but he had nominated Memphian Abe Fortas to replace Earl Warren as chief justice of the Supreme Court. There had been talk during the summer that Congress would not approve the nomination of Fortas.

Somehow the Colonel learned of Elvis's conversations with Scotty and D. J. about a possible European tour and a session in Scotty's Nashville studio. Elvis had told reporters earlier in the year that he wanted to tour Europe. There was no way Parker would allow that to happen. If the Colonel couldn't leave the country, no one would.

Back in Nashville, Scotty and D. J. waited for word of the tour.

LAS VEGAS TIGHTENS
THE NOOSE

Buoyed by the success of the 1968 NBC television special, Elvis prepared to record a new album. The next session was scheduled for January in Nashville, but Elvis didn't want to record there this time,
probably because he had talked to Scotty Moore about recording in
his studio and wanted to avoid a potentially awkward scene. No one
seems to know why he didn't follow through with Scotty, but Colonel
Parker's opposition is the likely reason. For years, the Colonel had
said no to any request that involved Scotty or Bill.[1]

Marty Lacker had recently become involved with Chips Moman at
American Recording Studios. Moman had built the studio after break-
ing away from the Stax Records family, and for the past several years he
had produced a phenomenal string of hits with artists such as Wilson
Pickett, Neil Diamond, Dusty Springfield, the Gentrys, and B. J.
Thomas. In 1969, Chips Moman was the hottest producer in America.

Lacker talked to Elvis about recording his next RCA album at
American Recording Studios, with Chips Moman as producer. Elvis
liked that idea. Not only did it get him off the hook with Scotty, it
plugged him in with a highly sought-after producer. But there was another reason Elvis wanted to record in Memphis.

None of the records that he recorded in Memphis had ever gone
to Number One. For a man so identified with Memphis music never

to have recorded a Number One record in the city was an embarrassment to him. Besides, he hadn't recorded in Memphis since 1955
and wanted another shot at it.

Lacker had a harder time convincing Moman. Elvis hadn't had a hit
in years, Moman argued. Why should he stop work with artists who
were making hit records to work with someone who was not? It took
some doing, but Lacker finally persuaded him to work with the King.
Parker was furious. Instead of going to Memphis to supervise the session, he sent Tom Diskin and Freddie Beinstock from Hill and
Range. The Colonel still had a healthy fear of the city and only went
there when absolutely necessary.

Billboard magazine, which managed to get a reporter into the
studio for an interview with Elvis, duly noted the Memphis session.
"This is where it all started for me," said Elvis, who had never allowed a reporter into the studio with him (the reporter was there
at Moman's invitation). "It feels good to be back in Memphis
recording."

Colonel Parker knew nothing about Moman, other than that as a
teenager he had hitchhiked to Memphis from Georgia and had made
a name for himself as a guitarist, producer, and gambler of considerable skill. It was that latter talent that the Colonel would appreciate
when Diskin and Beinstock informed Moman, after several songs had
been recorded, that Elvis would have to have a piece of the publishing on the two songs Moman brought to the session. It was a standard
industry kickback. Moman bristled at that suggestion.

"I'll tell you what," Moman said, rolling the dice. "If you feel that
way, we'll just wrap this session up right now and consider these songs
very expensive demos."

Diskin and Beinstock relayed the message to the Colonel.

Moman had the Colonel over a barrel. If he raised a ruckus about
the session, Elvis would find out that the Colonel was strong-arming
publishers and songwriters into giving up their rights, something the
producer felt the Colonel would just as soon not do. Even if the
Colonel pushed the issue and Moman carried out his threat to walk,
that would have been an acceptable loss for him to take. Moman had
other artists lined up for sessions. He would just call out, "Who's
next?"

Somehow Elvis got word of what was occurring. He went to Moman and asked him how they could resolve it. Moman was blunt: the Colonel's people, the publishers, would have to leave the studio.

"It's done," said Elvis.

Faced with Elvis's involvement in the dispute, the Colonel folded his cards. He told Diskin to let it go, that he would make sure that the two songs in which Moman had a financial interest—"Suspicious Minds" and "In the Ghetto"—would never be released. There was more than one way to skin a Georgia cracker. The Colonel had a saying: "I can't stop you from starting, but I can stop you from finishing."

Chips Moman and Steve Binder were the only two people to ever get the best of the Colonel in a deal. Binder did it by out-finessing him over the specifics of the television special. Moman did it by out-bluffing him—a gambler's move, straight and simple. The American sessions were the best of Elvis's career since his early work at Sam Phillips's studio. From those sessions came "Suspicious Minds," "Kentucky Rain," "Gentle on My Mind," "Any Day Now," and "In the Ghetto."

For the first time in Elvis's career he had a producer who pushed him. Most of the tracks were pre-recorded by Moman's 827 Thomas Street Band, so that when Elvis arrived in the studio Moman's energies went into working with the singer on his vocals.

"When he went at it, he was either on or off," says Moman. "If he was off, it was better to do it another day. A lot of people don't understand how I could get him to do so many takes. I would have him sing a song twenty or thirty times, over and over. I'd ask him to back up and fix little lines that he would miss. But he went through it without a problem."[2]

Some members of Elvis's entourage interpreted his cooperation with Moman as a sign of weakness and chided him for it. "Why you lettin' that guy push you around?" they asked. Some seemed to perceive Elvis's work ethic as somehow diminishing their own manhood. Their behavior was strange, but to Elvis's credit he totally ignored them.

Priscilla had never seen him so excited about a session. Often he took cassettes of the day's work back to Graceland to play for her. They listened to the songs over and over again, with Elvis excitedly pointing out what he liked best about each song.

Not invited to the sessions were Scotty Moore, D. J. Fontana, and the Jordanaires. The first Scotty learned of the sessions was when he read about them in the newspaper. It was devastating news, for he had been patiently waiting to hear from Elvis about the world tour and the upcoming session in his Nashville studio. Now he knew the session would never take place. Later that month came news that Elvis would be performing at Las Vegas. Scotty was contacted about performing with Elvis in Las Vegas, but when he asked about the world tour, he was told there would be no world tour.

Scotty, D. J., and the Jordanaires had all found steady work in Nashville studios, and running off to Las Vegas for a couple of weeks would require them to cancel sessions already on the books. They got together and figured out what they would lose in canceled sessions if they played Vegas and they gave that figure to the Colonel.

If he would pay them what they would lose in canceled sessions, they would be happy to go to Vegas. The Colonel's reaction was not totally unexpected: he turned down their offer and formed a new band under the leadership of guitarist James Burton, a well-regarded session player based in Los Angeles.

The disappointment over the recording session that never took place, the world tour that never materialized, and the refusal of Colonel Parker to adequately pay him and the others for the Las Vegas engagement, so frustrated Scotty that he put away his guitar and did not perform for twenty-four years.[3] He would never see Elvis again.

☆   ☆   ☆

Almost immediately after finishing the sessions at American, Elvis began work on a new movie, *Change of Habit*, that co-starred Mary Tyler Moore and Ed Asner. Encouraged by the quality of his new songs, he told Colonel Parker that he didn't want to make any more movies for a while. His MGM contract expired with *Change of Habit*. It would be a good time to take a break and focus on his music.

Parker reluctantly agreed. He promised to go all-out in promoting the upcoming engagement in Las Vegas. By spring, Elvis was hearing nothing but good news. "In the Ghetto" had made it into the Top Ten, his first in over three years, and his *From Elvis in Memphis* album was being praised by critics as his best effort in years.

Coupled with that was news from the political front. That May, amid a growing scandal, Supreme Court Justice Abe Fortas was forced to resign, following published reports of his acceptance of money from a defense contractor.[4] Information about Fortas's ties to Las Vegas casinos was coming to light. Senator Robert Griffin of Michigan, who led the fight against Fortas's nomination as chief justice, disclosed that he had received death threats as a result of his opposition to Fortas.

Actually, the situation was even worse than it appeared in the press. The FBI was investigating Fortas for a wide range of crimes, including bribery, obstruction of justice, and unlawful practice of law.[5] There was really no one for Elvis to talk to about those developments, except Colonel Parker, and he was probably fearful of broaching that subject with him.

Elvis was on top of the world: his music was soaring, Johnson and Fortas were now history, the new president appeared to have pulled the teeth from the Las Vegas sharks, and he was feeling like his old rock 'n' roll self again. He thought the worst was over.

☆   ☆   ☆

The Las Vegas International Hotel was a monstrous giant by Vegas standards. Located on sixty-three acres, it stood thirty stories high and offered 1,519 rooms furnished in three different decors—Spanish, French, and Italian. There was a large room on the thirtieth floor, where guests could dance to orchestra music, but the hotel's crown jewel was its main showroom, the 2,000-seat Showroom Internationale.[6]

The International was the brainchild of financier Kirk Kerkorian, who had raised the $60 million needed to build what was billed as "the world's largest casino." With one thousand slot machines, twelve craps tables, and thirty-two blackjack tables, all spread out over thirty thousand square feet of floor space, it easily qualified for that title.

The International was Kerkorian's second Las Vegas hotel and casino. In 1967, he had purchased Bugsy Siegel's infamous Flamingo

Hotel for $12.5 million. Kerkorian had a history of past dealings with MGM and knew Colonel Parker from that association, but his most direct link was through Alex Shoofey, the man hired to manage the hotel.

Shoofey went to the International from the Sahara Hotel, where he had worked for the Colonel's old friend, Milton Prell. Las Vegas was nothing if not an enormous extended family in which everyone was somehow related by prior association.[7]

Added to that family was Parker's old friend, Bill Miller. He left Las Vegas in 1962 to purchase the Bal Harbour Hotel in Miami Beach, which he used as a base of operations to build a hotel in Havana, where Santo Trafficante and Carlos Marcello had built up a lucrative casino empire. When Fidel Castro shut down the casinos, Miller bought some beachfront land in the Dutch West Indies and built the Bonaire Hotel. In 1967, Miller returned to Las Vegas to become the entertainment director at the Flamingo. When Flamingo owner Kirk Kerkorian opened the International Hotel in 1969, Miller stepped into the position of entertainment director, a position he held until he retired in the mid-1970s and moved to Palm Springs.

Miller has a son, Jimmy—who achieved prominence in the 1970s in England as a record producer working with the Rolling Stones (he produced six albums, including *Sticky Fingers* and *Let It Bleed*)—and two daughters.[8]

After Elvis told Colonel Parker that he didn't want to do any more movies—and no one at MGM or Paramount begged him to change his mind (ticket sales to his movies had dropped drastically during the socially conscious 1960s and, more often than not, new releases were relegated to drive-in theaters)—he went to Las Vegas to discover what kind of deal he could get and left with a contract from the International.

The International's official opening was set for July 1. Shoofey and Miller thought Elvis would be perfect to launch the new hotel, but Parker didn't agree and argued against it. Elvis had put on too much weight and needed more time to get in shape. Shoofey asked the

Colonel what he thought about Barbra Streisand appearing the month before Elvis.

Parker liked that idea.

"Let the girl go first," he said.

Elvis was booked to perform twice a night for twenty days at the International, with the first show scheduled to begin at 8:15 P.M. on July 31. The second show was scheduled for midnight. Appearing with Elvis would be comedian Sammy Shore and the Sweet Inspirations.

As Elvis dieted and worked out the month before his Vegas engagement—and made life around Graceland thoroughly disagreeable with an unending barrage of temper tantrums—Colonel Parker camped out in Las Vegas, where he proceeded to work the town as he had done countless others during his stint with Royal American. He put up thousands of posters, attaching them to streetlight poles and buildings and taxis, and he placed full-page ads in Las Vegas's local newspapers.

When, a week before his opening, Elvis arrived in Las Vegas to rehearse, over six thousand telegrams, sent from all over the world, greeted him. Also there to greet him were Frank Sinatra and his daughter, Nancy, who after scoring a Number One hit in 1966 with "These Boots Are Made for Walkin'," had come a long way, professionally, since she had met him in New York upon his return from Germany.

Incredibly, Priscilla had never seen her husband perform live. He asked her to stay away from rehearsals that week so that she would get the full impact on opening night. She was kept in the dark about what was happening at rehearsals, but she could not avoid the growing sense of anticipation she felt in the hotel and around town. She was shocked at the massive scope of the Colonel's impressive publicity blitz.

Elvis knew he had to deliver. Rock 'n' roll had changed since that hot summer night in Memphis when he, Scotty, and Bill had brought it kicking and screaming into the world. At age thirty-four, he knew he couldn't compete with the Beatles and the Rolling Stones for the youth market. Many of America's under-thirty generation were headed that month for a massive festival in Woodstock, New York.

The last time Elvis performed in Las Vegas the audience was in its thirties, forties, and fifties; the audience was polite but clearly preferred the music of the older generation. Elvis left town thinking he had failed. This time, the audience was still in its thirties, forties, and fifties, and again it preferred the music of the older generation—only this time, it was the music of Elvis Presley. Las Vegas had finally caught up with the King.

Elvis didn't know what to expect when he walked onstage for his opening night performance. The room was packed with celebrities and news reporters. Said Elvis to the audience, "It's the first time I've worked in front of people for nine years, and it may be the last, I don't know."

Elvis flung himself into his material the way new-wave artists would later fling themselves into their audiences. He sang with abandon, doing a mix of old and new songs, including his current hit, "In the Ghetto." It was exactly what they had come to hear and *see*. Wrote an Associated Press reporter: "All the gyrations remembered from Presley's 1956 launching of rock 'n' roll and of himself were there— his legs spread apart, shaking his left leg, shaking his head so the hair flew like black straw, rotating the guitar, then a final thrust to the side, his body vibrating all over like a jackhammer."

Most of the reviews of his opening night performance were wildly enthusiastic. From the moment Elvis broke into "Jailhouse Rock," wrote John Carpenter for the *Los Angeles Free Press*, "there was no doubt in my mind or any who were there who was the head honcho of rock." Robert Christgau, writing for the *Village Voice*, said: "For sixteen songs he brought us all together, junketing freaks and aging squares, and we all responded to the same thing—him." Writing for the *Chicago Sun Times*, Kathy Orloff enthused, "Elvis is the king, long live the king."

Newsweek credited Colonel Parker for Elvis's success and guessed that the International was probably paying him a million dollars for the engagement (their estimate was off by about $750,000). The magazine marveled at his "staying power," and said it was "hard to believe he was thirty-four and no longer nineteen years old."

After the first show, Elvis held a press conference at which he was asked if he wanted to do more live shows after finishing his Las Vegas engagement. "I sure hope so," Elvis replied. "I want to. I would like to play all over the world."

Lord Sutch of Lord Sutch Enterprises told Elvis that he was there to make an offer of one million pounds sterling for one appearance in England at the Wembley Empire Stadium for two concerts.

"You'll have to ask him," Elvis said, glancing at Colonel Parker, who was sitting nearby in a white coat plastered with "Elvis In Person" stickers.

"Would you mind repeating that, please?" said Parker.

Lord Sutch repeated the offer.

"Just put down the deposit," Parker said.

"Alright, I will attend to it," said Lord Sutch. Then, to Elvis, he said, "Would you like to appear in England?"

"I definitely would like to appear in England as we have had so many requests," said Elvis. "And it will be soon, as we are now doing live concerts again."

At the end of the press conference, the Colonel stood up and told the reporters that they could now all be photographed with Elvis. "But if you take too long," he warned, "I'll have to charge you overtime."

After Elvis's comments about touring in Europe, Parker immediately started making arrangements for an American tour that would keep Elvis too busy to think about leaving the country. If the boy wanted to get out and mingle with the common folk, the Colonel would make certain it was with *American* common folk.

At the end of the monthlong run, the International announced that Elvis's shows had been attended by 101,500 people. With a fifteen-dollar minimum in place, that meant the hotel had taken in a million-and-a-half dollars from ticket sales alone, excluding related income from its casinos, restaurants, and room rentals.

Ever the tactician, Parker sent word midway through the engagement to a reporter he trusted at the *Commercial Appeal* in Memphis that Elvis had been offered five million dollars from a competing hotel for a ten-year contract. Without identifying its source for that information, the newspaper ran a story that contained a denial from the

Colonel. "We are happy with what is happening at the moment," he said. "Looking into the future for ten years is a long time."

United Press International picked up the story, which made its way back to local Las Vegas newspapers. Falling for the Colonel's calculated ploy, the International offered Elvis a five-year, one-million-dollar-per-year contract that specified two engagements per year, with each engagement consisting of fifty-seven shows. Just because the Colonel had sold his soul to Las Vegas didn't mean he couldn't outwit the International at every opportunity.

Even so, it was a bad deal for Elvis. The International's offer of $125,000 a week was below what other stars of Elvis's magnitude were receiving. When the fifty percent commission was deducted, half that one-million-dollar-a-year paycheck was going back into Las Vegas through the Colonel, who invariably lost it at the gaming tables.

The bottom line was that Elvis had become an indentured servant. For his servitude, he would receive $500,000 a year, with fifty to ninety percent of that going to Uncle Sam in taxes.[9] The Colonel had turned him into a $50,000-to-$200,000-a-year cabaret singer. There were lawyers and accountants in Memphis who made more than that preparing tax returns.

Back home in Memphis, Elvis relaxed and basked in the glow of his success. The Las Vegas engagement had exhausted him; he had had a difficult time sleeping the entire time he was there. There was more good news in the months after his return to Memphis. "Suspicious Minds," the song the Colonel had wanted removed from the album, had peaked at Number One, giving Elvis his first chart-topper in over seven years.

By the time Elvis returned to the International Hotel in January 1970 for the first of his twice-yearly appearances, the decision had been made to break up the engagements into two-week blocks. His first two-week appearance would begin January 26 and the second would begin February 23, thus giving him a two-week breather in the interim.

Variety called his show the "essence of Kabuki drama," a reference to his highly stylized karate punches and dramatic stage movements, all seemingly calculated to provide a sense of drama to music played by a band that *Rolling Stone* described as "bland and professional."

Dean Martin was there on opening night, and Elvis paid tribute to him by singing his big hit, "Everybody Loves Somebody." The show was a sellout as expected, but Elvis hardly seemed to notice. He went through the motions—above all else, he prided himself on his professionalism—but to those around him, he seemed preoccupied. When talking to the audience between songs, he sometimes complained that he was gaining weight and could no longer fit into his costumes. Other times he delivered cursory religious sermons to his impatient fans.

As promised, Colonel Parker busied himself arranging a concert tour. The first performance was in Houston, Texas, where he booked Elvis for three nights at the Houston Astrodome, doing two shows a night. Those performances, beginning only four days after he concluded his second two-week stint at the International, exhausted and depressed Elvis.

He returned to Memphis and checked himself into the Baptist Hospital for a three-day stay during which doctors discovered glaucoma in one of his eyes. Fearful he was going blind, he sank into an even deeper depression. For most of March and April, he spent much of his time sleeping, only leaving his bedroom for short periods to play with Lisa Marie.

The Colonel pressured him constantly during their telephone conversations to return to the studio to record new material. Elvis had released two albums of live material recorded at his previous Las Vegas engagements, but RCA, encouraged by the success of "Suspicious Minds," was impatient for new studio material.

That summer, Elvis returned to Nashville to record material for an album entitled *Love Letters from Elvis*. He had mixed feelings about returning to American Recording Studios in Memphis. Moman was a tough taskmaster and Elvis wasn't sure he would thrive in that environment at this point in his life. Colonel Parker made it clear that he was opposed to Elvis ever again working with Moman.

By the time Elvis returned to Las Vegas in August to honor his second set of engagements of the year, he realized that he was not going blind and he relaxed somewhat. Unfortunately, his reprieve from

emotional distress was short-lived. About a week before the engagement ended, Colonel Parker received an early afternoon telephone
call at his office in the International. The caller said Elvis was going to
be kidnapped that weekend. The Colonel didn't report the call to the
police; he called his lawyer in Los Angeles, Gregory Hookstratten.[10]

The following day, the wife of one of Elvis's bodyguards received
an early morning call at her home in Los Angeles from a man who
said he was looking for her husband. The caller said Elvis was going
to "get it" the following night. Forty-five minutes later, the man, who
spoke in a southern accent, called again and said that the killer had a
gun with a silencer. He described the assassin as a "madman." For
$50,000 in small bills, the caller said, he would disclose the killer's
identity.

This call, too, was reported to the Colonel's lawyer, who notified
the FBI. Agents were sent to Las Vegas and around-the-clock protection was ordered for Priscilla and three-year-old Lisa Marie at the
Presley home in Los Angeles. Elvis was told to stay in his room except
during showtime.

Elvis did his shows that night as planned, with the addition of a
massive security force comprised of FBI agents, hotel security officers, and Elvis's own private army of well-armed Memphis boys. At
Hookstratten's request, John O'Grady, a Los Angeles Police Department detective whom Elvis had befriended in calmer times, was
flown to Las Vegas to be the entertainer's chief bodyguard. The caller
was never heard from again. The remainder of the engagement at the
International played out without incident, but the episode left the
King unnerved.[11]

Elvis had no new movies scheduled, and he was in between albums
and personal appearances. With time on his hands, he began obsess-
ing on Colonel Parker and all the troubles the old man had brought
down upon him. In Las Vegas he had learned that he was wrong to
think that Abe Fortas's fall was an omen of good things to come. Presley was still just as obligated to the Las Vegas power brokers as he had
been before.

The only difference was that he would now be working for maybe as little as $50,000 a year. As the holidays approached, Elvis's temper flared again and again. No one could stand being around him. His relationship with Priscilla was disintegrating. He didn't like himself—or anyone else.

Less than a week before Christmas 1970, Priscilla walked into the living room at Graceland to find Elvis and Vernon engaged in a heated argument about the Colonel. "Goddamn, Daddy, call and tell him we're through," Elvis said, according to Priscilla in her autobiography. "Tear up the goddamn contracts and I'll pay him whatever percentage we owe him." Vernon asked if he was sure he wanted to do that.

"Goddamn right I am," Elvis responded.[12]

Furious, he stormed out of Graceland. Without telling Priscilla or Vernon where he was going, he drove himself to the Memphis airport. Using the name Jon Burrows, he bought an airline ticket to Washington, D.C. Upon his arrival he felt ill—and perhaps a little frightened, for it was the first time he had ever traveled alone. Without leaving the Washington airport, he bought a ticket to Los Angeles.

During a stopover in Dallas, he phoned Jerry Schilling, a friend who had worked for him in Memphis and then had moved to California to build a career as a manager. Elvis said that he needed Jerry's help in arranging a meeting with President Richard M. Nixon. Schilling was busy working on a film project, but it was hard to say no to his friend. After Elvis had rested for a couple of days, they set out for Washington together.

On the plane with them was Senator George Murphy of California. During the long nonstop flight, Elvis conversed with Murphy. He told the senator that he was going to Washington to meet with the president to obtain credentials as a federal agent. Elvis told Murphy, a Republican, that he was upset about all the drug use occurring in the entertainment industry and wanted to do something about it.[13]

"Do you have an appointment?" Murphy asked.

"No, sir," answered Elvis.

Murphy suggested that Elvis write a letter to the president and promised to deliver it himself. Encouraged by the senator's interest, Elvis wrote a five-page letter addressed to the president. In it, he explained who he was and requested a meeting to discuss "the problems our country is faced with." He said he wanted to volunteer his services to the president. "I wish not to be given a title or an appointed position," he wrote. "I can and will do more good if I were made a federal agent at large."[14]

Schilling had called Graceland before leaving Los Angeles and apprised Vernon and Priscilla of Elvis's plans. They agreed Schilling needed reinforcements. Sonny West, along with five other bodyguards and Elvis's longtime friend, former Shelby County Sheriff Bill Morris, met them in Washington.

Elvis got the meeting he desired with the president. As he entered the White House, he told Secret Service guards that he had a commemorative Colt .45 as a gift for the president. He was allowed to proceed unchallenged into the Oval Office with the weapon. Nixon posed for photographs with Elvis, and, after talking to him for a while, agreed to supply the entertainer with a badge from the office of the Bureau of Narcotics and Dangerous Drugs.

Elvis was elated. At the end of the meeting, he shocked the president, who was not known to be physically demonstrative, by abruptly hugging him good-bye. Then he looked the president in the eye and broke down in tears.

Encouraged by his welcome at the White House, Elvis asked Bill Morris to arrange a similar meeting with FBI Director J. Edgar Hoover. Morris phoned the director's office from the hotel, introduced himself as the former sheriff of Shelby County, and explained the reason for the requested meeting.

One of Hoover's aides informed him of the request in a memorandum. He reminded the director that Senator Murphy had already called about the entertainer's unusual request. After a review of Elvis's file, the aide said: "Presley's sincerity and good intentions notwithstanding he is certainly not the type of individual whom the Director would wish to meet. It is noted at the present time he is wearing his hair down to his shoulders and indulges in the wearing of all sorts of exotic dress."

Instead, the aide recommended that a tour of the building be arranged for Elvis and his entourage, who would be advised that it was simply impossible for the director to meet with them.[15]

Elvis returned to Memphis with exactly what he wanted: publicity photos of himself and President Nixon, national press attention of the meeting, and—most importantly—credentials that identified him as a federal agent. Over the years, that trip has come to be considered an embarrassment to the entertainer's reputation as the King of Rock 'n' Roll. It has been blamed on everything from Elvis's excessive drug use to his dislike of the Beatles.

Clearly, such interpretations are unfair and unfounded. Elvis's use of uppers and downers had escalated dramatically in recent years, but to blame the trip on mood-altering drugs is a stretch.

Even less credible were government reports that Elvis had made the trip to offer the president a plan for combating the "evil influence" of the Beatles. FBI memos show that he talked to Nixon in negative terms about the Beatles, but Elvis had a penchant for telling people what he thought they wanted to hear, especially when he thought his life would be affected by the conversation. If Elvis truly felt that way about the Beatles, he would not have paid the group the ultimate compliment of performing two of their songs, "Yesterday" and "Hey Jude," at his Las Vegas opening.

Elvis felt betrayed by the Colonel, who had drained off half his income. That was the topic that he and Vernon were arguing about when Priscilla walked into the room. Elvis wanted to pay off the Colonel and get him out of his life. Vernon was deathly afraid to tangle with Parker.

When Elvis stormed out of Graceland that day and headed straight to the airport, all he apparently had in mind was getting to the only person he felt he could trust: the president of the United States. Nixon had gone against the Las Vegas mob and broken Abe Fortas. To Presley's way of thinking, Nixon was the only person who had the power to extricate him from the mess in which he now found himself.

As the hour-and-a-half flight from Memphis to Washington turned into an excursion of several days, Elvis had time to think the matter through. He didn't want to get involved in a federal investigation, nor did he want to get Parker in trouble. What he wanted from a meeting with Nixon was the public association and the badge. Maybe that would be enough to protect him from the wolves at the door.

The Washington trip shows an Elvis who was fighting for survival. He was stressed by the recent death threat and his realization that he had become an indentured servant to Vegas hotel casinos. He was guzzling uppers and downers, but he was *not* the drug-crazed loony tune that people have made him out to be. You don't have to be crazy to fly to Washington and demand meetings with the president and the director of the FBI: not if your manager is named Colonel Tom Parker.

☆   ☆   ☆

As Elvis prepared for his January 1971 engagement at the International, the Colonel busied himself lining up projects to keep his boy busy. His relationship with Elvis was on shaky ground, and it unsettled him to hear his client talk to reporters about doing an overseas concert tour.

Parker and Elvis had little communication during this time. Their personalities could not have been more different—and their personal belief systems stood poles apart—but their reaction to what was becoming an unbearably stressful situation for both of them was similar. Elvis retreated further into his ever-expanding world of prescription medication, feeding his newly acquired addiction with an insidious mixture of uppers and downers; Parker retreated into the blue-velvet isolation of the casino, where he lost himself in the fluorescent-lighted fantasy world of the Big Score, feeding an addiction that cost him nearly $20,000 a week. Self-destructive addictions may have been the only thing the two men had in common at that point in their lives.

While in Las Vegas, Elvis's behavior became more and more erratic, his dependence on drugs apparent to everyone around him, including the Colonel, who never lifted a hand to stop it. He viewed Elvis's drug use in the same way that owners of strip clubs view drug use among dancers: they don't supply the drugs, for that would be illegal, but neither do they prohibit their use. A medicated Elvis was good for business; it kept him out of trouble.

By the time he had completed fifty-seven shows at the International, Elvis was exhausted from the physical stress of the twice-daily performances and demoralized by his deteriorating marriage. But the Colonel pushed him to record more songs for RCA, and after only about a week's rest at Graceland, he went to Nashville to work on material for a new album. For most of the spring and summer, Elvis stayed in the studio.

Colonel Parker stayed in Las Vegas, where he worked out of the three-room suite he had been given on the fourth floor of the International. Then it was back to Nevada in July for another series of performances, only this time at the Sahara Tahoe Hotel at Stateline, Nevada. Elvis did twenty-eight shows, often stopping during his performance to read aloud from Bibles handed to him from the audience.

No sooner did he finish his engagement at the Sahara Tahoe than it was time to return to the International for another fifty-seven consecutive shows, only it was no longer the International: it was now the Las Vegas Hilton, having been bought out by Barron Hilton of the prestigious Hilton hotel group. At first, Barron Hilton was outraged when he learned that Colonel Parker had moved into the hotel and had been assigned free office space, accommodation, and room service. Elvis only played the hotel eight weeks a year. Why should his manager be taken care of so extravagantly by the hotel?

When it was explained to him that Parker was more than just an eccentric talent manager and was one of the casino's best customers—to the tune of one million dollars a year—Hilton quickly did the math. The hotel was paying Elvis one million dollars a year to perform and Colonel Parker was losing one million dollars a year at the tables. Hilton changed his mind about Parker and rolled out the red carpet. He could have the entire fourth floor if he wanted it.

By November, Parker had booked Elvis for a series of one-nighters in civic centers and auditoriums, from Minneapolis, Minnesota, to Tuscaloosa, Alabama. He performed before sellout crowds and most critics gave him rave reviews. Wrote *Rolling Stone* magazine: "The magnificence of Presley's performance lies in its presentation of him as royalty. . . . He is the one and only performer who can simply revel in it and us with him."

For the first time in years, there was an industry buzz about Elvis. Among those drawn to the economic benefits of the entertainer's revived career was Paul Lichter, the young entrepreneur who had first met Elvis and the Colonel backstage after his 1968 "Comeback" television special.

Lichter had stayed in touch with Elvis and the Colonel, beginning with the entertainer's 1969 Las Vegas opening, when a friend at RCA Records asked him to present Elvis with several gold records. It was a publicity stunt, Lichter knew that, but it would get his photograph in the trades and give him another excuse to talk to Elvis and the Colonel.[16]

When he arrived at the hotel, Parker told him to go to his room, stay there and wait for his telephone call. "There I was in Las Vegas for the first time, and pretty excited about it, and I spent the first day and a half in my room," he says. "He told me if I missed the call, that was it."

Lichter was afraid he would miss the call if he left his room. He ordered room service and as the casino downstairs hummed with activity and the city's wicked charms proceeded at full speed without him, he watched television and sat near the telephone, waiting for it to ring.

When the call finally came, he rushed downstairs and was escorted past two armed guards into a room where Elvis and the Colonel were holding court with a gaggle of reporters and photographers. He presented the gold records to Elvis and stood there for two minutes shaking Presley's hand as the strobe lights flared. Then he was escorted from the room. It ended as quickly as it had begun.

Later, Elvis invited Lichter to his suite. During the presentation Elvis had asked where he was from and he had said Philadelphia. That rang a bell with Elvis. He wanted a Cadillac station wagon like the one Dean Martin had purchased and the only place you could get them, he had heard, was in Philadelphia. He thought Lichter could help him get the car.

After that initial meeting—Elvis invited him to stay at the hotel for a month, all expenses paid—Lichter decided to get out of the management business and into the Elvis Presley business. When Elvis started touring again, Lichter hit the road as well, selling twenty-five-dollar subscriptions to his newly created Elvis Presley Unique Record Club.

To get photographs for his record club subscribers and for a bi-monthly magazine, the *Memphis Flash*, he hired a team of photographers to follow Elvis on tour. They snapped photos of him coming and going out of public places, and Lichter used them for his publications.

The Colonel did not think too highly of Lichter's efforts and asked his attorney to send threatening letters, which Lichter ignored. He had every right to take pictures of Elvis in public places and he knew there was nothing the Colonel could do to stop him.

One day Lichter was relaxing at the Hilton swimming pool, when Tom Diskin, whom he had met on previous occasions, approached and told him that the Colonel wanted to talk to him. "The entire fourth floor of the hotel was his office, which was intimidating in itself," says Lichter. "When I went into the meeting, he said, 'I like you and you remind me of me. I can't stop you from starting, but I can stop you from finishing.' I thanked him, but I realized I was doing nothing wrong and I continued doing it."

Al Dvorin, who made rock 'n' roll history during this period when he started punctuating Elvis's concerts with the memorable phrase, "Ladies and gentlemen, Elvis has left the building," viewed Lichter's promotional battles with the Colonel with amusement. "The Colonel got a kick out of him," he says. "One day he said to me, 'If I wasn't on the inside, I would be the first one working on the outside.'"[17]

Parker considered entrepreneurs like Lichter bootleggers, although technically they were not. They took photographs in public places and sold them in magazines or booklets on public property outside the venues where Elvis performed. It was all strictly legal, but the Colonel didn't like the idea of other people profiting from his boy's popularity, especially if he himself was not getting a cut of the profits.

Parker's first response to the "bootleggers" was to have his attorneys send threatening letters. Sometimes it worked. Other times it didn't. As the problem increased during the early 1970s, Parker took a more defensive stance by having announcers tell the audience before each performance that no professional photographs or recordings would be allowed during the performance. Later, that restriction would be printed on the tickets themselves.

That battle culminated in 1975 at the Omni Theater. As usual, Lichter had his people on the outside hawking flyers for his Elvis Presley products. Unknown to Lichter, Parker had hired a squad of bikers to provide security for the concert. Lichter's vendors were roughed up and their flyers were dumped into the street. Then it turned really ugly with gunfire.

"Bullets went boom, boom, boom," says Lichter. "I'm not saying the Colonel did it, but the motorcycle lunatics he hired definitely did it. So we ceased. Money is money, but bullets is bullets."[18]

Throughout Lichter's battle with Parker, he maintained a friendship with Elvis and often ran into the Colonel backstage or in the dressing room. "He never reacted to the fact that he was sending me letters," Lichter recalled. "He told me in later years that it was never him in the first place. He said it was Vernon." When asked if he believed that, Lichter laughed. "No, it was the Colonel every step of the way."

After Parker died, his widow, Loanne, asked Lichter if he wanted the file her husband had put together on him. As it turned out, the Colonel kept an extensive file of newspaper clippings and other information about his merchandising rival.

Lichter was impressed.

As 1972 began, it became apparent that Elvis was coming unraveled. When he found out about Priscilla's three-year affair with Mike Stone, the karate instructor, she took Lisa Marie and moved to Los Angeles. Elvis reacted violently and threatened to kill Stone. He went on emotional binges that were so intense they frightened even his battle-hardened bodyguards. His stage performances came under criticism because of his emotional outbursts and his long, rambling sermons.

Elvis told the Colonel to have lawyers file for divorce.

Life for both Elvis and his manager became an absolute nightmare, as the entertainer medicated himself with tranquilizers such as Quaalude and Percadan, and fasted for long periods. The Colonel's response was to intensify his boy's recording and touring schedule. It was the last thing Elvis needed, but, in fairness to Parker, he may have felt it was better for Elvis's emotional equilibrium to keep him before his fans.

Within a month of finishing fifty-seven soldout shows at the Las Vegas Hilton, Elvis was back out on the road. From April until the first of August, when he returned to the Las Vegas Hilton for sixty-three shows, he performed almost constantly, with shows in New York, Michigan, Ohio, Virginia, Indiana, North Carolina, Georgia, Florida, Arkansas, Texas, New Mexico, Wisconsin, Illinois, and Kansas.

That April, as Elvis was beginning his grueling tour, Barron Hilton approached Parker with an offer he couldn't refuse. The hotel would pay him $50,000 a year for three years as payment for his services as the hotel's "Talent and Publicity Consultant."[19] In exchange for his new "consultant's" title, which Elvis apparently never knew about—certainly he never signed off on it, as he had done on other deals made by his manager—Parker agreed to keep Elvis under contract to the hotel for the same one-million-dollar-a-year fee. It was a terrible deal for Elvis; other Las Vegas performers received much more.

In a letter to the Colonel that set out the specifics of the deal, Barron Hilton said he appreciated Parker's efforts on behalf of the hotel. "It is our belief that the efforts made by you to publicize the Hilton Hotels throughout the country were extremely beneficial, and we should like to retain your services to help publicize our hotels in the future," he wrote. "We look forward to a long and mutually beneficial association with a truly outstanding individual."[20]

No matter how Parker and Hilton described their little arrangement, it was a clear conflict of interest for a manager to sign on as a paid consultant with his client's employer. It is what anyone familiar with Las Vegas business practices would call a kickback. The hotel got Elvis at a cut-rate price and Parker got his nest nicely feathered.

Holding court in his fourth-floor office at the Hilton, the Colonel was surprised one day when Alex Shoofey, who had stayed on after the hotel changed hands, brought a Japanese promoter to meet him. The promoter wanted to arrange for Elvis to perform in Japan. Hearing that, the Colonel stiffened and replied that he needed two million dollars on his desk the following morning. The Japanese gentleman smiled and told him that would be no problem.

Once it became clear that the promoter would be able to get the money, the Colonel said he didn't want to go to Japan. What he really wanted, he said, was to make a movie. How about one million dollars for him to set that up? All the money would go to him. How about that? Again, the Japanese agreed. One million dollars would be fine. To Shoofey's disbelief, Parker told the Japanese to forget it. He just wasn't interested in doing anything outside the good old U.S.A. Eventually, Shoofey understood and escorted the perplexed Japanese gentleman from the office.

As 1973 approached, Colonel Parker lined up an exhaustive schedule for Elvis, beginning in January with the live satellite broadcast of *Elvis: Aloha from Hawaii*, which was viewed by an estimated one-and-a-half billion people. He got the idea for the ninety-minute Hawaiian concert while watching President Nixon's visit to China, which was broadcast by satellite. When he looked at Nixon being greeted by his Chinese hosts, all before a worldwide television audience, bells started ringing. Ever the manager, Parker instantly thought, "Elvis . . . satellite . . . Hawaii."

The show was an enormous success, and exposed Elvis, for the first time, to audiences in Japan, Thailand, the Far East, China, and Australia. In Japan alone the show received a ninety-eight percent share of the television audience. The following day, the taped version of the show was rebroadcast in twenty-eight countries in Europe.

Once again, the wily old Colonel—he was now sixty-three—made history, this time by spotting the enormous promotional potential of the new technology. Had the Internet existed then, he no doubt would have utilized it in innovative ways to promote Elvis's career. Whatever his shortcomings, Parker surely possessed a genius for promotion.

Within a week after the Hawaii concert, Elvis was rehearsing in Las Vegas for a fifty-four-performance run at the Las Vegas Hilton. At the end of the engagement, a physically and emotionally drained Elvis asked for some time off. The Colonel suggested he go to Memphis for four weeks to recharge his batteries.

Meanwhile, his manager set up a relentless schedule of concerts, beginning with an April performance in Phoenix, Arizona, and continuing all the way through June. Before the year was out, Elvis would give 169 performances in twenty cities. It would have been a tough schedule for a young man in good health, but for someone in Presley's physical condition—and nearing the age of forty—it was excruciating and bordered on managerial abuse.

While Elvis was on the road, the Colonel executed a new scheme. On March 1, 1973, he signed a mysterious series of contracts with RCA Records that sold Elvis's master tapes and the rights to all royalties received from them to the record company in what is commonly called a "buyout" agreement. It is the type of agreement that a manager would customarily arrange for an artist who is retiring and does not expect to live long enough to benefit from the royalty schedule currently in effect. Or one without heirs to benefit from royalties paid after his death. It was a way to close the books on Elvis Presley. There were six agreements in all.[21]

The first agreement committed Elvis to a new seven-year recording contract with RCA Records. His current contract was not up for another two years, and the reason for signing a new agreement has never been fully explained.

The second agreement transferred the rights of Elvis's master tapes and his royalties to RCA Records for a sum of $5 million.

The third agreement was among RCA, Elvis Presley, and All Star Shows, the company that the Colonel had established to exploit merchandising opportunities associated with Elvis's career. Under the terms of that agreement RCA agreed to pay Elvis and All Star Shows $100,000 upon the expiration of the new seven-year recording contract.

The fourth agreement was among RCA, RCA Record Tours (the company that had hired Parker's future wife, Loanne), and All Star Shows. Under the terms of that contract RCA agreed to use Colonel Parker in the "planning, promotion and merchandising" of the tour agreement with Elvis Presley. For those services, RCA would pay All Star Shows $675,000, with $75,000 payable the first year and $100,000 payable in each successive year. In addition, RCA Record Tours agreed to pay All Star Shows $675,000, payable on the same schedule outlined by the record company.

The fifth agreement, signed by RCA, All Star Shows, and Colonel Parker, stipulated that RCA would pay All Star Shows $50,000 over five years for the services of Colonel Parker. Elvis signed the agreement, but did not benefit financially from it. The sixth agreement was between All Star Shows and RCA Record Tours. It stipulated that All Star Shows was bound to furnish the services of Colonel Parker to assist RCA Records in planning and promoting the concerts arranged by the tour agreement. For those services, RCA Records agreed to pay All Star Shows $350,000, payable at $50,000 over seven years.[22]

The total effect of the six agreements was that Elvis Presley received payments totaling $4,650,000 and Colonel Parker received payments totaling $6,200,000, with an additional ten percent payable to him from the net profits of the concerts arranged by RCA Record Tours. At that time, Elvis was in a fifty percent tax bracket, which meant that he realized $2,325,000 from what amounted to a buyout of his life's work.

At stake was his catalogue of over seven hundred chart songs, which would have provided an almost certain lifetime annuity. It was a shameless betrayal of Elvis's long-range best interests. Elvis signed some of the documents, but there is no indication that he understood what he was signing.

The following year, Parker made yet another strange agreement with RCA. Under this agreement, RCA agreed to distribute an album entitled *Having Fun on Stage with Elvis*, recorded for Parker's Boxcar Enterprises label. The contract called for an advance of $100,000, payable to Parker, and a fifty-cent per album royalty.[23] Apparently, Elvis did not receive any of the advance. With those agreements, Colonel Parker treated Elvis as if he was already dead and gone—and as if he had no heirs who could benefit from his estate.

When asked about RCA's buyout agreement with Colonel Parker, Jean Aberbach, who worked for Freddie Beinstock at Hill and Range, told author Albert Goldman that Parker's life, at that point, was being controlled by his gambling addiction. Said Aberbach, who had a close working relationship with the Colonel: "He was forced to do many things that he otherwise might not have done. He was forced to go in directions in which he otherwise might not have gone."

As far as the buyout was concerned, Aberbach said it "certainly fit in with his need to come up with money because there are certain people to whom you cannot owe money."

Not only was 1973 pivotal in Elvis's career, it was yet another landmark year for organized crime. It was the year in which Flamingo Hotel owners pleaded guilty to underworld connections with mobster Meyer Lansky. Three years later the FBI would raid the Stardust for evidence of a mob connection. The long-running myth that the mob had been pushed out of Las Vegas was just that—a myth.

Las Vegas had changed radically since Colonel Parker first tapped into its entertainment potential in the 1940s while managing country crooner Eddy Arnold. At that time, the city was little more than a glorified bus stop for dedicated sons of the Wild West. Not until the Flamingo opened in 1947 under the leadership of mobster Bugsy Siegel did organized crime get a stranglehold on the city.

Throughout the 1950s the Teamsters invested millions with the Chicago mob, which channeled the money into Las Vegas, usually through Meyer Lansky, to finance the construction of new casinos. By the late 1960s, when Howard Hughes started buying up casinos from mob-connected investors, the story circulated that Hughes had put the mob out of business. Nothing could have been further from the truth.

Even though the mob sold out to Hughes, the wiseguys who ran the operations stayed at the casinos. The real profit in operating a casino had always been in the money that was skimmed off the top of each night's proceeds and then passed along, tax free, in brown paper bags to mob bosses.

What changed in the 1970s was how the money was handled. Brown paper bags were exchanged for offshore bank accounts. The goal was the same: to keep large cash deposits from the prying eyes of the FBI, IRS, and federal prosecutors. Once the cash was deposited in offshore banks, it could be re-channeled into legitimate businesses owned by the mob through the use of legal transfers such as checks and money orders.

To investigate the use of offshore banks by organized crime and other so-called "white collar" offenses, the Justice Department coordinated a massive undercover operation called Strike Force. Involved were investigators in at least nine cities: New York, Miami, Jacksonville, Memphis, Boston, Houston, Milwaukee, Indianapolis, and Charlotte, North Carolina.

Early on, four men attracted Strike Force's attention: Nigel Winfield, Lawrence Wolfson, Frederick Pro, and Philip Kitzer.[24] The men were thought to be associates in "The Fraternity," a loosely knit, clandestine organization composed of thirty to forty of the world's top con men. They communicated by telephone, telex machines, mail, and personal visits for the purpose of assisting each other in various scams and moneymaking ventures.

For several years, the FBI had monitored Wolfson's activities with New York and New Jersey Mafia families. By the mid-1970s, the fifty-eight-year-old Wolfson had relocated to Miami, where, according to a report in the December 15, 1977, *Miami Herald*, he was spotted meeting at the Miami Heart Institute with Sam "The Plumber" De-Calvacante, the reputed head of the New Jersey Mafia family, and Sebastian "Buster" Aloi, a member of the Joseph Columbo crime family of New York. Of the four, it was Frederick Pro who had the most interesting background. A veteran of the armed forces, he had once studied for the priesthood at St. Charles Seminary in Lansdowne, Pennsylvania.[25]

In the spring of 1976, Winfield was tipped off, almost certainly by someone close to Elvis, that the entertainer owned a Lockheed Jetstar that was not being used. Attempts to sell the aircraft, Winfield was informed, had been unsuccessful. Since $600,000 was still owed on the aircraft, Elvis was anxious to do something with it.

The previous year, Vernon had arranged for Elvis to purchase a plush Boeing 707 once owned by financier-fugitive Robert Vesco, then under indictment for conspiracy to block a Securities Exchange Commission probe of his finances. Elvis put down a $75,000 deposit on the plane and told reporters that he would be using it for upcoming business flights to Europe and the Far East. Shortly after the deal was consummated, Elvis received an anonymous telegram from Panama threatening to hijack the plane. That threat, coupled with the seizure of the plane by authorities in New Jersey, caused Elvis to back out of the deal.[26]

Several months later, Elvis purchased a Gulfstream turbo-prop aircraft, valued at $1.2 million, as a gift for Colonel Parker, and a 109-passenger Convair 880 for himself. The Gulfstream was delivered to Parker, who did not like to fly, and he promptly sold it. The gift was described as a goodwill gesture, but it was more likely a part of the deal to acquire the Convair 880. By that time, the Colonel had told Vernon that if he and Elvis ever had a parting of the ways, Elvis would owe him a considerable amount in unpaid commissions. Most likely, Elvis got the Gulfstream at a cut-rate price. Since it was valued at $1.2 million, he could claim that amount, not the actual price, as payment toward his debt with Parker.

Since Winfield had spoken with Vernon Presley in recent years regarding other aircraft sales (most likely during the Gulfstream-Convair-Boeing 707 negotiations), he called Presley's father and told him that he wanted to introduce him to a man who could solve his problems with the Jetstar. The man's name was Frederick Pro.[27]

The way Winfield described it over the telephone, it sounded like a good deal. On June 24, 1976, Winfield, Pro, Wolfson, and three other men flew to Memphis to meet with Vernon and two of Elvis's Memphis attorneys, Beecher Smith and Charles Davis. Under the terms of the sale-lease agreement proposed by the men, the following would transpire: they would purchase the Jetstar from Elvis by borrowing enough money from the Chemical Bank of New York to pay off the remaining $600,000 debt and they would spend $350,000 upgrading the aircraft, elevating the value of the aircraft to nearly one million dollars. Then they would lease the aircraft back to Elvis for seven years at a monthly rental of $16,755. In turn, Elvis would sublease the aircraft to them for $17,755 per month, thus providing Elvis with a $1,000-a-month profit.

The following day, Vernon agreed to the proposal. Pro took the keys to the Jetstar and left for New York. Immediately after takeoff, Pro contacted Kitzer on the aircraft's air-to-ground telephone and announced that he had conned Elvis out of the aircraft. Previously, Kitzer had told Pro that obtaining the aircraft would be "mission impossible."[28]

Pro requested the use of his colleague's offshore banks to complete the deal. The reason why it was so important to obtain the Jetstar was never established, but, considering the players involved, it certainly was not to profit from the relatively small amount of money involved.

By October, it was clear to Beecher Smith that Vernon had been taken for a ride. Smith read an article in the *Wall Street Journal* that said the FBI was investigating organized crime's ties to several offshore banks. One of the banks mentioned in the article was Kitzer's Mercantile Bank and Trust.

Smith was familiar with the bank because Pro had issued checks on that bank for some of the expenses associated with the Jetstar deal. Armed with that information, Smith went to the U.S. Attorney's office in Memphis, thus setting in motion an FBI investigation of the men involved in the Jetstar scam.

Unknown to Smith, he and Vernon inadvertently had stepped right in the middle of the Strike Force investigation. When FBI agents went to Graceland in October 1976 to interview Elvis and Vernon about the scam, Elvis, who had been on the road for most of the year, showed them the badge that Nixon had given him and offered to help in any way he could. The agents questioned them about their contact with Pro and others, but they never told Elvis and Vernon that they had become involved in a worldwide organized crime probe.

By the spring of 1977 Elvis and Parker were feuding openly. The *Nashville Banner* reported that the Colonel was ready to "sell" Elvis's management contact. Quoting unidentified sources close to Elvis, the newspaper stated that Parker had made that decision because of "health and financial" reasons. It said certain West Coast "businessmen" had expressed an interest in the contract. "The Colonel isn't necessarily broke," said the source. "He just needs some money, like about a cool million he lost in December alone."

The newspaper said the Colonel had closed his offices in Los Angeles and Las Vegas, and was referring all business inquiries to his garage office in Madison. That report was consistent with what Presley bodyguard Sam Thompson told authors Charles Thompson and

James Cole. That spring the Colonel told Sam that he was going to sell the management contract because Elvis "was a lot of trouble—and it was getting to be more trouble than it was worth."

Parker denied both the newspaper story and Thompson's allegations, but if it was true that his monthly gambling losses had escalated to one million dollars, as the newspaper reported, then he was probably on the verge of losing his share of his management contract with Elvis. If that happened, then the only way he would be able to explain why he was no longer involved in Elvis's management would be to "sell" that contract to the holder of the remaining twenty-five percent share.

Elvis was an absolute mess by midsummer. He weighed nearly 260 pounds and his bloated appearance shocked his fans and those who had not seen him in recent years. He was in and out of hospitals for an almost constant stream of ailments, and was medicating himself for depression and anxiety. His personal physician Dr. George Nichopoulos prescribed 8,805 amphetamine, sedative, and narcotic pills in the first seven months of the year, according to a subsequent police investigation. Elvis's speech was often slurred during his personal appearances, and his onstage behavior became increasingly erratic and punctuated with rambling musings of a religious nature.

Despite his client's condition, Colonel Parker booked him for fifty-five concert appearances that year. Since his concerts were grossing more than $100,000 each, that would add up to $5.5 million before expenses and taxes were deducted. The Colonel had his boy out on the road almost continuously from mid-February until the end of June, when Presley ended that tour with a performance at the Market Square Arena in Indianapolis, Indiana. He and several band members became ill after the performance and were hospitalized overnight.

Elvis attempted to recuperate at Graceland. He was seriously ill, but continued to take diet pills to lose weight. He slept for most of July, rarely leaving his bedroom. In early August he pulled himself together long enough to go to Libertyland amusement park to attend a private party for Lisa Marie.

A couple of days later, he attended a private showing of the new James Bond movie, *The Spy Who Loved Me*, at a Memphis theater.

He was spotted packing a PK Walther automatic at the movie theater, but that was not unusual; he almost always carried an assortment of pistols, which he concealed beneath his jacket, in his pockets, and in his boots.

Of all the things Elvis had on his mind—his deteriorating health; the recently published "tell-all" book by three of his former body-guards; his divorce from Priscilla; his inability to settle into another relationship; his mind-numbing concert schedule; his bickering with the Colonel—it was probably the Strike Force probe that concerned him most. The investigation was proceeding at a glacial pace. Several months earlier, they had sent two undercover agents, posing as underworld operatives, to New York with Philip Kitzer. In a sting that resembled something from the James Bond movies of which Elvis was so fond, the three men caught a National Airlines flight in Miami bound for New York.

None of the three men sat together during the flight, and none spoke to each other or acknowledged that they were acquainted. They continued the ruse when they arrived in New York and checked into the Mayflower Hotel, where the two undercover agents separated from Kitzer and rendezvoused with an FBI agent.[29]

Kitzer took the two undercover agents to another room at the hotel, where he introduced them to Frederick Pro. Kitzer told Pro that the two men were "good guys to know" and would be able to work out any problems that Pro had with the "outfit," meaning mob families in New York and New Jersey. It was during that meeting that Pro revealed the extent of his worldwide operations and joked about how he had "conned" Elvis out of his Jetstar.

Based on the conversations that occurred in the Mayflower, all of which were recorded by the FBI, the Strike Force managers concluded that they would be able to release the Pro-Kitzer-Wolfson case to the U.S. Attorney in Memphis for prosecution.

FBI files do not indicate how much information was passed along to Elvis and Vernon, but almost certainly they were notified that prosecutors would soon be going to the grand jury to ask for indictments. When that happened, it would be necessary for both of them to testify before the grand jury. Certainly, their testimony would be needed for the trial itself.

Since Elvis's next scheduled concert was in Portland, Maine, on August 17, Colonel Parker went there several days in advance to set up the promotional materials for the concert. He had always been a firm believer in the economic value of concert concessions. He put more value on the trinkets that were sold at the concerts than he did on the musical content of the performance.

On August 15, Elvis spent time with Lisa Marie, who had come for a short visit, but when she went to bed, he stayed up all night, playing racquetball and visiting with his current girlfriend, Ginger Alden. By 6 A.M., August 16, everyone in the house except Elvis and Alden had turned in. She told him that she had had enough and was going to bed.

Elvis said he wasn't ready to turn in. Alden was the last person to see him alive that morning. As she got into bed, she saw him heading toward the bathroom.

"Don't fall asleep," she said.

Later that afternoon, Colonel Parker received a telephone call at his hotel suite in Portland: Elvis was dead.

8

THE KING IS DEAD: LONG LIVE THE MANAGER

As Elvis was being rushed to the Baptist Hospital, Assistant U.S. Attorney Hickman Ewing was in federal court in Memphis prosecuting topless nightclub kingpin Arthur Baldwin on cocaine and firearms charges. One of the lead stories in the morning newspaper had been about the trial.

Its theme of sex, guns, and drugs had generated considerable public interest. Memphians seemed incredulous that anyone would suggest that women, good *Memphis women,* would strip for money. That would *never* happen in Memphis, they argued–not in the King's backyard—proving once again that denial was a prerequisite to living in a metropolis with the foresight to call itself the Bluff City.

To the fair-headed Ewing, who would achieve fame in the 1990s as Special Prosecutor Kenneth Starr's lead prosecutor in the Arkansas-based Whitewater investigation, the dark-haired, smooth-talking Baldwin was as transparently evil as they came. "While we were on break, about three in the afternoon, someone came into the courtroom and said they had taken Elvis to the hospital and he had died," recalls Ewing. "Baldwin, who had never said a word to me in his life, came over to me and said, 'Well, Mr. Ewing, I hate to wish old Elvis any bad luck, but at least it will take the publicity off of me for a few days'—and it did. Then a few days later the jury convicted him."[1]

Ewing never let on to Baldwin, but federal authorities were caught off guard by Elvis's sudden death. Ewing was involved in the Jetstar case, and his office was within weeks of approaching the grand jury for indictments.

After receiving news of Elvis's death, Colonel Parker immediately phoned Vernon Presley and told him he would fly to Memphis for the funeral, but would need to take care of some business before doing that. They would have to work together to make sure unscrupulous people did not try to cash in on Elvis's death. There was still lots of money to be made, and it would be a damned shame if the family lost out during this time of grief.

Before leaving Maine, Parker called RCA and spoke with executives there. In light of Elvis's death, they would need to draw up a new promotions-and-marketing agreement. One month later, RCA sent the agreement to Parker in care of All Star Shows in Madison. It stipulated that RCA would retain the Colonel's services at least until October 1979 for a fee of $675,000.

Fearing that fleet-footed bootleggers would capitalize on the Elvis Presley name, Parker called Harry "The Bear" Geissler, the high-rolling novelties dealer whose company, Factors, had made a name for itself marketing *Star Wars*, Farrah Fawcett, and Sylvester Stallone products. Parker and Geissler struck a deal over the telephone. The following day the Colonel flew to New York to pick up the agreement, which provided for a $100,000 advance on signing, then he headed straight to Memphis. Elvis had been dead for less than twenty-four hours and the Colonel already had made $775,000.[2] He was on a roll.

On the morning of August 17, 1977, the big news in Memphis was the death of Elvis Presley. "Death Captures Crown of Rock and Roll" read the banner headline in the morning newspaper, the *Commercial Appeal*. The newspaper quoted Elvis's personal physician, Dr. George Nichopoulos, as saying the forty-two-year-old entertainer had probably died of a heart attack, but the precise cause of death would not be known until a postmortem examination could be completed.

Elvis's cousin, Donna Presley Early, was in her grandmother's bedroom with her Uncle Vernon and two other family members when Colonel Parker—wearing a baseball cap, khaki pants, and a bright blue shirt—walked in. They were consoling each other, especially the grandmother, Minnie Mae, whom Elvis had nicknamed "the Dodger."

The family was discussing what songs should be sung at the funeral. "Colonel Parker was there in the room, but he didn't have too much to say," says Early. "He wasn't the type of person who showed his emotions, so he wasn't weeping or anything, but he was obviously upset." By contrast, Vernon was distraught and frightened. "They've killed my son," he said over and over again. "They've killed my son."[3]

Again, Parker stepped in to handle the funeral arrangements. Did Vernon ask him to place a Star of David on Elvis's gravestone as Elvis had wanted done for his mother? No one seems to know. The odd thing about it is that Vernon approved lettering that read "Elvis Aaron Presley." That's odd because Elvis's middle name was Aron. Did Vernon not know how to spell his son's name? The "error" was probably because Vernon chose the Jewish spelling of the name. Aaron, of course, was the brother of Moses and the first high priest of the Hebrews. Vernon had his shortcomings, but he almost certainly knew that one cannot get much more Jewish than "Aaron." He must have figured that this slight deception was between him and God.

Parker was asked to be a pallbearer, but he declined, saying he had been on the road and lacked the right clothes. No one suggested he go to a Memphis store and purchase what he needed because no one really cared whether he attended the service. During the wake Parker talked to Vernon about the Factors deal and said he would need authorization to continue representing the Presley estate.[4] It is not clear when Vernon signed the papers for the Factors deal, but court records show that it went into effect on August 18, the day of the funeral.

Parker wore the same baseball cap, blue shirt, and khaki pants to the funeral. His wife, Marie, did not attend, but hundreds of fans and celebrities did, including James Brown, Caroline Kennedy, Ann-Margret, George Hamilton, Sammy Davis Jr., Chet Atkins, and Tennessee Governor Ray Blanton, who was about to become the target of a Justice Department probe instigated by Hickman Ewing.

The following week, *Newsweek* published a four-page spread on the entertainer. It called him "more than a pop superstar," and said he had changed forever the course of popular music. Noting the

hordes of fans who had descended upon Memphis, the magazine reported that Parker had arranged for vendors to be placed outside
Graceland to hawk Elvis Presley T-shirts for five dollars each. Said a
thirty-seven-year-old housewife from Waldorf, Maryland, who had
rushed to Memphis for the funeral: "Whatever's written about [Elvis],
true or false, makes no difference to me. I have no other idols."

☆   ☆   ☆

Immediately after the funeral, the Colonel returned to Los Angeles, where he quickly began consolidating his holdings on the Presley
estate. He negotiated with RCA Records to produce a two-record set,
Elvis in Concert. Under the terms of that agreement the Presley estate would be advanced $225,000 and Colonel Parker would be ad-
vanced $225,000, plus an additional $50,000 for his All Star Shows.[5]

Four days after the funeral, Vernon signed an agreement that allowed Parker to become the estate's manager. The agreement stated,
"As executor of Elvis's estate, I hereby would appreciate it if you will
carry on according to the same terms and conditions as stated in the
contractual agreement you had with Elvis dated January 22, 1976,
and I hereby authorize you to speak and sign for me in all these matters pertaining to this agreement. I will rely on your good judgment
to keep the image of Elvis alive for his many fans and friends."[6]

James Kingsley, a reporter with the *Commercial Appeal* who had
formed a close friendship with Elvis, called Parker at his Los Angeles
office to inquire about the agreement. "I will be busy looking after
Elvis's estate," Parker told him. "It used to be it was Elvis and the
Colonel. . . . Now, it will be Elvis and the Colonel and Vernon Presley." Kingsley asked about the Elvis T-shirt vendors outside Graceland, but Parker told him that the family had not been involved.

On the day of Elvis's demise, the Memphis Police Department reported the cause of death as either heart failure or an accidental drug
overdose, then later that day denied that a drug overdose was a possibility. Dr. Jerry Francisco, the chief medical examiner, subsequently
declared "cardiac arrhythmia" as the cause of death. He said there
was no evidence of chronic drug use, and declared that "the most
likely conclusion after all tests are complete is natural causes."

In the weeks after Elvis's death the Justice Department intensified its Jetstar investigation and its case against the mob-connected group of con men known as the "Fraternity." According to confidential FBI documents, the group was responsible for "billions of dollars in fraudulent financial transactions" that had occurred in banks around the world. The report listed the names of over thirty banks, which were listed as either "subjects," meaning they were part of the conspiracy, or "victims," meaning they had received fraudulent financial transactions from the "subject" banks.[7]

On October 13, the facts of the Jetstar case were presented to the Memphis grand jury, which returned sealed indictments on six men.[8] With FBI agents already in place, two of the men, Frederick Pro and Philip Kitzer, were arrested immediately after the seventeen-count indictment was opened in federal court on October 18. Arrest warrants were issued for the other four men, all of whom were promptly apprehended. After the suspects made bail, FBI agents advised Vernon of the new developments and suggested he take extra precautions to ensure his safety.[9]

When Elvis's death negated his upcoming August appearance at the Las Vegas Hilton, the Colonel's office privileges at the hotel were revoked. Barron Hilton no longer required his services as a $50,000-a-year consultant. As a result, the Colonel began working out of his Los Angeles office. With him was Loanne Miller, who had become his full-time assistant in 1975. He kept his distance from Memphis, consulting with Vernon by telephone when necessary.

As the new year began, individuals and corporations beseiged Vernon with claims against the estate. Elvis's bank, the National Bank of Commerce, sued his grieving father to collect $1.4 million on three different notes. Ginger Alden's mother sued Vernon for nearly $40,000 because she alleged that Elvis had promised to pay off her house note.

Even Priscilla filed a claim against the estate. Probate court records show that she asked for $356,000 as the balance of the cash portion of her $725,000 divorce settlement. The amount was supposed to have been paid in monthly installments of $6,000, with the balance due by August 1, 1982.

The April before Elvis's death, Vernon, acting on his son's behalf, had signed a promissory note on the Graceland mansion for $494,024 to guarantee payment of the monthly installments to Priscilla. California law stipulated that divorce payments required a security deposit when the paying spouse lived in another state.

Priscilla's claim also asked for half the money received from the sale of the furnishings in the couple's former Los Angeles home, the value of which was placed at $500,000; a five percent share of the stock in Elvis Presley Music and Whitehaven Music; and $4,000-a-month support for the care of Lisa Marie.

All of which was bad news for Vernon. According to the financial report filed by the estate in probate court, Elvis had three accounts, totaling $1.9 million, at the National Bank of Commerce. The most intriguing item in the report was the disclosure that Elvis was a stockholder (696 shares), along with Frank Sinatra, in the Del Webb Corporation, a publicly held company that was involved in operating several Las Vegas casinos.[10] In 1969, when Elvis began his Las Vegas bookings, Del Webb owned the Thunderbird and the Sahara.

Exactly when Elvis acquired his stock is not known, but it was obviously sometime between 1969 and 1977. He was not in the habit of purchasing stock, so it is doubtful that the Del Webb stock was the result of a cash transaction. More likely, he and Parker were given the stock as part of a barter deal.

Another claim against the estate was generated by 1103 Imports, a wholesale diamond business with offices in the Thunderbird. The company said it was owed over $13,000 for jewelry that Elvis had purchased in November and December 1976.[11]

Besides the money problems, the upcoming trial in the Jetstar case was continuously hanging over Vernon's head. He was the key witness in the case. The right word from him on the witness stand and the dominos could be toppled, creating a ripple effect that would wash not only into the clandestine fortress of the Fraternity, but into the inner sanctum of America's top organized crime families.

In the last years of Elvis's life, when he started wearing bullet-proof vests and carrying an arsenal of firearms, people mocked him and laughed behind his back. They said he was paranoid and strung out on drugs. No one took his fears seriously. Vernon was now experiencing a similar reaction. Every time he said anything about Elvis's death not being natural, people looked away, even family members, as if Elvis's embarrassing paranoia had spread to Vernon, infecting him with nonsensical thoughts.

When Frederick Pro failed to show up for a routine scheduled court hearing in February 1978, Assistant U.S. Attorney Hickman Ewing issued a warrant for his arrest. The FBI again advised Vernon to take special precautions. Pro was now a fugitive and anything might happen. Meanwhile, Philip Kitzer plea-bargained with the U.S. Attorney in Louisville, where he also had been indicted under related racketeering charges.[12]

In May, Frederick Pro was apprehended in Los Angeles and transported to New York, where he faced racketeering charges related to the offshore banks. After several months of negotiations, Pro arranged a plea-bargain agreement, whereby all outstanding charges against him were transferred to the New York jurisdiction.[13]

Now it was two down, four to go, but that was hardly a comfort to Vernon. The cases against Pro and Kitzer had effectively been swept under the carpet. Vernon was grateful he had been spared a court appearance, but there were still four cases to go and it was becoming increasingly apparent that someone had the clout to move the cases out of Memphis. Elvis's name and connection to the Jetstar case had been kept out of the newspapers, but so had the names of the organized crime families involved and any mention of the Fraternity. Vernon was not a sophisticated man, but he knew he was in trouble.

Shortly after Elvis's death, Colonel Parker commissioned sculptor Carl Romanelli to create a statue of the entertainer for the lobby of the Las Vegas Hilton. In September, Vernon and Priscilla met in Las Vegas for the statue's dedication. It was a six-foot-tall bronze likeness of the King that depicted him with a guitar. Looking thin and frail, Vernon posed for photographs with Priscilla and Barron Hilton. The stress clearly showed on his tormented face.

The Colonel registered Vernon with the William Morris Agency for media interviews at $25,000 a pop, but, not surprisingly, there were no takers. That same month Parker worked with Factors's owner, Harry Geissler, to crack down on vendors who were selling unauthorized Elvis souvenirs. Attorneys for Geissler sent out what is known in legal circles as a "scare letter." The letter threatened to sue anyone who did not file a "full accounting" of unauthorized sales. Few vendors took the letter seriously.

In November 1978 Parker signed yet another agreement with RCA Records. In this one, the record company agreed to pay him $175,000 for "extra services in preparing product promotion costs merchandising." Parker signed the agreement, but Vernon, who apparently was not informed of its existence, didn't.[14]

By January 1979, the probate court judge, Joseph Evans, realized something had to be done to protect Lisa Marie's rights in the estate. He appointed Priscilla, the National Bank of Commerce, and Elvis's accountant, Joseph Hanks, to oversee the management of Lisa Marie's inheritance.

That same month, Elvis's cousin, Donna Presley Early, began working for Vernon in his office at Graceland. She had grown up in Missouri, but by the age of ten she had begun regular summer visits to Graceland to spend time with her uncle. Now he needed help in the office from someone he could trust and she was happy to oblige.

"Uncle Vernon was a rather stern type of person, and I didn't get to know him closely until I started working for him—and then we became very close," said Early.

One day she was alone in the office, when Vernon came in and sat down at the desk next to hers. He put his feet up on the desk and let out a plaintive sigh. He gazed out into the Meditation Garden, where Elvis was buried. "I can't believe my baby is lying out in that cold ground and the SOBs that did it are out there walking around," he said.

Early thought, well, he's just grieving. She said: "Yeah, I know. It's awful to think he's out there and we're still here."

Vernon gave her a hard look. "No, you don't understand what I'm saying."

"What are you talking about?" she asked.

"I'm talking about Elvis's death and the people who killed him."

"What do you mean?"

"I mean Elvis was murdered."

Early reached for the telephone, saying, "We need to call the police."

"No, put the phone down."

"We need to tell somebody," she said.

"No, we need to handle this the way Elvis would have wanted us to handle it."

Early knew what that meant. She had been in Las Vegas when Elvis received the death threats for which the FBI was called in. "I was in the room," she says. "Elvis said, 'I've told the guys that if this guy gets me, for them to get him because I don't want some SOB sitting up on the witness stand becoming famous for killing Elvis Presley.'"

Vernon continued the conversation: "I'll handle it in-house, the way Elvis would have wanted it done."

"Do you have proof?" she asked.

"I know who did it and I have the proof."[15]

Early went home that day—she lived with her parents in a mobile home parked behind Graceland—and told her mother about her conversation with Vernon. "She said, 'Yeah, I know. He's mentioned that to me.'"

"Shouldn't we do something?"

"No, let Vernon handle it," her mother said. "If they can get to Elvis, they can get to you."

Vernon never handled it. Several months after that conversation, he died of what the medical examiner determined was a heart attack—the same ruling made in Elvis's death. The end came on June 26—the Colonel's birthday. Vernon could not have given him a worse gift. Did Vernon have proof that Elvis was murdered? In view of the FBI probe, Parker's ties to unsavory elements in Las Vegas, the continuous stream of death threats throughout Elvis's career, and the historical climate for murder in Memphis, it would be a mistake to discount Vernon's allegations as the ravings of a bereaved father. Coincidence has its place in life, but not many investigative reporters and law enforcement officials give it much credence when lives and fortunes are at stake.

Once again, the Elvis Presley estate was thrown into chaos. Colonel Parker flew to Memphis for the funeral. Songs recorded by Elvis played over a loudspeaker as Vernon was laid to rest in the Meditation Garden at Graceland. Parker met with Priscilla and said he would need a letter to continue acting as the estate's manager.

The following day, Priscilla sent the letter, co-signed by Hanks and a representative of the National Bank of Commerce, to Parker in care of All Star Shows in Madison. The letter thanked him for the work that he had done for the estate and stated that, as co-executors of the estate, all three wanted "things to continue as they have and as set forth under the letter of August 23, 1977 from Vernon Presley."

Vernon's death threw the Jetstar case into another tailspin. The death of the government's star witness meant further delays as prosecutors scrambled to build a case that could go to trial without Vernon's testimony. That spring, two of the other men jumped bail and went into hiding, causing yet another delay in the trial as FBI agents searched for the missing defendants.

☆   ☆   ☆

As the months went by, Priscilla became more involved in the finances of the estate. She was stunned at how badly Elvis's money had been managed. Debts exceeded cash on hand and—other than the house and a small amount of stock—most of Elvis's assets were tied up in man-toys such as automobiles, motorcycles, airplanes, and firearms (including several machine guns). Simply put, there was very little money.

Priscilla went to Hanks and the representative from the bank. Together they petitioned the probate court judge to appoint a guardian *ad litem* for Lisa Marie. The judge chose a young Memphis lawyer with a name that seemed straight out of a Tennessee Williams play— Blanchard Tual.

On May 5, 1980, Tual was instructed to act as Lisa Marie's guardian and to investigate the estate's finances, with the view of protecting her interests. He was specifically instructed to investigate Colonel Parker's relationship with Elvis and his financial dealings with the estate after the entertainer's death.

All summer everyone was on pins and needles.

Finally, after a five-month investigation during which Parker initiated no new Elvis-related projects, Tual submitted his report to the court. "All agreements entered into between Parker and Presley from 1967 forward . . . were unfair in that the amount of commissions were excessive," wrote Tual, in what amounted to a blistering attack against the Colonel. "Parker, both during Presley's life and in his role in the administration of the estate, has been guilty of self-dealing and overreaching and has violated his duty both to Presley, when Presley was alive, and to the estate."[16]

By allowing Parker to have free rein in controlling the finances of the estate, Tual said, the court had "literally cost the estate, and ultimately Lisa Marie Presley, millions of dollars." Tual asked the court to remedy the situation by ordering that all royalties from Elvis's financial investments be sent directly to the estate and not to Parker; that Parker's fifty percent commission be terminated by the court; and that the estate file suit against Parker in federal court to prevent him from disposing of any assets from Boxcar Enterprises. It was the first time the Colonel had ever been publicly attacked.[17]

The report caught the Memphis news media off guard. A number of attorneys in Memphis had made careers from bombast and fiery courthouse-step pronouncements, but the bookish, mild-mannered Tual was not one of them. Colonel Parker was the most intimidating figure in show business. No one, not even Elvis, had ever dared challenge him. The report was a bombshell.

Memphis newspapers had always enjoyed a good relationship with the Colonel, but when reporters tried to reach him for comment on the report—*Tell us it ain't so, Colonel!* went the refrain—he would not return their telephone calls. The national media also pursued him for his reaction, but he succeeded in eluding everyone. Spokesmen at his office said he was ill and had gone home to recuperate.

The *Commercial Appeal* sent reporter William Dawson to Los Angeles to track down the elusive Colonel. Dawson first went to the RCA Records office in Hollywood. He had been told by sources that Parker had a small suite of offices on the seventh floor, but when he arrived, he discovered that Parker's name was not included in the lobby directory.

A security guard told him that Parker seldom came into the office and there was no one there at the moment. Even if someone had

been in the office, said the security guard, it would have done the reporter no good since the Colonel and his staff received visitors only
by appointment.

Eventually, the reporter located the Colonel's home in Palm
Springs. It was a white house with blue trim, set back away from the
street behind a white wall with blue wrought-iron fencing. A sign
warned visitors that the fence was electrified. The reporter received
no response when he pushed the button to the intercom, but after
standing around for a while at the gate, he saw two women peer out
from behind a door on the side of the house.

One of the women stepped outside and asked what the reporter
wanted. He said he wished to speak to the Colonel. The woman said
she was a nurse and was there to care for the Colonel's wife, who was
ill. She said the Colonel was in Los Angeles and could not be reached.
The second woman is presumed to be Loanne Miller. The reporter
was never able to talk to the Colonel, but he returned to Memphis
and wrote a story about the "Cloak of Secrecy" that surrounded the
manager.

In December, Tual returned to court and asked the judge to give
him the power to widen his investigation. Beecher Smith, the attorney representing Priscilla and the co-executors, protested, saying it
was their responsibility—not Tual's—to look after the interests of
Elvis's twelve-year-old daughter.

Tual charged that Smith had tried to "sandbag" his investigation.[18]
He said that he felt the executors of the estate, with the exception of
Priscilla, were "afraid" of Colonel Parker. He described his September report as only a "first step," and said there were many things in
the case that needed "looking into." It was a contentious hearing.

Ablaze with righteous indignation, Tual passionately defended Lisa
Marie and her interests. Reporters described Smith as sometimes
"trembling" as he stood before the judge; he pleaded with the court
to terminate Tual's investigation. He criticized Tual's report and accused him of overreacting.

Fired back Tual: "Not one time did I use the word 'negligence,'
though I could have done so; not one time did I use the words 'gross
negligence,' though I could have; I never used the word 'malpractice,'
though I could have."

Judge Evans listened to Tual's argument, and he listened to Smith's argument. Elvis Presley was probably the most famous entertainer in the world. Colonel Parker was almost as famous himself. No one in music circles knew Evans from a hole in the ground, but he had been given the responsibility of protecting the interests of a little girl who truly seemed to need protection.

Finally, Judge Evans, in a moment of exemplary southern jurisprudence, granted Tual the power to require Parker to provide the court with a full accounting of his finances, including tax information. The authority granted to Tual also gave him the power to examine the records of Boxcar Enterprises and the Colonel's financial dealings with Factors. It was the legal equivalent of a football coach sending his prize fullback into the game with instructions to *go, boy, go!*

Colonel Parker was not the only person associated with Elvis who came under attack. As Judge Evans was making waves in probate court, Elvis's personal physician, Dr. George Nichopoulos, was brought before the state medical board on charges that he had overprescribed addictive drugs to nine patients, including Elvis.

Nichopoulos testified about Elvis's drug abuse, confirming suspicions that the entertainer had become addicted to a wide assortment of drugs. After a stay in California, where he received injections of Novocain, Demerol, and steroids for a strained back, Elvis returned to Memphis addicted to Demerol and was admitted to Baptist Hospital for detoxification, said Nichopoulos. The physician defended the large quantity of medication that he had prescribed by saying that he was trying to control Elvis's drug problem by administering a therapeutic reduction.

The medical board acquitted Nichopoulos of the most serious charges, but found him guilty of overprescribing addictive drugs. His license was suspended for three months and he was placed on probation for three years. Sitting in the public seating throughout the hearing were investigators for the district attorney general's office. Unknown to Nichopoulos, the attorney general had decided to initiate a criminal investigation of Elvis's drug use and of the physician's activities. It would be the only criminal investigation associated with Elvis's death.

Since some members of Elvis's inner circle had moved to the West Coast, investigators Larry Hutchinson and David McGriff flew to Los Angeles with Bobby Armstead, a police department sergeant, to interview potential witnesses. On their list were former bodyguard Red West, former road manager Joe Esposito, and former Elvis girlfriend Linda Thompson.

"Everyone in California has an agent," says McGriff, laughing at his recollection of the hoops that they had to jump through to set up the interviews. "We thought that was comical. . . . It gave the impression that everyone was busy and I'm not sure that was the case."[19]

The last person on their list was Colonel Tom Parker. To their surprise, they were able to reach him without any trouble. He agreed to meet them at their Beverly Hills hotel room. After what they had gone through trying to set up interviews with the others, they were pleasantly surprised by his attitude.

At the appointed time, Parker, dressed in casual clothes and clutching a massive cigar, arrived at the hotel room. He did not come alone. Accompanying him was George Fenneman, the announcer who had co-starred with Groucho Marx on a popular 1950s television show, *You Bet Your Life*. McGriff and Hutchinson did not realize it, but Parker had come prepared to play a high-stakes game of chance.

It was unthinkable for him to even consider evading an opportunity to roll the dice with the Memphis investigators. For this performance the Colonel would play the role of Groucho and his friend George Fenneman would play himself. The name of the show was *You Bet Your Life* (the Colonel was, in effect, doing exactly that) and the running joke was the same one-liner Groucho and Fenneman had used on their show: "Say the secret word and win a hundred bucks."[20]

The Memphis detectives grilled the Colonel about his knowledge of his client's drug use. He said he really didn't know much about that. He spent most of his time in California and Las Vegas. They inquired about Elvis's relationship with his entourage. Was there someone on the inside encouraging his use of drugs?

Parker said he really didn't know. They asked if he had any personal contact with Elvis during the two years his client was in the army. Not really, he said. Elvis called him two or three times, and maybe sent a couple of letters.

The Colonel told the investigators that when Elvis visited him at his Palm Springs home in 1974, he thought something might be wrong. He said Elvis admitted to taking drugs, but admonished the Colonel not to interfere.

Throughout the interview the Colonel was amiable, giving the investigators the impression that he had nothing to hide. At the conclusion of the interview he invited the detectives to drive back to Palm Springs with him. Parker was having dinner at George Hamilton's home and was certain the famous actor would be happy to have them as guests. The detectives declined the invitation.

"I found Parker to be an absolute gentleman," McGriff said in a 1997 interview with the author. "He was extremely calm, relaxed, almost as if he was going to tell us what he had to tell us and was very comfortable doing it. Never did I detect him getting uncomfortable or trying to disguise his answers. I walked away from that interview with a conviction that the Colonel had pretty well told the truth to what we had asked—of course, there may have been fifty great questions that I didn't ask that he may have had trouble with."

Say the secret word and win a hundred bucks!

The detectives never said the secret word during the interview. They returned to Memphis convinced that there was no reason to call the Colonel as a witness for the upcoming trial of Dr. George Nichopoulos. They were certain Parker had not encouraged Elvis's drug use and was so removed from the day-to-day life of the entertainer that the manager had nothing to contribute to the case.

It is interesting to speculate how things might have been different if the detectives had said the secret word and the Colonel had opened his treasure chest of revelations about Elvis's drug use. He might have been a con man, but he never welched on a bet. It is not beyond the realm of possibility that the Colonel had a wager riding on the interview. Fenneman not only contributed an element of drama, he also served as a witness.

Based on the investigative work of the detectives, a Memphis grand jury indicted Nichopoulos in May. At the trial, noted Tennessee attorney James Neal, who had distinguished himself as a Watergate prosecutor, represented the physician. Neal depicted Nichopoulos as a caring and dedicated doctor who had tried his best to administer to his patient's needs. The jury found Nichopoulos not guilty and he resumed his medical practice.

When the author interviewed McGriff in 1997, he was still working as a cop, assigned to the Drug Task Force, a special investigative arm comprised of officers from the FBI, the Drug Enforcement Agency, the county sheriff's office, and the Memphis police department. In fact, the scheduled interview was delayed because McGriff was on an undercover stakeout when the author arrived in town.

After calling in a replacement, McGriff received permission from his superior officer to meet the author at an East Memphis restaurant. When asked if he felt justice had been served in the case, McGriff pondered the question for a moment, then said, "I won't comment as to who justice was and was not done to. Justice was not done," he said.

☆   ☆   ☆

Colonel Parker did not run from Blanchard Tual, nor did he attempt to fight the court order, but he did ask Tual to sign a confidentiality agreement before releasing his financial records. Tual kept his thoughts to himself during the months in which he delved further into the financial structure of the Presley estate and the entertainer's relationship with the Colonel. He held no press conferences and politely declined requests for interviews.

Whatever Priscilla and the Colonel expected from the court-appointed guardian, it is probably a safe bet that they were shocked by the depth and intensity of his final eighty-five-page report to the court, which was filed on July 31, 1981. The headline in the next morning's *Memphis Press-Scimitar* set the mood: "Report Says Manager's Deals Defrauded Elvis."[21]

Tual reported to the court that his investigation showed that Colonel Parker and RCA Records had together defrauded the Presley estate out of $2.7 million. He was especially critical of the six agreements signed during the 1973 RCA "buyout." Said Tual: "The executives at RCA had to have realized that the side deals to Parker were in effect a pay off to Parker . . . for keeping Elvis under control in future years with no audit."

Tual urged the court to order the Presley estate not to enter into any new agreements and to stop payment on Parker's current requests for money. He also suggested that the estate file suit against RCA in an effort to stop the 1973 buyout agreement and to audit RCA's dealings with the estate.

"Colonel Parker knowingly violated [Elvis's trust] and continued to abuse it until Elvis's death," said Tual. "There is evidence that both Parker and RCA are guilty of collusion, conspiracy, fraud, misrepresentation, bad faith and overreaching. . . . [The agreements] were unethical, fraudulently obtained and against all industry standards. These actions against the most popular American folk hero of this century are outrageous and call out for a full accounting from those responsible."

As it had been for much of the proceedings, the Presley estate was speechless. Beecher Smith, attorney for the estate, told reporters that he had no comment. Jack Magids, a Memphis attorney whom Parker had hired to represent him, publicly declared that the Colonel denied all the allegations made in the report.[22]

Judge Joseph Evans digested the contents of the report, then on August 14—two days before the anniversary of Elvis's death—read his ruling to a courtroom packed with Elvis fans, some of whom had driven long distances. Said Evans: 'The court finds that the compensation received by Colonel Parker is excessive and shocks the conscience of the court."

With that, he ordered the estate to file suit against Colonel Parker within forty-five days to recover "such sums as shall be determined due and owing to the estate." As a special incentive, the judge ordered that Tual should be an associate counsel in the lawsuit.

Afterward, James Chisum, a reporter for the *Commercial Appeal*, spoke to some of the court spectators. "They ought to hang him," one woman said.

"Who?" asked Chisum.

"Parker," she said.

The following day, the Colonel broke his long, self-imposed silence by telephoning James Kingsley at the *Commercial Appeal*. "I am prepared to fully defend myself regarding all of the allegations which have been made against me, and I will take other proper legal actions which may be available to me," he told the reporter. Parker said he was "shocked" by Tual's report and he denied any wrongdoing.

Subsequently, the Colonel did an interview with Randell Beck, a reporter with the *Memphis Press-Scimitar*. After attacking Tual's knowledge of the music industry, he contradicted the guardian's description of Elvis as an easily manipulated individual. Parker said Elvis was moody and undependable. "Sometimes it was such a heartache to keep [him] going," he said.

For the first time in his life, the great Colonel Parker was against the ropes, put there by an unknown Memphis lawyer who was either too fearless—or too damned stupid—to comprehend the enormity of his actions. It was David and Goliath, and the aging, rotund Colonel knew that no one would mistake him for David.

Making the Colonel's prospects look even worse were news reports that Factors owner Harry "the Bear" Geissler pleaded guilty in a Delaware court to charges of mail fraud involving corporations dealing with *Superman: The Movie, Star Wars*, and *Grease*. The entertainment newspaper *Variety* reported that Geissler had filed more than two hundred lawsuits in an effort to protect the Presley image, but an appellate court had stripped away that presumed authority by ruling that a celebrity's exclusive right of publicity to his image cannot be inherited and ends with his death.

By 1982, Priscilla had filed two lawsuits against Parker: one, filed in Memphis, sought to revoke the Colonel's fifty percent share of Elvis's royalties; the other, filed in San Francisco, accused him of defrauding the estate of more than $5 million. Both lawsuits were ordered by Judge Joseph Evans.

The Presley estate was not the only entity filing lawsuits. RCA Records filed a lawsuit in New York that asked the court to find valid its 1973 buyout agreement. In the lawsuit RCA asked the court to prohibit the Presley estate from suing RCA for lost royalties. Listed as defendants were everyone involved with the Memphis court proceedings—Priscilla Presley, Joseph Hanks, the National Bank of Commerce, Blanchard Tual, and Colonel Parker.

The only major player in this drama not being sued was Judge Joseph Evans.

The Colonel responded with a lawsuit of his own. On March 12, 1982 the seventy-two-year-old Parker filed a lawsuit in Nevada state court that challenged the Presley estate for control of Elvis's assets. Listed as defendants were Priscilla Presley, the National Bank of Commerce, and Joseph Hanks. In the lawsuit Parker characterized his relationship with Elvis as that of "partner" and described their business arrangement as a "joint venture."[23]

It was not a new strategy for the Colonel. From day one, he had sent out letters signed "Elvis and the Colonel," and he had done advertising that included references to "Elvis and the Colonel." He was more than a manager. He was the long-suffering "partner" in a decades-old joint venture.

Said Parker in the lawsuit: "In recognition of the Colonel's unique skills, in appreciation for the Colonel's loyalty to Elvis, and as an inducement to the Colonel to continue and to expand the Colonel's services, Elvis and the Colonel agreed that from and after January 2, 1967, Elvis and the Colonel would share equally in all profit participations provided under Elvis's movie contracts and in all royalties over the guaranteed payments arising from the recording agreement with RCA."

Parker charged that the co-executors of the estate were interfering with his continued operation of the joint venture. He asked the Nevada court to give him the authority to control the assets of the estate for the purpose of "winding down" the affairs of the joint venture. Furthermore, he said he had advanced Elvis a total of $1.6 million from the receipts of the joint venture out of the goodness of his heart because the entertainer had needed the money more than he did at the time. Now he wanted the money, even if it did not at the moment exist—and even if it belonged to a twelve-year-old girl whose father had died under traumatic circumstances.

It was during this time that Parker acknowledged to the probate court that he was born Andreas Cornelis van Kuijk. He said he had immigrated illegally to the United States from Holland in his youth to enlist in the U.S. Army. He said he had neither Dutch nor American citizenship. This story is identical to one that two Dutch journalists, working independently of each other, published in Holland. The two journalists differed over Parker's actual name, but they agreed on many of the details sworn to in the court documents presented by Parker.

Unfortunately, none of the statements given by Parker about his ancestry can be documented. Certainly, there is no record that he ever served in the army under the names of either Tom Parker or Andreas Cornelis van Kuijk.

If the story is not true, then why would Parker intimate that it was? Obviously, he thought it was in his best interest to perpetuate an unprovable myth. Legally, it was to his advantage to claim to be a stateless person, immune, he would argue, from lawsuits in an American court. Personally, it insulated him from future claims from actual family members, who most logically still lived in Russia. As a con, it was brilliant.

Lost in the headlines of the battle over the Presley estate was the still meandering Jetstar case, which had undergone a series of delays, none of which were really fought with much enthusiasm since they had lost their star witness. The two defendants who had pleaded guilty, Frederick Pro and Philip Kitzer, had already served their time and been released. The remaining defendants were still out on bail, reporting once a week to their bonding companies. It had been five years since the grand jury handed down its indictments and the Justice Department had discovered no new evidence in the case.[24]

Besides the Jetstar case, there were other significant developments in the early part of the 1980s that affected Colonel Parker, however indirectly. On April 7, 1982, as prosecutors were preparing for the Jetstar case, former Supreme Court Justice Abe Fortas died, effectively closing the books on his case.

During this same period the Justice Department closed in on Louisiana Mafia don Carlos Marcello. A federal probe code-named Brilab (short for bribery and labor) ensnared him and charged him with attempting to bribe a federal judge who was about to preside over a racketeering and extortion case involving some of Marcello's associates.

Marcello was convicted on April 19, 1983, and sentenced to ten years at a federal penitentiary in Texarkana, Texas. With time off for good behavior, he was released in 1989 and allowed to return to Louisiana, where he died in 1994.[25]

After discovering just how little the estate was worth, Priscilla Presley looked for ways to enhance its value, even as she was battling with the Colonel in court. Expenses for the upkeep of Graceland, closed upon Vernon's death in 1979, exceeded $30,000 a month. That cost had to be paid from the income derived from continuing record royalties, which had dwindled to a little over $340,000 a year.

Since the deaths of Elvis and Vernon, Priscilla had sought counsel from a variety of friends and associates. When one of her primary advisors, Texas financier Jester Maxfield, was killed in a plane crash in September, she went to Kansas City to meet with one of his employees—Jack Soden, a thirty-five-year-old stockbroker.

Priscilla laid out all of the estate's financial problems before Soden. The estate wasn't poor; it wasn't rich. It was sort of dog-paddling its way from one year to the next. She needed a plan that would allow the estate to become profitable. Otherwise, Lisa Marie would have little to show for her father's illustrious career.

Soden suggested Priscilla open Graceland to the public.

That sounded like a good idea to Priscilla. She carried it back to the other co-executors, and together they decided Graceland would become Memphis's newest tourist attraction. They hired Jack Soden to oversee the project. By June of the following year, the thirteen-acre Graceland estate had opened its gates to fans of the late entertainer—at $7.50 a head. For four dollars extra, fans could also tour the bus and the airplanes.

"The thought of selling Graceland was never a consideration," Priscilla told Steve Tompkins, a reporter for the *Commercial Appeal*. "Opening [Graceland] was the last thing I wanted to do. . . . I think that we waited as long as we could, hoping there would be other revenue to help us out."

The estate spent $500,00 preparing the mansion for public exhibit, but response was so great that the initial investment was recouped within the first five weeks of operation. During the first year more than 300,000 people visited Graceland. By the end of the decade, it was drawing some 600,000 visitors annually. Not surprisingly, Jack Soden was installed as the executive director of Graceland.

In November 1982, when it was apparent that Graceland would be a successful tourist attraction, it was announced—prematurely, as it turned out—that Colonel Parker and the Presley estate had reached an out-of-court settlement in their long battle over control of the entertainer's remaining assets. There were still some matters to be ironed out between the two parties, and there was still work to be done on the RCA Records lawsuit.

In June 1983, Colonel Parker, RCA Records, and the estate formally ended their legal wrangle. Under the terms of the agreement the Colonel's managerial relationship with the estate was severed. He was allowed to keep all royalties that he received prior to 1982.

The estate agreed to purchase Parker's share of Boxcar Enterprises for $225,000, Boxcar's "Always Elvis" trademark for an additional $100,000, and the company's other assets for $25,000. RCA agreed to pay the estate $110,000 annually for ten years; it also agreed to pay the Colonel $2 million for more than 350 movie and television clips, and all master copies of recordings made by Elvis.[26]

In essence, Parker agreed to settle for a little over $2.3 million. After all the name calling and threatening legal gestures, all three parties—Priscilla, the Colonel, and RCA—decided to end the dispute on amicable terms, with Priscilla and RCA continuing their working relationship.

The Colonel was sent packing, but not without a secret agreement, according to sources, that prohibited the estate and the Colonel from ever discussing the other party in public without the other party's permission.[27]

☆   ☆   ☆

For the remainder of the 1980s the Colonel kept a low profile. He was not in good health. He had suffered a heart attack several years back, and in 1981 he broke his right shoulder when he fell down in the elevator at the RCA Building in Los Angeles. As he lay in the doorway of the elevator, unable to get to his feet, the door repeatedly slammed into his helpless body, striking him with sufficient force to break his shoulder.

On Parker's seventy-seventh birthday, Barron Hilton threw a party for him on the thirtieth floor of the Las Vegas Hilton. About one hundred people attended the party, including Priscilla and her parents, Mr. and Mrs. Joseph Beaulieu, comedian Rodney Dangerfield, and Al Dvorin.

"I may be seventy-seven, but I don't feel it," he told the guests. "I just let my body tell me what to do."

Not attending the party was Marie Parker, his critically ill wife. About five months after the party, on November 25, 1986, she finally succumbed. She had been seriously ill for several years. She died at their home in Palm Springs and was buried in the mausoleum at the Spring Hill Cemetery in Madison, Tennessee. Her crypt is located several vaults up from ground level in the open-air portion of the mausoleum. The inscription reads simply: "Marie Frances Parker, May 18, 1908–November 25, 1986." There are no phrases of endearment. No "rest in peace" or "loving wife."

The vault adjacent to Marie's crypt is unmarked and unoccupied, and was presumably meant for the Colonel.[28] There is something forlorn about Marie's final resting place, something that speaks to the eternal loneliness of her strange journey through life on the arm of the Colonel.

During the legal fight with RCA the Colonel had used Marie's failing health as a reason why he could not travel to New York to be deposed. In an affidavit he said that Marie was in a "virtually comatose condition" and was under continuous medical supervision.

A year later, after becoming increasingly reclusive, the Colonel made a rare visit to Memphis to visit Graceland, where he stayed for two days as a guest of Jack Soden. From Memphis, he went to visit Marie's final resting place and to inspect his office in Madison. He decided to convert the office into a museum to display artifacts squirreled away during his long career.

While in Nashville, he stopped by a local print shop to pick up several Elvis posters he had ordered for an upcoming exhibit in Las Vegas. Pat Embry, a reporter for the *Nashville Banner*, met him at the print shop and arranged a hasty interview with him there in the store. He told Embry about his trip to Graceland and said, "You can tell 'em the Colonel said they're doing a beautiful job at Graceland."

In August the Colonel, then seventy-eight years of age, emerged in Las Vegas on the tenth anniversary of Elvis's death. Looking bloated and feeble, but wearing a snappy white cowboy hat, he held a news conference at the Las Vegas Hilton Hotel, where he had put together an exhibit in the $2,500-a-night Elvis suite.

For five dollars, the public could view his weeklong exhibit of photos, placards, and memorabilia. Nothing was for sale. It was for viewing only. The Colonel told the Associated Press that although Elvis had been dead for ten years, he was shedding no tears. "There's nothing to cry about, everything is too happy," he said. "I'm the spokesman for him now that he's gone, and it helps me sell some of his memorabilia."

In the final years of his life Colonel Parker seldom made personal appearances and granted few interviews. In a 1990 interview with Woody Baird, an Associated Press reporter in Memphis, he said there was nothing he could have done to keep Elvis away from drugs. Said Parker: "He made his own decisions and you could not change them."

What seemed to aggravate him the most was the constant stream of tabloid articles that proclaimed Elvis to be alive and well. In a 1995 interview with Mike Weatherford of the *Las Vegas Review-Journal*, he said fans had been telling him recently of weekly conversations with Elvis during seances. The fans offered to send the Colonel a plane ticket so he could attend one of the seances and speak to Elvis himself. Parker told them, "Here's my new number—the next time Elvis shows up, give it to him and have him call me."

Three years after Marie died, Colonel Parker married his longtime assistant, Loanne Miller. She was about twenty-five years younger than the Colonel, but had worked with him at the Las Vegas Hilton at RCA Record Tours, and since 1975 as his personal assistant.

The Colonel never lost his zeal for Elvis, or at least his zeal for promoting Elvis, but when Graceland grew into the multi-million-dollar enterprise that it became by the 1990s, the Colonel's tacky photo-and-poster displays seemed out of place, and he seemed to know that. Elvis had finally become too big for the Colonel.

When the U.S. Postal Service issued an Elvis Presley stamp in 1992, the Colonel stood in line in Las Vegas to be among the first to purchase the stamps. He looked ancient, his face splotchy, and his bulbous, 300-pound body misshapen by the ravages of old age. He moved slowly, with the aid of a walking stick, and seemed on the verge of teetering over as he ambled along at his own pace.

One day he put away his cigar, just did it cold turkey. It happened while he was reading the Sunday newspaper. He saw an advertisement that said, "Stop smoking for $200." After he read the ad, he shouted out to Loanne, who was in another room, "We just made $200!"

"How's that?" she said.

"I just stopped smoking."[29]

Off and on for weeks, the Colonel called friends and asked them to come to Las Vegas to visit him. Because it was over the Christmas holidays and into the New Year, no one could get away. Most had families and businesses to run. It was inconvenient to visit. "Is it important?" they asked.

"Well, no," he answered. "Just come by when you can."

The Colonel watched Elvis's sixty-second birthday anniversary come and go. Elvis Presley Enterprises celebrated the January 8 birthday in Memphis, as always, but the big event of the year would not occur until August 16, the twentieth anniversary of the entertainer's death. Parker knew he would not live to participate in that observance.

The Presley estate, still under Priscilla's control, had a love-hate relationship with Parker. The estate endured some rough times to win control of Elvis's assets, but when all was said and done, he was still "The Colonel," the man most closely associated with the career of the late entertainer. The estate knew it had nothing to gain—and everything to lose—by perpetuating a public feud with him.

The estate's attitude toward Parker was similar to the army's "don't ask, don't tell" policy toward homosexuals. The estate's secret pact with Parker stipulated that neither party would ever publicly comment on the affairs of the other. Neither one would question the conduct or motives of the other, and neither one would tell what they knew about the other.[30]

The estate had strong reasons for entering into such an agreement. Elvis's popularity exploded after his death. When Graceland was opened to the public, more than 300,000 fans paid to tour the mansion in the first year. Each year after that, Graceland drew, on average, 500,000 visitors.

Only one home in America drew more visitors: the White House. Whatever the estate's private feelings about Parker, it had a major investment to protect. That investment was best served by not tearing down the reputation of the man most closely associated with Elvis's career.

That financial consideration was reason enough to protect the reputation of Parker, but it wasn't the only one. Almost from the beginning, there had been rumors that Parker "had something" on Elvis, that he was blackmailing the entertainer with information of a devastating nature.

Whether Parker actually told any Elvis associate that he had incriminating information on the entertainer has never been documented, but he certainly made people *believe* he did. Then there were the stories about his alleged connections to organized crime figures in Louisiana, Tennessee, Florida, and Las Vegas. Without ever saying outright that he had high-level mob contacts, he made people *believe* that he did.

Parker played up those fears masterfully. Faced with the reality of his long, public association with Elvis—and the rumors of the damage that he could inflict on the entertainer's reputation if provoked— Priscilla could see no advantage in calling the old man's bluff. It was easier to reconcile with him than to fight him.

In the final week of his life Parker continued to call his friends. He didn't make it seem urgent, so they kept putting him off. On Monday, January 20, 1997, Dr. Charles W. Ruggeroli, a cardiologist who had been treating Parker for congestive heart problems, admitted him to Las Vegas's Valley Hospital. The Colonel's final illness had arrived without warning.

Loanne had been in another room when she heard a thud. She called out, asking if the Colonel was all right, but he didn't answer. When she went into the living room to see about him, she found him slumped in his chair, a pile of Christmas fan letters heaped on his lap. He had been responding to the letters when he collapsed.

The old man's health had been slipping all year and the former 300-pounder was nowhere near that weight. Loanne sent him to the hospital and the following morning he suffered a stroke. At 9:58 A.M. Dr. Ruggeroli pronounced him dead. Loanne was at his side.

Reaction to Parker's death was curious. "Parker Has Left the Building" read the headline in *Entertainment Weekly*. The magazine called him "the most notorious rock manager in history." *Time* magazine identified him as "Elvis Presley's impresario," the man who "masterminded the King's career" and took oversized percentages.

In Nashville, where Parker and Marie maintained a home for many years, reaction was more sedate. The *Nashville Banner* called him the "ingenious mind" behind Elvis, and the *Tennessean* called him "the most famous manager in popular music history."

In Las Vegas, former Hilton Hotel publicist and longtime associate Bruce Banke told a reporter for the *Las Vegas Review-Journal* that Parker was "the most incredible promoter that I have ever met." Entertainer Wayne Newton told the same newspaper that when Elvis died, half of Parker's existence went with him. Now, with Parker's death, he said, "The passing is complete."

The Elvis fan magazines were not so kind. In an obituary entitled "Sonofobituary" published in *Now Dig This*, Gordon Minto depicted Parker as a court jester. "Sadly, it seems, there are few who will mourn him," he wrote. "The world of pop music has lost its most notorious and talked about manager ever. For sure there will never be anyone like him again. . . . Cynics might say it is truly the end of an error [*sic*]."

The image that emerged of the Colonel in his final years is remarkably different from the one that stuck with him for most of his life. Words like intimidating, gruff, threatening, and egomaniacal no longer seemed to apply.

Paul Lichter had several run-ins with the Colonel over the years as a freelance vendor of Elvis memorabilia, but what sticks with him most about the Colonel is the way he responded to Lichter's young son, Tristan. "The Colonel showered gifts on the kid," he says. "He was an extremely generous man."

Once Tristan told the Colonel that he was a fan of Michael Jackson. "Soon as the Colonel knew that, he sent Tristan this great picture of the Colonel and Michael Jackson on the balcony of his apartment in Las Vegas," says Lichter. "Then Michael Jackson sent Tristan a platinum record from *Thriller*, with an invitation to a party—all because of the Colonel."[31]

Sharing Lichter's view of the Colonel's gentler, more caring side is his longtime associate Al Dvorin, who looked after the day-to-day operations of many of the tours. "He had me give out the checks," says Dvorin. "I paid people more than they earned, because that was his way of helping them. When one of the promoters we worked with fell on hard times, it was the Colonel who took care of him. . . . He was a good buddy, a good pal, so don't pay attention to the phony baloney you read in the newspapers."

Where the Colonel comes under the most criticism is not for his lack of generosity, but for the way that he managed Elvis's career. Rolling Stones guitarist Keith Richards says it was "really scandalous what Parker did to Elvis." Others agree. Frances Preston, head of Broadcast Music, Inc., feels that Parker was "neglectful" in the manner he handled the entertainer's finances. "He took an astronomical fee for managing Elvis, much larger than is the norm for management, and for that Elvis's affairs were not properly handled," she says. "Elvis's drug situation could have been better controlled by Parker. He just had a hands-off attitude toward it."[32]

To Marshall Grant, "The biggest tragedy in American music is Parker's mismanagement of Elvis Presley." For those who knew Elvis in the beginning, who saw the bright promise of his career, what the Colonel did to him remains unforgivable. "As a manager, I never had much respect for [Parker]," says Grant. "I know the Colonel's gone and all that, and I don't [like to] speak of someone who's in his grave, but there's nothing that suffices for the truth. To me, the Colonel was not a manager. Elvis made himself. . . . I don't know why Elvis didn't say, 'Hey, that's enough!' If Colonel Parker had been doing his job, he would have made damn sure Elvis was in every corner of the globe, whether [Parker] had a passport or not. I know a lot of managers who don't travel with the artists. He was afraid someone would steal Elvis from him the way he stole him from Bob Neal."

Grant thinks Parker knew about Elvis's drug addiction all along. "Of course, he did. No question about it. And he didn't do anything about it. He could have tried to help him along. The only thing he was interested in was the money [Elvis] was generating for him. He never turned one hand to help the situation."[33]

Colonel Parker was not a religious man. There is no public record that he ever acknowledged the existence of a higher power. It surprised no one that he wanted his funeral services conducted in the Las Vegas Hilton instead of a church. Certainly, he couldn't have it done in a synagogue. It was fitting that his send-off to another world take place in a casino.

Services were held at 2:30 P.M. on the Saturday following his death. The glitzy hotel marquee said good-bye to the Colonel in fitting fashion—one of the few times *his* name had been up in lights. Loanne invited a number of VIPs to the service, but few came, with the exception of old-timers like Eddy Arnold. In all, about one hundred and sixty people attended the service.

Perhaps the biggest surprise was the presence of Priscilla Presley, the last person one would expect to see at a memorial service for the Colonel. Of course, the person whom they had all come to see, perhaps stretched out in an ornate, covered-wagon casket hoisted on the shoulders of a team of nimble-footed midgets, was Colonel Tom Parker. But he was noticeably absent, having been cremated prior to the service.

Most of the friends Parker telephoned in the days before his death came to the service. Most felt badly they had not seen him again in life. As they talked among themselves, they realized that many of them had received the same telephone call from their friend in the final weeks of his life.

In the year after his death, Priscilla refused to be interviewed about her reasons for attending the funeral. Had she, too, received a telephone call to which she had not responded? At one point during the services, she broke down, sobbing, her voice rising for all to hear, "This was not part of the deal!"

Was Priscilla weeping because Parker had finally expired after several years of bad health? Or was she weeping because he had promised to free her from bondage at his death and she suddenly realized that was not going to happen? Had she forgotten she was attending a funeral in a casino where the odds are always with the house?

Everything went smoothly at the service, although there was an awkward moment when an inquiring magazine writer was asked to leave the room. One by one, several of Parker's friends and associates stood to eulogize him. Looking over their shoulder was a life-size picture of the Colonel wearing a cowboy hat. When Loanne rose to speak, soft violin music filled the room. She told the mourners that she thought a monument should be built to honor the Colonel's memory. Not surprisingly, no one passed a collection plate.

One of the speakers, John O'Reilly, chairman of the Las Vegas Chamber of Commerce, told of how Parker once worked as a Santa Claus in a Las Vegas store and told a little girl to ask her mother for a hamburger because he was hungry. Said O'Reilly: "Where do you begin to celebrate the memory of a man that's been so dear to us? If the Colonel was here, I know he'd have the thoughts that would guide us."[34]

Later that day, his ashes were interred at Las Vegas's Palm Memorial Gardens. No sooner had the mourners left the Las Vegas Hilton than hotel officials switched the outside marquee to advertise an upcoming heavyweight prize fight. To the surprise of many, the Colonel did not choose to be placed alongside Marie, who was entombed in the mausoleum in Spring Hill Cemetery in Madison, Tennessee. Like the service at the casino, the burial was closed to the public.

In his will, Parker stipulated that upon his death nine friends and associates would receive cash amounts ranging from $2,500 to $30,000. Included were former Presley associates Jerry Schilling and Joe Esposito. Everything else he owned was left to Loanne, who was named executrix of his estate. In his will, Parker acknowledged that he might have living family members, including "brothers, sisters, nephews, nieces and cousins," but he said he had taken that into consideration in preparing the document. He left them nothing.

As the mourners departed that day, it was with the feeling that something had been left unresolved. Those who had expected a sealed envelope, an explanation, or a reason for it all, left empty-handed.

In a way, Parker made sure he would have the last word. The way things worked out, no one could be certain he would not reach out from the other side—one year, ten years, or twenty years hence—with messengers bearing sealed envelopes with devilish words that would radically alter their lives.

There are those who believe Colonel Parker will someday rise like a giant, lumbering Phoenix, accompanied by an army of tap-dancing midgets and, perhaps, even the King himself, to reclaim his throne as the Greatest Showman on Earth. It will take years, perhaps decades, for the full extent of Parker's tangled business dealings to emerge. His true identity may never be known for certain.

During his lifetime many people feared the Colonel. They feared saying something that might offend him, feared incurring the wrath of his friends, feared the unknown that seemed to hover over the Colonel like a dark cloud. Over the years, the Colonel protected Elvis from those who would harm him, and he should be given credit for that. But in the end, the Colonel's greatest gift to Elvis may have been in succumbing to death, for only with Parker's passing has it become apparent that there was a rational reason for Elvis's erratic behavior in his final years.

Parker was a marketing genius who revolutionized American popular culture. You cannot look at television, listen to music, or watch a motion picture without seeing his oversized fingerprints. But, like other geniuses in American history, he was possessed of dark, destructive impulses that contributed to the demise of the very source of his creative power—Elvis Presley.

One cannot look at Colonel Parker without seeing the worst—and the best—of America as a nation. Perhaps that is how the game is played. If so, no one ever played it better than the man who went by the name of Tom Parker.

NOTES

CHAPTER 1

1. Probate Court of Shelby County, Tennessee (file A-655). It was during the disposition of the Elvis Presley estate that Tom Parker was first identified, for the record, as Kuijk. He left that assertion unchallenged and, in fact, maintained in other legal proceedings that he was not a U.S. citizen and thus could not be forced to provide information requested by an American court proceeding.

2. In his book, *Elvis and the Colonel*, Dutch author Dirk Vellenga wrote that he located Andreas van Kuijk's surviving family members and interviewed them about Andreas's early years in the Netherlands.

3. McKennon, *A Pictorial History of the American Carnival*; Bogdan, *Freak Show*.

4. McKennon, *A Pictorial History of the American Carnival*.

5. McKennon, *A Pictorial History of the American Carnival*.

6. McKennon, *A Pictorial History of the American Carnival*.

7. Interviewed by the author in 1997 on the eve of his 78th birthday.

8. *Commercial Appeal; Memphis Press-Scimitar*.

9. White, "Sinners in Dixie"; *Collier's* (January 26, 1935); Prudential Insurance Company reports, 1910–1940; *Commercial Appeal* (crime reports 1910–1950); Lee, *Beale Street*; Harkins, *Metropolis of the American Nile*. Readers desirous of in-depth information about early Memphis history, particularly as it relates to crime, may find it in two books by the author—*Dixie's Dirty Secret* and *Goin' Back to Memphis*.

10. McKennon, *A Pictorial History of the American Carnival*.

11. How the slot machines got there—and elsewhere in Louisiana— was researched by author John H. Davis, who tracked Costello's entry into the bayou state in his book, *Mafia Kingfish: Carlos Marcello and the Assassination of John F. Kennedy*.

12. Author interview with U.S. Immigration and Naturalization Service historian; *The World Book Encyclopedia* (1964 edition).

13. U.S. Immigration and Naturalization Service; *The World Book Encyclopedia* (1954 edition).

14. Jahoda, *River of the Golden Ibis*.

15. Thomas A. Parker Selective Service file.

16. Author interview with Debbie Taylor, Tampa Humane Society (1997); Hopkins, *Elvis;* various news and magazine articles.

17. Thomas A. Parker Selective Service file.

18. Thomas A. Parker Selective Service file.

CHAPTER 2

1. Swindell, *Spencer Tracy*; Ponti, *Hollywood East*.

2. Thomas A. Parker Selective Service file.

3. General pre-induction physicals remained largely unchanged for the duration of World War II, the Korean War, and the Vietnam War. This description of Parker's pre-induction physical was recreated from interviews with other inductees and based on the author's own experience with the same physical.

4. Selective Service System guidelines.

5. Thomas A. Parker Selective Service file.

6. Arnold, *It's a Long Way from Chester County*; Streissguth, *Eddy Arnold*.

7. Arnold, *It's a Long Way from Chester County*.

8. Thomas A. Parker Selective Service file.

9. Sindler, *Huey Long's Louisiana*.

10. Martin, *Dynasty: The Longs of Louisiana*; Jeansonne, *Leander Perez: Boss of the Delta*. Other information in this chapter about Jimmie Davis, Leander Perez, and Huey Long came from a variety of sources, including newspaper articles, Allan Sindler's *Huey Long's Louisiana*, and Glen Jeansonne's *Leander Perez: Boss of the Delta*.

11. Davis, *Mafia Kingfish*.

12. Time-Life Books, *Mafia*.

13. Davis, *Mafia Kingfish*; Time-Life Books, *Mafia*. Other information in this chapter about Carlos Marcello, Santo Trafficante, and Meyer Lansky came from a variety of sources, including Time-Life Books' *Mafia*, and Curt Gentry's *J. Edgar Hoover: The Man and the Secrets*.

14. KWKH's Louisiana Hayride souvenir booklet.

15. Interview with Al Dvorin.

16. *Nashville Tennessean; Nashville Banner.*

17. *Nashville Tennessean* (May 7, 1953).

18. K. J. Evans, "Mr. Entertainment." *Las Vegas Review-Journal,* 1999. Nat Freedland. "Star-Making for Las Vegas." *Entertainment World,* May 8, 1970.

19. Streissguth, *Eddy Arnold.*

20. *Nashville Tennessean.*

21. Snow, *The Hank Snow Story.* Other information in this chapter about Hank Snow was derived from the Associated Press, *Commercial Appeal, Nashville Banner,* and other sources.

22. Snow, *The Hank Snow Story.*

23. Interview with Scotty Moore. Moore's account of Elvis's first recording session at Memphis Recording Studio, owned by Sam Phillips, differs substantially from Phillips's account. The author has used Moore's account since it has been verified by Moore's wife, Bobbie Moore, and by Phillips's associate, Marion Keisker. The author has interviewed Sam Phillips on several occasions and feels he is sincere in his recollections. The author accounts for the differences in Phillips's story and the recollections of others by concluding that Phillips, a non-musician, is less inclined to recall events based on specific instances relating to the music. He is more likely to recall those events relating to the business aspects of the sessions.

24. Interview with Bobbie Moore.

25. Interview with Bobbie Moore.

26. Interview with Scotty Moore.

27. Interview with Scotty Moore; Moore and Dickerson, *That's Alright, Elvis.*

28. The author has examined the contract, the original of which is in the possession of Scotty Moore.

29. Interview with Frank Page; Hopkins's interview with Page, Special Collections, University of Memphis. All quotes in this chapter and elsewhere in the book attributed to Marion Keisker were obtained from interviews done by Jerry Hopkins and donated to the Special Collections room at the University of Memphis Library, where they are available to researchers.

CHAPTER 3

1. Scotty Moore–Elvis Presley management contract dated July 12, 1954; reproduced in *That's Alright, Elvis* (p. 66).

2. The original letter is in Scotty Moore's archives.

3. Interview with Jerry Hopkins, University of Memphis Library.

4. Interview with D. J. Fontana.

5. Interview with Scotty Moore.

6. Snow, *The Hank Snow Story*.

7. Interview with Scotty Moore.

8. Highway 82, which ran east-west across Mississippi from Greenville to the Alabama–Mississippi state line, was regarded as the boundary for crime families in New Orleans and Memphis.

9. Senator Kenneth McKellar Collection, Memphis and Shelby County Library; John D. Martin Collection, Memphis and Shelby County Library; detailed information about the Memphis underworld can be found in Dickerson, *Dixie's Dirty Secret*.

10. Interview with Evelyn Black Turveville.

11. Interview with Bobbie Moore.

12. Interview with June Carter Cash.

13. Interview with Marshall Grant.

14. Interviews with Scotty Moore and D. J. Fontana.

15. Guralnick, *Last Train to Memphis*.

16. Alanna Nash, with Billy Smith, Marty Lacker, and Lamar Fike. *Elvis Aaron Presley: Revelations from the Memphis Mafia*. New York: HarperCollins, 1995, pp. 2–3.

17. Keisker, *Memphis: 1948–1958*; Keisker interview with Jerry Hopkins.

18. Marion Keisker interview with Jerry Hopkins, University of Memphis.

19. *Memphis Press-Scimitar*.

20. Sam Phillips interview, Special Collections, University of Memphis Library; interviews with Sam Phillips and Kemmons Wilson, Gruber, *Memphis: 1948–1958*; author interviews with Kemmons Wilson associates who asked not to be identified; additional information in Dickerson, *Goin' Back to Memphis*.

21. Snow, *The Hank Snow Story*.

22. Snow, *The Hank Snow Story*.

23. *New York Times* (December 30 and 31).

24. *New York Times* (December 30 and 31); *Commercial Appeal* (December 29 and 30); 1972 Mississippi Code (annotated), Volume 2, Title 3; Mississippi Department of Archives and History, Jackson, Miss.; Governor Paul B. Johnson Collection at the University of Southern Mississippi in Hattiesburg, Miss.; additional information in Dickerson, *Dixie's Dirty Secret*.

25. Mississippi Rep. A. C. "Butch" Lambert.

26. *Nashville Tennessean*, November 30, 1956.

27. Interview with Scotty Moore; Moore and Dickerson, *That's Alright, Elvis*.

28. Elvis Presley FBI files.

29. Evans, *Las Vegas Review-Journal*, 1999.

30. Associated Press, *Nashville Banner*, August 15, 1983.

31. Jerry Hopkins Collection, Special Collections, University of Memphis, "Elvis Presley's Personal Appearances," June 1970.

CHAPTER 4

1. Statistics and a Mississippi case study can be found in Dickerson, *North to Canada* (chapter 3).

2. Elvis Presley Selective Service file.

3. Elvis Presley Selective Service file.

4. United Press International, August 4, 1955.

5. Elvis Presley estate probate court files.

6. *Commercial Appeal*.

7. Interview with Hal Kanter.

8. Interview with Scotty Moore.

9. Interview with Gordon Stoker.

10. Elvis Presley Selective Service file, which contains notification and classification records of thirty-two men, including Presley.

11. Interview with Jack Clement.

12. Interview with Brenda Lee.

13. Elvis Presley FBI file; Allen, "Elvis Given Sixty-Day Reprieve," *Commercial Appeal*, December 28, 1957.

14. Scotty Moore's archives.

15. Nash, *Elvis Aaron Presley: Revelations from the Memphis Mafia*, p. 4.

16. Interview with Scotty Moore; Moore and Dickerson, *That's Alright, Elvis*.

17. The interview was recorded by radio and television and reported by wire services.

18. In a July 1989 ruling, U.S. District Judge William Barbour of Jackson, Miss., found that the commission had engaged in a wide-ranging conspiracy to deprive southerners of their constitutional rights. Dickerson, in *Dixie's Dirty Secret*, catalogued a variety of crimes committed by the commission.

19. In *Mafia Kingfish*, author John Davis gives an account of Kohn's attempt to prosecute Carlos Marcello; additional information can be found in Time-Life Books, *Mafia*.

20. Interview with Al Dvorin.

CHAPTER 5

1. Elvis Presley FBI file (the author does not refer to page numbers because the 663-page file was not paginated by the FBI).
2. Elvis Presley FBI file.
3. Interview with Scotty Moore.
4. Scotty Moore's archives.
5. Letter, Walter Jenkins to Colonel Parker, 12/22/59, Senate Masters, Box 142, LBJ Library.
6. Letter, Lyndon Johnson to Colonel Parker, 12/29/59, Senate Masters, Box 142, LBJ Library.
7. Letter, Lyndon Johnson to Colonel Parker, 12/10/59, Senate Masters, Box 142, LBJ Library.
8. Elvis Presley FBI files.
9. Elvis Presley FBI files.
10. Elvis Presley FBI files.
11. Marion Keisker, Hopkins Collection, University of Memphis.
12. Marion Keisker, Hopkins Collection, University of Memphis.
13. Godbout, *New York Times*, March 4, 1960.
14. Mitchell, *Commercial Appeal*, March 3, 1960.
15. Marion Keisker, Hopkins Collection, University of Memphis.
16. Interview with Scotty Moore.
17. Associated Press, November 9, 1960, reported on Louisiana Governor Jimmie Davis's efforts to fight school desegregation and his threat to call out the state militia.
18. Davis, *Mafia Kingfish*.
19. Interview with Scotty Moore; Moore and Dickerson, *That's Alright, Elvis*.
20. Burk, *Memphis Press-Scimitar*, February 27, 1961.
21. *Commercial Appeal*.
22. Interview with a Parker associate who asked not to be identified.
23. Hopkins, Elvis.
24. Wilder, *Tampa Tribune*, August 4, 1961.
25. Meffert, *Tampa Tribune*, July 16, 1961.
26. Marion Keisker, Hopkins Collection, University of Memphis.
27. Interview with Hal Kanter.
28. Letter, Lyndon Johnson to Colonel Parker, 12/15/62, "VP Masters," Box 38, LBJ Library.

CHAPTER 6

1. The author contacted Trude Forsher in 1997 to interview her for this book, but she said she would do no interviews unless she was paid

for her time, an offer the author declined. Forsher, who was living in a California nursing home, was pleasant about it. She chuckled that her paid-interview rule was in keeping with the standards the Colonel had established over the years of not giving the media anything for which it did not pay.

2. Parker, *Elvis: The Secret Files*; Hal Wallis interview, DeGolyer Institute of American Studies at Southern Methodist University, Dallas, Texas.

3. Interview with Scotty Moore.

4. Letter, LBJ Library. Letter, Walter Jenkins to Colonel Parker, 12/6/63, "WHCF," Box 54, LBJ Library.

5. Hopkins, *Elvis*.

6. Clayton and Heard, *Elvis Up Close*.

7. Knott, "Elvis' Acting Still Limps After Ten Years, Twelve Movies," *Commercial Appeal*, June 16, 1966.

8. Barber, *Memphis Press-Scimitar*, February 15, 1964.

9. Ibid.

10. Ibid.

11. Elvis Presley FBI files.

12. Elvis Presley FBI files.

13. Letter, Scotty Moore to Colonel Parker, April 1, 1964, Scotty Moore archives.

14. Interview with Evelyn Black Turveville; Moore and Dickerson, *That's Alright, Elvis*.

15. Interview with Evelyn Black Turveville.

16. Before Abe Fortas left for Yale University, where he received his law degree, he worked his way through college in Memphis by playing fiddle in a band named the Blue Melody Boys. In Memphis, he was known as "Fiddlin' Abe."

17. Information about Abe Fortas's links to Las Vegas casinos through the Great American, and possible links to the Parvin Foundation through Supreme Court Justice William Douglas, was obtained from a variety of sources, including Curt Gentry's *The Man and the Secrets*; a November 12, 1968, Scripps-Howard story by Dan Thomasson and Nicholas Norrock on Fortas's link to a real estate shelter in Virginia; a May 6, 1969, story by Thomasson on Douglas's directorship of the Albert Parvin Foundation, whose stock portfolio included a casino owned by Meyer Lansky. Whether Fortas and Douglas were both involved in the Parvin Foundation has been lost to history since the Fortas-Douglas FBI files have been destroyed, according to a telephone conversation between the author and FBI officials. Abe Fortas's FBI file, obtained by the author in 1998, suggests a history of illegal activities by the Supreme Court justice.

18. Williams, *Commercial Appeal*, January 18, 1966.

19. *Memphis Press-Scimitar*, May 1, 1964; *Commercial Appeal*, May 7, 1966.

20. Elvis Presley probate court files (No. A-655).

21. Elvis Presley probate court file.

22. Presley, *Elvis and Me*.

23. Gov. Paul B. Johnson Collection, University of Southern Mississippi library.

24. Moore and Dickerson, *That's Alright, Elvis*.

25. Interview with Scotty Moore.

26. Interview with Paul Lichter.

27. Elvis Presley FBI files.

CHAPTER 7

1. Interview with Scotty Moore.

2. Interview with Chips Moman.

3. Interview with Scotty Moore; Moore and Dickerson, *That's Alright, Elvis*.

4. Abe Fortas FBI files.

5. Abe Fortas FBI files.

6. Las Vegas International Hotel press release.

7. Champlin, *Los Angeles Times West Magazine*, October 19, 1969; information about Bill Miller was obtained from Nat Freeland's "Star-Making for Los Angeles" in the May 8, 1970, issue of *Entertainment World*.

8. Evans, "Mr. Entertainment," *Las Vegas Review-Journal*; Freedland, "Star-Making for Las Vegas," *Entertainment World*; Champlin, "Las Vegas," *Los Angeles Times West Magazine*, October 19, 1969.

9. Elvis Presley probate court files.

10. Elvis Presley FBI files.

11. Elvis Presley FBI files.

12. Presley, *Elvis and Me*.

13. Elvis Presley FBI files.

14. Elvis Presley FBI files.

15. Elvis Presley FBI files.

16. Interview with Paul Lichter.

17. Interview with Paul Lichter.

18. Interview with Paul Lichter.

19. A copy of Barron Hilton's letter to Colonel Parker offering to pay him $50,000 a year for three years as payment for his services as a "consultant" can be found in the files of the Elvis Presley probate court proceedings.

20. Barron Hilton's letter.
21. Elvis Presley probate court files.
22. Elvis Presley probate court files.
23. Elvis Presley probate court files.
24. Nigel Winfield was president of Commercial Air Transport Sales of Miami; Lawrence Wolfson did business as Transworld Industries and Leasco; Frederick Pro was president of Air Cargo Express and assorted other companies, including a Florida-based holding company named Parker-West; Philip Kitzer was an executive of Seven Oaks Finance of Minneapolis, Minnesota, and a partner in three off-shore banks—the Mercantile Bank and Trust of St. Vincent in the British West Indies, the First National City Bank and Trust Company of Granada, West Indies, and the Seven Oaks Finance Bank in Kent, England. All information in this book about the FBI investigation of the Jetstar fraud was obtained from FBI files, the office of the Florida secretary of state, and cited newspaper articles.
25. Elvis Presley FBI files.
26. Elvis Presley FBI files.
27. Elvis Presley FBI files.
28. Elvis Presley FBI files.
29. Elvis Presley FBI files.

CHAPTER 8

1. Interview with Hickman Ewing in 1991 when he was U.S. attorney for the Western District of Tennessee.
2. Elvis Presley probate court files.
3. Interview with Donna Presley Early; Vernon Presley's comments are derived from Early's recollections.
4. Kinsley, "Parker Continues as Elvis Manager," *Commercial Appeal*, August 25, 1977. A copy of Vernon Presley's agreement with Parker can be found in the Elvis Presley probate court files.
5. Elvis Presley probate court files.
6. Elvis Presley probate court files.
7. The list can be found in the Elvis Presley FBI files.
8. Frederick Pro, Lawrence Wolfson, Philip Kitzer, Raymond Baszner, Gabriel Caggiano, and Roy Everett Smith, per Elvis Presley FBI file.
9. Elvis Presley FBI file.
10. Triplet, "Partial List of Elvis's Assets, Graceland Inventory Filed," *Commercial Appeal*, November 23, 1977.
11. Triplel, "Partial List of Elvis's Assets, Graceland Inventory Filed."

12. In April he was transported under armed guard to Memphis, where he pleaded guilty to fraud charges in the Jetstar case. In all, he received ten years imprisonment.

13. Elvis Presley FBI files. Details of Pro's plea bargain agreement were never made public, but eleven of the charges against him in Memphis were dismissed by the Justice Department. Pro was fined $20,000 and sentenced to four years imprisonment, a term that was later reduced by one year.

14. Elvis Presley probate court files.

15. Interview with Donna Presley Early.

16. Elvis Presley probate court files.

17. Chism, "RCA, Parker Accused of Plot to Cheat Elvis," *Commercial Appeal*.

18. "Judge Widens Lawyer's Powers in Elvis Estate Case," *Commercial Appeal*.

19. Interview with David McGriff.

20. George Fenneman died on May 29, 1997.

21. *Memphis Press-Scimitar*, August 1, 1981.

22. "Silence Follows Probate Court Report on Cheating of Elvis," *Commercial Appeal*, August 3, 1981.

23. *Thomas Andrew Parker v. Joseph Hanks, Priscilla Presley, and the National Bank of Commerce*, Eighth Judicial District Court of the State of Nevada in the County of Clark, A211531 and A213589.

24. Following a jury trial in July 1982, Lawrence Wolfson, Nigel Winfield, Gabriel Caggiano, and Raymond Baszner were each found guilty of conspiracy. The Justice Department dropped all of the other charges. Their sentences averaged two years and their fines ranged from $2,000 to $10,000. It was hardly a spectacular finish to a case that involved billions of dollars, the most famous entertainer in the world, and underworld connections that ranged from the Fraternity to La Cosa Nostra. For those convicted, it amounted to little more than a slap on the wrist. No one was particularly surprised. Without Elvis or Vernon Presley on the witness stand, the case had lost its punch.

25. Time-Life Books, *True Crime: Mafia*.

26. Beck, "Elvis estate, Colonel Parker end battle," *Memphis Press-Scimitar*, November 16, 1982; Bloom, "Colonel Parker settles for $2 million," *Memphis Press-Scimitar*, June 20, 1983; "Elvis estate will settle with Parker," *Commercial Appeal*, November 17, 1982.

27. Interview with individuals who asked not to be identified.

28. The author visited the vault in 1998.

29. Interview with former associates who asked not to be identified. Information about Colonel Parker's funeral service was compiled from interviews with his friends and acquaintances, almost all of whom asked

not to be identified by name. Information about his death and the aftermath was obtained from a variety of sources, including the Nevada Bureau of Vital Statistics, the Clark County Coroner's office, and news accounts. Refusing to comment on Parker were Valley Hospital, where he died, and the Hilton International Hotel, which responded with a letter that stated it could not comment on any aspect of the Colonel's life without permission of his widow.

30. Sources associated with the Presley estate.
31. Interview with Paul Lichter.
32. Interview with Frances Preston.
33. Interview with Marshall Grant.
34. Associated Press, January 26, 1997.

SELECT BIBLIOGRAPHY

BOOKS

Arnold, Eddy. *It's a Long Way From Chester County*. Old Tappan, N.J.: Hewitt House, 1969.

Bogdan, Robert. *Freak Show: Presenting Human Oddities for Amusement and Profit*. Chicago: University of Chicago Press, 1988.

Bronson, Fred. *The Billboard Book Of Number One Hits*. New York: Billboard Publications, 1985.

Brown, Peter, and Steven Gaines. *The Love You Make: An Insider's Story of the Beatles*. New York: Signet, 1976.

Cotton, Lee. *Did Elvis Sing In Your Hometown?* Sacramento, Calif.: High Sierra Books, 1995.

Cusic, Don. *Eddy Arnold: I'll Hold You in My Heart*. Nashville: Rutledge Hill Press, 1997.

Davis, John H. *Mafia Kingfish: Carlos Marcello and the Assassination of John F. Kennedy*. New York: McGraw-Hill, 1989.

Dawson, Joseph. *The Louisiana Governors*. Baton Rouge: Louisiana State University Press, 1990.

Dewitt, Howard A. *Elvis: The Sun Years*. Ann Arbor, Mich.: Popular Culture, Ink, 1993.

Dickerson, James. *Coming Home: 21 Conversations About Memphis Music*. Memphis: Scripps Howard, 1986.

———. *Goin' Back to Memphis: A Century of Blues, Rock 'n' Roll, and Glorious Soul*. New York: Schirmer Books, 1996.

————. (with Scotty Moore). *That's Alright, Elvis: The Untold Story of Elvis's First Guitarist and Manager, Scotty Moore.* New York, Schirmer Books, 1997.

————. *Dixie's Dirty Secret: The True Story of How the Government, the Media, and the Mob Conspired to Combat Integration and the Vietnam Antiwar Movement.* Armonk, N.Y.: M.E. Sharpe, 1998.

————. *North to Canada: Men and Women Against the Vietnam War.* Westport, Conn.: Praeger, 1999.

Editors, *Mafia.* Alexandria, Va.: Time-Life Books, 1993.

Esposito, Joe. *Good Rockin' Tonight.* New York: Simon & Schuster, 1994.

Facts On File Yearbook. New York: Facts On File, 1966.

Gentry, Curt. *J. Edgar Hoover: The Man and the Secrets.* New York: Plume, 1991.

Goldman, Albert. *Elvis.* New York: McGraw-Hill, 1981.

Gruber, J. Richard. *Memphis: 1948-1958.* Memphis: Memphis Brooks Museum of Art, 1986.

Guralnick, Peter. *Last Train to Memphis: The Rise of Elvis Presley.* New York: Little, Brown, 1994.

Hannaford, Jim, and G.J. Rijff. *Inside Jailhouse Rock.* Holland: Jim Hannaford Productions, 1994.

Harkins, John E. *Metropolis of the American Nile.* Oxford, Miss.: Guild Bindery Press, 1991.

Hopkins, Jerry. *Elvis: A Biography.* New York: Simon & Schuster, 1971.

Jahoda, Gloria. *River of the Golden Ibis.* New York: Holt, Rinehart and Winston, 1973.

Key, V. O., Jr. *Southern Politics.* New York: Random House, 1949.

Lee, George W. *Beale Street: Where the Blues Began.* College Park, Md.: McGrath, 1969.

McAleer, Dave. *The All Music Book of Hit Singles.* London: Carlton Books, 1994.

McKennon, Joe. *A Pictorial History of the American Carnival* (Volume 1). Sarasota, Fla.: Carnival Publishers, 1971.

Miller, William D. *Memphis During the Progressive Era.* Memphis: Memphis State University Press, 1957.

Murphy, Bruce Allen. *Fortas: The Rise and Ruin of a Supreme Court Justice.* New York: Morrow, 1988.

Nash, Alanna, with Billy Smith, Marty Lacker, and Lamar Fike. *Elvis Aaron Presley: Revelations from the Memphis Mafia.* New York: HarperCollins.

Ownbey, Jack, and Bob Burris. *The Hank Snow Story.* Chicago: University of Illinois Press, 1994.

Parker, John. *Elvis: The Secret Files.* London: Anaya Publishers, 1993.

Pierce, Patricia Jobe. *The Ultimate Elvis*. New York: Simon & Schuster, 1994.

Ponti, James. *Hollywood East*. Orlando, Fla.: Tribune Publishing, 1992.

Presley, Priscilla Beaulieu, and Sandra Harmon. *Elvis and Me*. New York: G.P. Putnam's Sons.

Preston, Patricia Tunison, and John Preston. *Frommer's Comprehensive Travel Guide: Tampa & St. Petersburg*. New York: Prentice Hall Travel, 1991.

Reeves, Miriam. *The Governors of Louisiana*. Gretna, La.: Pelican Publishing, 1962.

Rijff, Ger J., and Jan van Gestel. *Fire in the Sun*. Amsterdam: Tutti Frutti Productions, 1991.

Shaw, Arnold. *Dictionary of American Pop/Rock*. New York: Schirmer Books, 1982.

Smith, Gene. *Elvis's Man Friday*. Nashville: Light Of Day Publishing, 1994.

Stambler, Irwin, and Grelun Landon. *The Encyclopedia of Folk, Country & Western Music*. New York: St. Martin's Press, 1969.

Streissguth, Michael. *Eddy Arnold: Pioneer of the Nashville Sound*. New York: Schirmer Books, 1997.

Swindel, Larry. *Spencer Tracy: A Biography*. New York: World Publishing, 1969.

Thompson, Charles C., and James P. Cole. *The Death of Elvis: What Really Happened*. New York: Delacorte, 1991.

Vellenga, Dirk, with Mick Farren. *Elvis and the Colonel*. New York: Delacorte Press.

Whitburn, Joel. *Billboard Top 1000 Singles (1955–1992)*. Milwaukee: Hall Leonard Publishing, 1993.

Wilson, Charles Reagan, and William Ferris. *Encyclopedia of Southern Culture*. Chapel Hill: University of North Carolina Press, 1989.

Worth, Fred, and Steve D. Tamerius. *All About Elvis*. New York: Bantam Books, 1981.

Wright, Fred W. *City Smart Guidebook: Tampa/St. Petersburg*. Santa Fe, N.Mex.: John Muir Publications, 1966.

NEWSPAPERS

The Commercial Appeal, Memphis, Tennessee.
The Memphis Press-Scimitar, Memphis, Tennessee.
The Nashville Banner, Nashville, Tennessee.
The Nashville Tennessean, Nashville, Tennessee.
The New York Times, New York, New York.

AUTHOR INTERVIEWS (ON THE RECORD)

June Carter Cash (1985)
Jack Clement (1985, 1996)
Al Dvorin (1998)
Donna Presley Early (1998)
Hickman Ewing (1991)
D. J. Fontana (1996, 1997)
Marshall Grant (1997, 1998)
Dan Grossi, Tampa Police Department
Hal Kanter (1997)
Brenda Lee (1997)
Paul Lichter (1998)
David McGriff (1997)
Chips Moman (1985, 1986, 1987, 1988)
Bobbie Moore (1996, 1997)
Scotty Moore (1995, 1996, 1997, 1998)
Frank Page (1997)
Sam Phillips (1985, 1986)
Frances Preston (1997)
Carl Sedlmayr Jr. (1997)
Gordon Stoker (1996)
Debbie Taylor, Tampa Humane Society (July 1997).
Evelyn Black Turveville (1996, 1997)
U.S. Immigration and Naturalization Service, historian (1998).

ARCHIVES, LIBRARIES, AND SPECIAL COLLECTIONS

Federal Bureau of Investigation
  Elvis Presley file
  Abe Fortas file
Selective Service System
  Thomas A. Parker file (Hillsborough County, Florida) Classification
    Record, page 101.
  Elvis A. Presley file (Shelby County, Tennessee)
Scotty Moore archives, Nashville, Tennessee
University of Memphis
  Special Collections, University of Memphis Library, Memphis,
    Tennessee. Interviews with Marion Keisker, Steve Sholes, Sam
    Phillips, Scotty Moore, Bob Neal, and Frank Page
Mississippi Department of Archives and History, Jackson, Mississippi

University of Southern Mississippi
  Governor Paul B. Johnson Collection, Hattiesburg, Mississippi
Memphis and Shelby County Library
  Senator Kenneth McKellar Collection, Memphis, Tennessee (by
    appointment only)
  John D. Martin Collection
Florida Secretary of State Archives, Tallahassee, Florida
Probate Court of Shelby County, Tennessee
Eighth Judicial District Court of the State of Nevada in the County of
  Clark
    *Thomas Andrew Parker v. Joseph Hanks, Priscilla Presley, and the
    National Bank of Commerce* (A211531 and A213589)
Lyndon Baines Johnson Library, Austin, Texas

ARTICLES

Adams, Malcolm. "Elvis Wants No Fancy Fuss When He Puts Up Uniform." *Commercial Appeal*. February 17, 1960.
Allen, Richard. "Elvis Given 60-Day Reprive—Army Won't Stop Career." *Commercial Appeal*. December 28, 1957.
———. "Presley To Net $9.86 On Final Army Pay." March 5, 1960.
Associated Press. "Jealous Ohioan Punches at Elvis." August 3, 1956.
———. "Elvis Shines in Vegas Appearance." August 2, 1969.
Barber, Tom. "The White Elephant." *Memphis Press-Scimitar*. February 15, 1964.
Beck, Randell. "Report Says Manager's Deals Defrauded Elvis." *Memphis Press-Scimitar*. August 1, 1981.
Blalock, Bill. "Presley's Invasion of State Has Everybody Cooperating." *Tampa Tribune*. July 22, 1961.
Bradford, Vernon. "State To Pay $8,000 To Help Finance Presley Film." *Tampa Tribune*. August 3, 1961.
Bruce, Russell. "It's Elvis 'the King of Swing' Now." Associated Press. February 4, 1956.
Burk, Bill. "Elvis Is 'Shocked' At Musicians Quitting." *Memphis Press-Scimitar*. September 21, 1957.
———. "Elvis Ambition: To Be Fine Actor." *Memphis Press-Scimitar*. February 27, 1961.
Carpenter, John. "Vegas Pays the King's Ransom." *Los Angeles Free Press*. August 29, 1969.
Champlin, Charles. "Las Vegas." *Los Angeles Times West Magazine*. October 19, 1969.

Chisum, James. "Elvis' Former Wife Files For Benefits of Divorce." *Commercial Appeal*. February 3, 1978.

Christgau, Robert. "Elvis in Vegas." *The Village Voice*. September 4, 1969.

Cronin, Peter, Scott Isler, and Mark Rowland. "Elvis Presley: An Oral Biography." *Musician*. October 1992.

Dalton, David. "Elvis." *Rolling Stone*. February 21, 1970.

Dickerson, James. "Presley Pal Still Pickin'." *CoverStory*. Vol. 2, No. 44 (1993).

Donahue, Michael. "That's All Right, Mama." *Mid-South Magazine*. August 11, 1981.

Edwards, Joe. "Originator says 'Elvis the Pelvis' disliked name." Associated Press. 1983.

Embry, Pat. "The Colonel." *Nashville Banner*. June 12, 1987.

Freedland, Nat. "Bill Miller: Star-Making For Las Vegas." *Entertainment World*. May 8, 1970.

Henry, Polly. "Tampa Beauty Home From Hollywood But Not For Long." *St. Petersburg Times*. July 11, 1961.

Holmes, Charles. "There Was No Favoritism In Armor Branch Service— Different 'After House.'" *Commercial Appeal*. February 28, 1960.

Godbout, Oscar. "Presley Flies In To Drop The 'Sgt.'" *New York Times*. March 4, 1960.

James, Steve. "The Acoustic Roots of Rock." *Acoustic Guitar*. July/August 1994.

Johnson, Robert. "The Elvis Diary." *16: The Magazine for Smart Girls*. May 1957.

Kingsley, James. "Threatening Telegram Pulls Presley Out of Deal For 707." *Commercial Appeal*. February 14, 1975.

———. "Elvis Buys Manager $1.2-Million Plane." *Commercial Appeal*. July 27, 1975.

Knott, John. "Elvis's Acting Still Limps After 10 Years, 12 Movies." *Commercial Appeal*. June 10, 1966.

KWKH, "Louisiana Hayride." A souvenir booklet (publication date unknown).

Lawson, Herbert. "Uncollectible Drafts on West Indian Bank Flood U.S. and Total Millions of Dollars." *Wall Street Journal*. October 19, 1976.

LeBrecque, Ron. "Poor Health Brings Mobsters Together." *Miami Herald*. December 15, 1977.

Martin, Neville. "The King and I." *Guitarist*. November 1992.

Meffert, Neil. "Elvis Comes To Yankeetown." *Tampa Tribune*. July 16, 1961.

Mitchell, Henry. "For Civilian 'Mr.' Tomorrow." *Commercial Appeal*. March 3, 1960.

————. "Elvis and Fans Share Thrills at his Joyous Homecoming." *Commercial Appeal*. March 8, 1960.

Nashville Banner. "Is Col. Parker Ready to 'Sell' Elvis Presley?" April 28, 1977.

Newsweek. "Return of the Pelvis." August 11, 1969.

Nolan, John. "Singer Still Bears Scars of Abuse in Childhood." Associated Press. May 18, 1979.

Orloff, Kathy. "Elvis Hasn't Lost It." *Chicago Sun-Times*. August 10, 1969.

Porteous, Clark. "Cotton Is No. 1 On City's Hit Parade." *Memphis Press-Scimitar* (May 10, 1954).

————. "Two Big Charity Shows." *Memphis Press-Scimitar.* February 25, 1961.

Randall, Nancy. "Elvis." *Nine-O-One Network*. July/August 1987.

————. The Men Who Shot Elvis." *Nine-O-One Network*. July/August 1987.

————. "Elvis—The Memory Lives." *Nine-O-One Network*. December 1987.

"Shaw, Arnold. "An Unrecorded Chapter of the Elvis Presley Story." *Billboard* (undated).

Scott, John L. "Subdued Presley Returns to Vegas." *Los Angeles Times*. August 2, 1969.

Scott, Vernon. "Famous Singer In Turnabout." United Press International. September 26, 1968.

Schumach, Murray. "Money No Object In Sinatra Show." *New York Times*. May 13, 1960.

Sims, Lydel. "Genuine Respect For Elvis Has Grown In Home Town." *Commercial Appeal*. March 8, 1960.

Thomas, Bob. "It Looks Like Romance For Presley and Ann-Margret." Associated Press. August 6, 1963.

Triplett, John. "Graceland Inventory Files." *Commercial Appeal*. November 23, 1977.

United Press International. "Presley Rejects Las Vegas Offer." August 11, 1969.

————. "Elvis Freed From Jet Contract." May 9, 1975.

White, Owen P. "Sinners in Dixie." *Collier's* January 26, 1935.

Wilder, Paul. "Dispute Over State Funds To Help on Elvis Presley Film Upsets His Manager." *Tampa Tribune*. August 4, 1961.

INDEX

ABOUT THE AUTHOR

James L. Dickerson is the author of *Faith Hill: Piece of My Heart, Going' Back to Memphis: A Century of Blues, Rock 'n' Roll, and Glorious Soul* (also available from Cooper Square Press), *Coming Home: 21 Conversations about Memphis Music, That's Alright, Elvis: The Untold Story of Elvis' First Guitarist and Manager* (with Scotty Moore), *Women on Top: The Quiet Revolution That's Rocking the American Music Industry,* and *Dixie Chicks: Down-Home and Backstage,* among many other books. A longtime Memphis resident, Dickerson now lives in Nashville, Tennessee.

GOIN' BACK TO MEMPHIS
A Century of Blues, Rock 'n'
Roll, and Glorious Soul
James L. Dickerson
284 pp., 58 b/w photos
0-8154-1049-2
$16.95

MICK JAGGER
Primitive Cool
Christopher Sandford
Updated Edition
352 pp., 56 b/w photos
0-8154-1002-6
$16.95

THE BLUES
In Images and Interviews
Robert Neff and Anthony Connor
152 pp., 84 b/w photos
0-8154-1003-4
$17.95

ROCK 100
The Greatest Stars of Rock's
Golden Age
David Dalton and Lenny Kaye
with a new introduction
288 pp., 195 b/w photos
0-8154-1017-4
$19.95

SUMMER OF LOVE
The Inside Story of LSD, Rock
& Roll, Free Love and High
Times in the Wild West
Joel Selvin
392 pp., 23 b/w photos
0-8154-1019-0
$15.95

ANY OLD WAY YOU
CHOOSE IT
Rock and Other Pop Music,
1967–1973
Robert Christgau
Expanded Edition
360 pp.
0-8154-1041-7
$16.95

DESPERADOS
The Roots of Country Rock
John Einarson
320pp., 31 b/w photos
0-8154-1065-4
$19.95

HE'S A REBEL
Phil Spector—Rock and Roll's
Legendary Producer
Mark Ribowsky
368 pp., 35 b/w photos
0-8154-1044-1
$18.95

TURNED ON
A Biography of Henry Rollins
James Parker
280 pp., 10 b/w photos
0-8154-1050-6
$17.95

DREAMGIRL &
SUPREME FAITH
My Life as a Supreme
Mary Wilson
Updated Edition
732 pp., 150 b/w photos,
15 color photos
0-8154-1000-X
$19.95

FAITHFULL
An Autobiography
Marianne Faithfull with
David Dalton
320 pp., 32 b/w photos
0-8154-1046-8
$16.95

MADONNA
Blonde Ambition
Mark Bego
Updated Edition
416 pp., 57 b/w photos
0-8154-1051-4
$18.95

ROCK SHE WROTE
Women Write About Rock,
Pop, and Rap
Edited by Evelyn McDonnell &
Ann Powers
496 pp.
0-8154-1018-2
$16.95

Available at bookstores;
Or call 1-800-462-6420

COOPER SQUARE PRESS
150 Fifth Avenue
Suite 911
New York, NY 10011